09/02
13.95

408 VACATION & SECOND HOME PLANS

TABLE OF CONTENTS

CREATIVE HOMEOWNER®

COPYRIGHT © 1999
CREATIVE HOMEOWNER®
A Division of Federal Marketing Corp.
Upper Saddle River, NJ

Visit our Web site at
www.creativehomeowner.com

Library of Con
Catalogue Card No.: 99-60679
IBSN: 1-58011-059-2

CREATIVE HOMEOWNER®
A Division of
Federal Marketing Corp.
24 Park Way
Upper Saddle River, NJ 07458

Manufactured and Printed in
the United States of America

Current Printing (last digit)
10 9 8 7 6 5 4 3

plan no. price code **C** ✖️🗜️ **total living area: 2,015 sq. ft.**

10515

Loft, Windows and Decks

The first floor living space of this inviting home blends the family room and the dining room for comfortable family living. The large kitchen shares a preparation/eating bar with the dining room. The ample utility room is designed with a pantry, plus room for a freezer, a washer and a dryer. Also on the first floor is the master suite with its two closets and five-piece bath which opens into a greenhouse. The second floor is highlighted by a loft which overlooks the first floor living area. The two upstairs bedrooms each have double closets and share a four-piece, compartmentalized bath. The photographed home may have been modified to suit individual tastes.

plan info

First Floor	1,280 sq. ft.
Second Floor	735 sq. ft.
Bedrooms	three
Baths	2(full), 1(half)
Foundation	crawl space

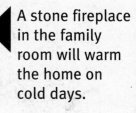

A stone fireplace in the family room will warm the home on cold days.

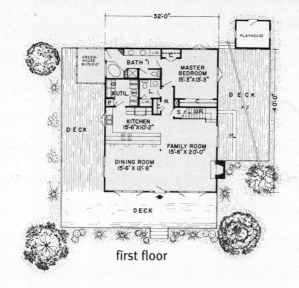

first floor

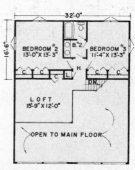

second floor

An open floor plan and multiple windows add spaciousness to this vacation retreat.

Loft Overlooks Foyer

Photography by Beth Singer

This hillside home, characterized by enormous rooms and two garages, is built on two floors. From the foyer, travel down one hall to a cozy bedroom, full bath, island kitchen, laundry and garage. Or, walk straight into the sun-filled Great and dining rooms with wrap-around deck. One room features a massive fireplace, built-in bookshelves, and access to the lofty study; the other contains a window greenhouse. In ultimate privacy, the master bedroom suite possesses a lavish skylit tub. On the lower floor are two additional bedrooms, a bath, and a rec room with bar that opens onto an outdoor patio. The photographed home may have been modified to suit individual tastes.

plan info

First Floor	2,367 sq. ft.
Second Floor	295 sq. ft.
Lower Floor	1,241 sq. ft.
Basement	372 sq. ft.
Garage/lower level	660 sq. ft.
Garage/main level	636 sq. ft.
Bedrooms	four
Baths	3(full)
Foundation	basement

The Great Room has lots of space and beauty. Enjoy the outdoor sunlight in your home from the abundant windows.

DECK

GREAT ROOM
17'-0"
X
24'-6"

DINING
16'-0"
X
13'-4"

HUTCH

WIND.
BENCH.

DECK

SLOPED CLG.
LEVEL CLG.
SLOPED CLG.

BOOKS

30" HIGH

MAST. BEDROOM
21'-2"
X
15'-4"

KITCHEN
17'-10"
X
15'-6"

BOOKS

DOWN

C.

H.

UP

DESK

CABINET

DRESSING AREA

FOYER

H.

C.

C.

BEDROOM 2
13'-8"
X
11'-2"

LAUND.

SHWR.

SKYLT. OVER TUB

C.

82'-6"

FIRST

60'-0"

GARAGE
23'-4"
X
25'-10"

DRIVEWAY

first floor

PATIO

REC. ROOM
17'-0"
X
25'-6"

BEDROOM 3
13'-6"
X
13'-4"

DRIVEWAY

UP

H.

BEDROOM 4
12'-0"
X
14'-10"

MECHANICS GARAGE
21'-2"
X
29'-4"

BAR AREA

BSMT.

B.

C.

BASEMENT/LOWER FLOOR

lower floor

second floor

LOFT/STUDY
16'-8"
X
15'-2"

ATTIC

RAILING

LOFT PLAN

OPEN TO FOYER

An
EXCLUSIVE DESIGN
By Karl Kreeger

This beautiful deck that extends across the rear of the home is a perfect place to entertain guests or to just relax.

price code **H**

total living area: **3,244 sq. ft.**

Unique Floor Plan

Photography supplied by Sater Design

Curved bay windows at the dining room and study give the front of this stucco house a custom design look. A formal living and dining room are off the main gallery hallway. Arches and a raised ceiling define the formal spaces. The living room has an abundance of glass looking toward the atrium and rear yard views. The dining room looks out to the front garden. The kitchen has a walk-in pantry, island eating and prep bar, a cooktop center and a desk space. The family nook has mitered glass giving one the feeling of eating outdoors. Glass corner sliding doors pocket back giving the leisure room an open feel with the covered lanai. The owner's wing is the entire right side of the home. It has a study, master suite and sumptuous vault. The study has ample built-ins and is perfect for a library or home office. The suite has a bayed sitting room to the rear yard views. Two secondary guest's suites are privately located away from the master side. No materials list is available for this plan. The photographed home may have been modified to suit individual tastes.

plan info

Main Floor	3,244 sq. ft.
Garage	810 sq. ft.
Bedrooms	three
Baths	3(full), 1(half)
Foundation	slab

This is the life! Indoor pool to relax all year round.

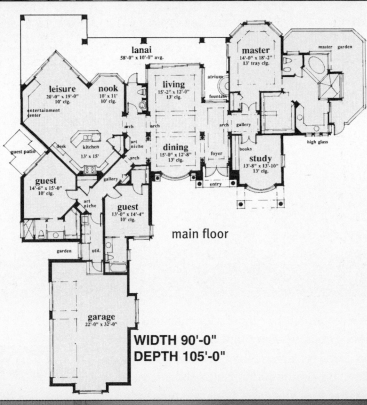

lanai
58'-0" x 10'-0" avg.

master
14'-0" x 18'-2"
13' tray clg.

master garden

leisure
20'-0" x 19'-0"
10' clg.

nook
10' x 11'
10' clg.

living
15'-2" x 12'-0"
13' clg.

atrium

fountain

entertainment center

kitchen
13' x 15'

desk

art niche

dining
15'-0" x 12'-8"
13' clg.

arch

gallery

high glass

guest patio

guest
14'-6" x 15'-0"
10' clg.

art niche

gallery

arch

foyer

books

study
13'-8" x 13'-10"
13' clg.

guest
13'-0" x 14'-4"
10' clg.

entry

garden

util.

main floor

garage
22'-0" x 32'-0"

WIDTH 90'-0"
DEPTH 105'-0"

Enjoy this luxurious bathroom and pamper yourself after a hard days work.

price code **C**

total living area: 1,764 sq. ft.

Year-Round Living

Photography supplied by Sater Design

An abundance of porches and a deck encourage year-round indoor outdoor living in this classic two-story home. The spacious Great room includes a cozy fireplace and is adjacent to the dining room. Both rooms have access to the screen porch/deck area and are perfect for formal or informal entertaining. An efficient kitchen and nearby laundry room make chores easy. The private master suite offers access to the screened porch and leads into a relaxing master bath complete with a walk-in closet, a tub and separate shower, double vanity and a toilet compartment. A second bedroom and a loft are on the second floor. No materials list is available for this plan. The photographed home may have been modified to suit individual tastes.

plan info

First Floor	1,189 sq. ft.
Second Floor	575 sq. ft.
Garage	658 sq. ft.
Bonus	581 sq. ft.
Bedrooms	three
Baths	2(full)
Foundation	post

Enjoy the warmth of the fireplace as you sit back and relax.

first floor

46'-0"

44'-6"

down

screened verandah
30'-8" x 8'-0"

sundeck
15'-0" x 11'-0"

kitchen

dining
10'-0" x 11'-0"
vault clg.

great room
15'-0" x 26'-7"
vault clg.

fireplace

laundry

up

master suite
17'-3" x 11'-0"
8' clg.

foyer

entry porch

down   down

garage

patio
46'-0" x 8'-0"

garage
24'-0" x 28'-0"

storage/bonus

up

second floor

br. 2
11'-1" x 13'-6"
8' clg.

open to great room below

attic access

loft/br. 3
13'-0" x 13'-6"
8' clg.

down

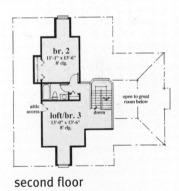

Open floor plan design topped off with beautiful hardwood floors.

Multi-Level Contemporary

Photography by John Ehrenclou

The features of this multi-level contemporary home lend character to both the exterior and interior. A wooden deck skirts most of three sides. The variety in the size and shape of the doors and windows adds charm. Inside, the living room forms a unique living center. It can be reached from sliding glass doors from the deck or down several steps from the first floor inside. It is overlooked by a low balcony from the entryway and dining room on the lower level and from the second floor landing. Large windows on both the right and the left keep it well lit. Ceilings slope upward two stories. A partial basement is located below the design. The photographed home may have been modified to suit individual tastes.

first floor

Bedroom/Den 12'-0" x 11'-0"
Cl
Bath
Kitchen 8'-0"x 9'-0"
Cl
up
dn
Entry
dn
Dining Area 12'-0" x 11'-0"
Living 16'-0"x 14'-0"
Deck
Deck
32'
30'

second floor

Bedroom 12'-0" x 13'-0"
Cl
Bath
Cl
dn
Skylights
Balcony
Bedroom 12'-0"x 20'-0"
Cl
Open to Living
30'

plan info

First Floor	769 sq. ft.
Second Floor	572 sq. ft.
Basement	546 sq. ft.
Bedrooms	three
Baths	2(full)
Foundation	basement

LINWOOD
custom cedar homes

Creative Homeowner Press in cooperation with the Garlinghouse Company is pleased to present a special section of Cedar Homes from the Linwood Homes Collection. You will find these homes on the next 11 pages. Once you have perused this section, please refer to page # 346-347. There will be described your options if you are interested in building one of these fine homes. Enjoy!

total living area: 1,860 sq. ft.

Carlyle

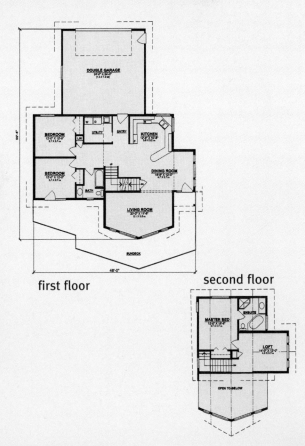

B road projecting roof lines distinguish the design of this gorgeous three bedroom home. Both stone and a wide profile cedar siding have been used to create a striking exterior effect. The master bedroom, with corner tub ensuite and adjacent loft, is located on the private second level. The huge country kitchen, separate dining area, vaulted living room with prow front, and wrap around sundeck ensure comfortable living on the main level.

first floor

second floor

plan info

Bedrooms	three
Baths	2(full)
Foundation	crawl space or basement

Sierra

for more info: see page 346-347

T his distinctive four bedroom home features exceptional use of glass and the privacy of a second floor master bedroom with a walk in closet and a full ensuite. Amenities on the main floor include the vaulted living room, open dining room and a delightfully large country kitchen. Three bedrooms, another full bath, and the utility room complete this superb floor plan.

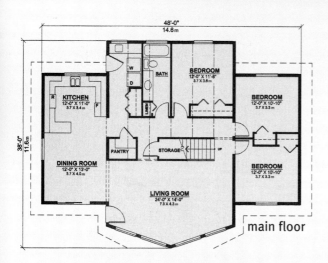

main floor

second floor

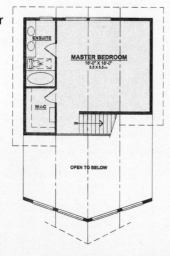

plan info

Bedrooms	four
Baths	2(full)
Foundation	crawl space or basement

LINWOOD
custom cedar homes

total living area: 1,187 sq. ft.

Sitka

This unique get away retreat features two very private bedrooms. Many picture windows and skylights facilitate the flow of natural light from all directions. The stunning spiral staircase adds architectural interest to this truly one of a kind home design.

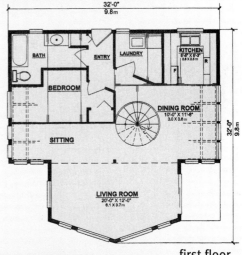

first floor

plan info

Bedrooms	two
Baths	1(full)
Foundation	crawl space or basement

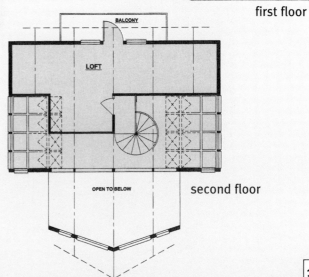

second floor

for more info: see page 346-347

Montblanc

T his convenient three bedroom chalet has all of its bedrooms located on the second floor. The master bedroom boasts his and hers closets and a private front facing balcony. The layout of the living areas with sundeck permits individual family members to enjoy their privacy.

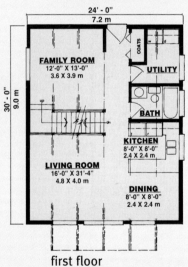

24' - 0"
7.2 m

30' - 0"
9.0 m

FAMILY ROOM
12'-0" X 13'-0"
3.6 X 3.9 m

COATS

UTILITY

BATH

KITCHEN
8'-0" X 8'-0"
2.4 X 2.4 m

LIVING ROOM
16'-0" X 31'-4"
4.8 X 4.0 m

DINING
8'-0" X 8'-0"
2.4 X 2.4 m

first floor

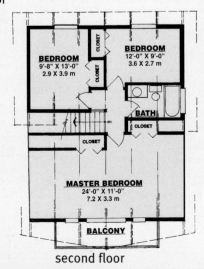

BEDROOM
9'-8" X 13'-0"
2.9 X 3.9 m

CLOSET

BEDROOM
12'-0" X 9'-0"
3.6 X 2.7 m

CLOSET

BATH

CLOSET

CLOSET

MASTER BEDROOM
24'-0" X 11'-0"
7.2 X 3.3 m

BALCONY

second floor

plan info

Bedrooms	three
Baths	2(full)
Foundation	crawl space or basement

LINWOOD
custom cedar homes

total living area: 2,026 sq. ft.

Vail

This distinctive three bedroom chalet design offers indoor elegance and intimacy with the outdoors through an extraordinary wall of windows. The second floor consists of a huge master bedroom, with a full ensuite and a walk in closet. On the first floor are two more bedrooms, a full bath, utility room, comfortable living room, dining and kitchen areas.

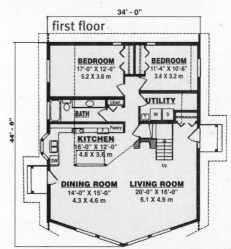

first floor

34' - 0"

44' - 8"

BEDROOM
17'-0" X 12'-0"
5.2 X 3.6 m

BEDROOM
11'-4" X 10'-8"
3.4 X 3.2 m

UTILITY
T | W D

Linen

BATH

Pantry

KITCHEN
16'-0" X 12'-0"
4.8 X 3.6 m

DW

Up

DINING ROOM
14'-0" X 15'-0"
4.3 X 4.6 m

LIVING ROOM
20'-0" X 16'-6"
6.1 X 4.9 m

plan info

Bedrooms	three
Baths	2(full)
Foundation	crawl space or basement

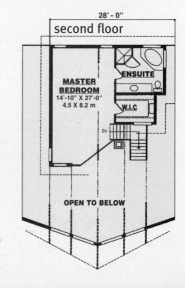

second floor

28' - 0"

MASTER BEDROOM
14'-10" X 27'-0"
4.5 X 8.2 m

ENSUITE

W.I.C

Dn

OPEN TO BELOW

LINWOOD
custom cedar homes

for more info: see page 346-347

total living area: 2,158 sq. ft.

Hampstead

The inherent beauty of wood extends throughout every room of this spectacular, architecturally designed home. All the bedrooms, including the large, private master bedroom with full ensuite and a spacious walk in closet, are located on the upper floor. First floor highlights include a grand foyer entrance that separates the front facing living and dining rooms. A large functional kitchen with eating area adjoins the family room.

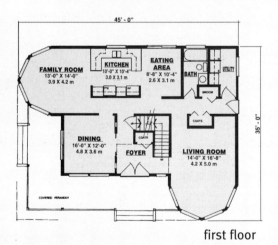

first floor

second floor

plan info

Bedrooms	four
Baths	3(full)
Foundation	crawl space or basement

for more info: see page 346-347

total living area: 2,240 sq. ft.

Stratford

This gorgeous four bedroom home offers room for family enjoyment and privacy too. Amenities on the first floor include a spacious living room with a corner fireplace, a family room, a large kitchen with skylights, three bedrooms and a full bath. The private second floor master suite also has a fireplace, a private balcony, a corner tub, shower, and a walk in closet.

first floor

plan info

Bedrooms	four
Baths	2(full), 1(half)
Foundation	crawl space or basement

second floor

LINWOOD
custom cedar homes

for more info, see page 346-347

total living area: 1,841 sq. ft.

York

The appealing design of this stately three bedroom home offers privacy and lifestyle. The large island kitchen, utility, bath, and vaulted living and dining areas are located on the main level, as is the secluded master bedroom. Highlights of the master bedroom include an enormous walk in closet and access to the screen room. Two more bedrooms and a full bath are set in the second floor. Also an expansive loft that overlooks the wall of windows in the living area below.

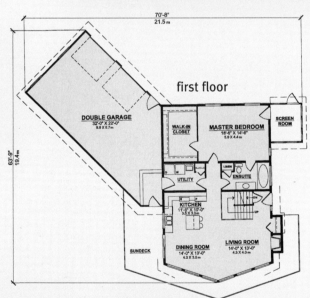

first floor

70'-8"
21.5 m

63'-9"
19.4 m

DOUBLE GARAGE
32'-0" X 22'-0"
9.8 X 8.7 m

WALK-IN CLOSET

MASTER BEDROOM
18'-6" X 14'-6"
5.6 X 4.4 m

SCREEN ROOM

UTILITY

LINEN

ENSUITE

KITCHEN
11'-6" X 10'-0"
3.5 X 3.0 m

DINING ROOM
14'-0" X 10'-0"
4.3 X 3.0 m

LIVING ROOM
14'-0" X 13'-0"
4.3 X 4.0 m

SUNDECK

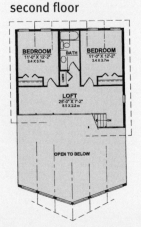

second floor

BEDROOM
11'-0" X 12'-2"
3.4 X 3.7 m

BATH

BEDROOM
11'-0" X 12'-2"
3.4 X 3.7 m

LOFT
28'-0" X 7'-2"
8.5 X 2.2 m

OPEN TO BELOW

plan info

Bedrooms	**three**
Baths	**2(full)**
Foundation	**crawl space or basement**

LINWOOD
custom cedar homes

for more info: see page 346-347

Highgrove

The impressive foyer of this spectacular one bedroom ranch leads to the massive vaulted Great room. The Great room features a fireplace and a magnificent prow of windows. Dual covered porches, one off the master bedroom and another off the kitchen, extend the living areas to embrace gracious outdoor living. Other amenities include a walk in closet, separate shower and tub in the master bedroom, an enormous country kitchen with pantry, a uniquely designed dining area, and a utility/mudroom that is also accessible from the yard.

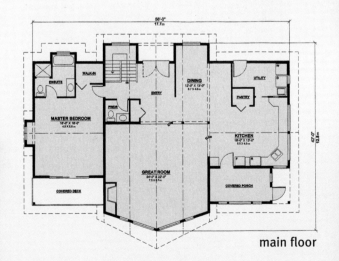

main floor

plan info

Bedrooms	**one**
Baths	**1(full), 1(half)**
Foundation	**crawl space or basement**

LINWOOD
custom cedar homes

for more info: see page 346-347

Chesapeake

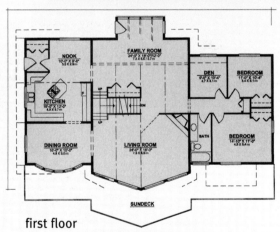

first floor

This handsome three bedroom home with family room offers ample space for everyone to enjoy their individual pursuits. On the second floor is the totally private master bedroom, with full ensuite. Also on the second floor find a cozy loft that opens onto the living areas below. There is a huge sundeck that extends the generous indoor living areas, which include a breathtaking prow of windows and a sunny breakfast nook.

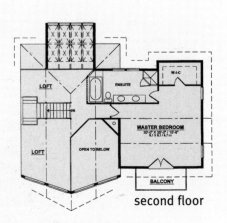

second floor

plan info

Bedrooms	three
Baths	2(full)
Foundation	crawl space or basement

for more info: see page 346-347

total living area: 2,032 sq. ft.

Woodstock

This attractive home features a spacious entrance, two very private bedrooms, three baths, laundry area, and a marvellous kitchen. The master bedroom with ensuite and huge walk in closet is situated in its own wing. The second bedroom with bath is located on the secluded second floor. Adjacent to it is a loft that is open to the living area below. There is a large sundeck that is accessible from both the vaulted great room and the main floor master bedroom.

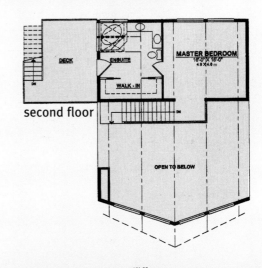

second floor

plan info

Bedrooms	**two**
Baths	**3(full)**
Foundation	**crawl space or basement**

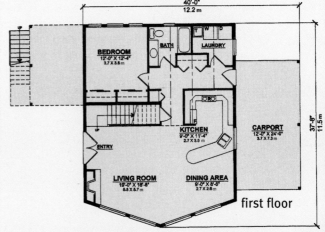

first floor

LINWOOD
custom cedar homes

for more info: see page 346-347

total living area: **1,312 sq. ft.**

Extra Touches of Style

You don't have to sacrifice style when buying a smaller home. Notice the palladian window with a fan light above at the front of the home. The entrance porch includes a turned post entry. Once inside, the living room is topped by an impressive vaulted ceiling. A fireplace accents the room. A decorative ceiling enhances both the master bedroom and the dining room. Efficiently designed, the kitchen includes a peninsula counter and serves the dining room with ease. A private bath and double closet highlight the master suite. Two additional bedrooms are served by a full hall bath.

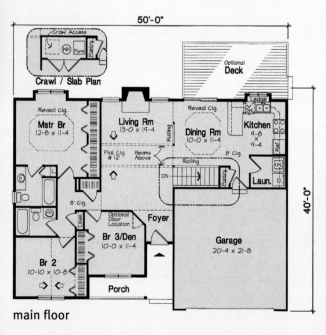

main floor

plan info

Main Floor	**1,312 sq. ft.**
Basement	**1,293 sq. ft.**
Garage	**459 sq. ft.**
Bedrooms	**three**
Baths	**2(full)**
Foundation	**bsmt, slab or crawl space**

Dramatic Ranch

The exterior of this ranch home is all wood with interesting lines. More than an ordinary ranch home, it has an expansive feeling driving up to it. The large living area has a stone fireplace and decorative beams. The kitchen and dining room lead to an outside deck. The laundry room has a large pantry, and is off the eating area. The master bedroom has a wonderful bathroom with a huge walk-in closet. In the front of the house there are two additional bedrooms with a bathroom. This house offers convenient one floor living and has nice big rooms.

main floor

plan info

Main Floor	1,792 sq. ft.
Basement	818 sq. ft.
Garage	857 sq. ft.
Bedrooms	three
Baths	2(full)
Foundation	basement

An EXCLUSIVE DESIGN *By Karl Kreeger*

plan no.

91033

price code (A) ✖ **total living area: 1,249 sq. ft.**

Neat and Tidy

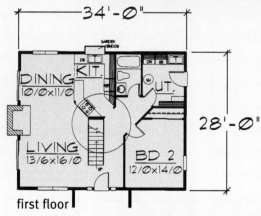

34'-0"

28'-0"

GARDEN WINDOW

DINING 10/0x11/0

KIT.

UT.

LIVING 13/6x16/0

BD 2 12/0x14/0

first floor

This compact house has plenty of closets and storage areas where you can stow away the gear you usually need on vacation. The utility room is also larger than most, and opens directly outside, so there's no reason for anyone to track in snow or mud. Sliding glass doors lead from the two-story living room and dining room out to a paved patio. Tucked into a corner, the kitchen is both out of the way and convenient. A handsome stone fireplace adds a functional and a decorative element to both the interior and the exterior of the home. A downstairs bedroom will sleep either children or guests. Beyond the railed loft, a master suite with a full bath and a walk-in closet provides the owner of this home with every comfort. This plan is available with a basement or crawl space foundation. Please specify when ordering.

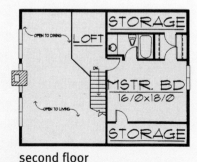

STORAGE

LOFT

OPEN TO DINING

MSTR. BD 16/0x18/0

OPEN TO LIVING

STORAGE

second floor

optional basement plan

plan info

First Floor	952 sq. ft.
Second Floor	297 sq. ft.
Bedrooms	two
Baths	2(full)
Foundation	basement or crawl space

C price code

plan no.

94262

Louisiana Style

Exposed rafters, lattice panels and a deep covered porch make a strong architectural statement. The covered entry porch runs the width of the home, creating an outdoor haven for cozy family gatherings. Inside, decorative arches and columns make a grand entrance to the living and dining areas. The gourmet kitchen provides a pass-through to the formal dining room, while a focal point fireplace warms the Great room. A secluded master suite nestles to the back of the plan, with private access to a sun deck and French doors to the covered porch. The bayed sitting area offers space for reading and brings sunlight into the homeowner's retreat. His and her walk-in closets provide plenty of storage, while a garden tub enjoys a bright bay in the master bath. No materials list is available for this plan.

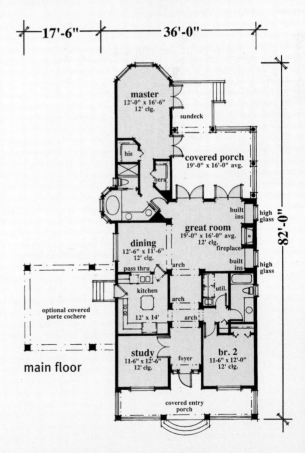

main floor

plan info

Main Floor	1,792 sq. ft.
Bedrooms	two
Baths	2(full)
Foundation	crawl space

price code **A** total living area: **1,328 sq. ft.**

Rustic Exterior

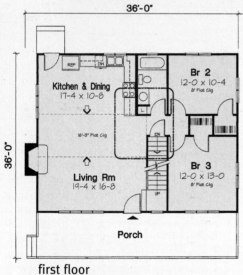

36'-0"

36'-0"

Kitchen & Dining
17-4 x 10-8

16'-3" Flat Clg

Br 2
12-0 x 10-4
8' Flat Clg

Living Rm
19-4 x 16-8

Br 3
12-0 x 13-0
8' Flat Clg

Porch

first floor

Although rustic in appearance, the interior of this cabin is quiet, modern and comfortable. Small in overall size, it still contains three bedrooms and two baths in addition to a large, two-story living room with exposed beams. As a hunting/fishing lodge or mountain retreat, this compares well.

Open to Living Room Below

DN

Flat Clg @ 7'-6"
Master Br
12-0 x 13-4

second floor

crawl space/slab plan

plan info

Main Floor	1,013 sq. ft.
Upper Floor	315 sq. ft.
Basement	1,013 sq. ft.
Bedrooms	three
Baths	2(full)
Foundation	bsmt, slab or crawl space

total living area: 1,307 sq. ft. Detailed Charmer

A price code

plan no. 20161

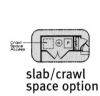

slab/crawl
space option

An
EXCLUSIVE DESIGN
By Karl Kreeger

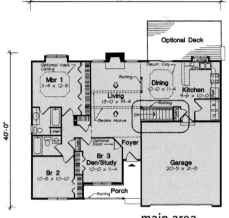

50'-0"

40'-0"

Optional Deck

Mbr 1
11-4 x 12-8

Living
13-0 x 19-4

Dining
10-0 x 11-4

Kitchen
4-8 x 10-0

Foyer

Br 3
Den/Study
10-0 x 11-4

Br 2
10-8 x 10-10

Garage
20-5 x 21-8

Porch

main area

The living room is complete with high sloping ceilings and a beautiful fireplace flanked by large windows. The large master bedroom shows off a full wall of closet space, a private bath and an extraordinary decorative ceiling. Just down the hall are two more bedrooms and another full bath. The dining room has a full slider out to the deck. Along with great counter space, the kitchen includes a double sink and an attractive bump-out window. The adjacent laundry room, optional expanded pantry and a two-car garage make this Ranch a charmer.

plan info

Main Area	1,307 sq. ft.
Basement	1,298 sq. ft.
Garage	462 sq. ft.
Bedrooms	three
Baths	2(full)
Foundation	bsmt, slab, or crawl space

total living area: 1,710 sq. ft. Classic Design

B price code

plan no. 92625

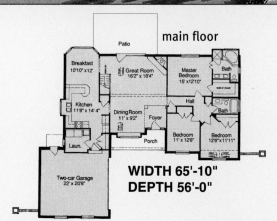

main floor

Patio

Breakfast
10'10"x12'

Great Room
16'2" x 18'4"

Master
Bedroom
15'x12'10"

Bath

Kitchen
11'8" x 14' 4"

Dining Room
11' x 9'2"

Foyer

Hall

Bath

Laun.

Porch

Bedroom
11' x 12'6"

Bedroom
12'6"x 11'11"

Two-car Garage
22' x 20'8'

WIDTH 65'-10"
DEPTH 56'-0"

Brick and wood trim, multiple gables and wing walls enhance the outside; while the interior offers features that are designed for entertaining guests. Sloped ceilings, a corner fireplace, windows across the rear of the Great room and a boxed window in the dining room are visible as you enter the foyer. The kitchen provides plenty of counter space, and a pantry. In the master bedroom you will find a bath with a whirlpool tub, double sink, shower and walk-in closet. No materials list available for this plan.

plan info

Main Flr.	1,710 sq. ft.
Basement	1,560 sq. ft.
Garage	455 sq. ft.
Bedrooms	three
Baths	2(full)
Foundation	basement

Comfortable Living

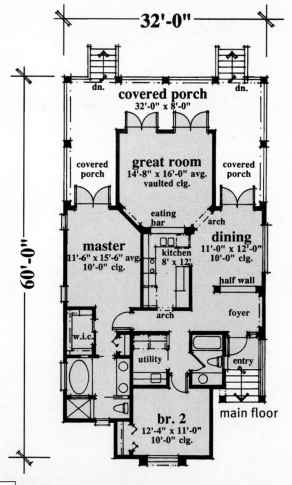

32'-0"

60'-0"

dn.   dn.

covered porch
32'-0" x 8'-0"

covered porch

great room
14'-8" x 16'-0" avg.
vaulted clg.

covered porch

eating bar

arch

master
11'-6" x 15'-6" avg.
10'-0" clg.

kitchen
8' x 12'

dining
11'-0" x 12'-0"
10'-0" clg.

half wall

foyer

arch

w.i.c.

utility

entry

br. 2
12'-4" x 11'-0"
10'-0" clg.

main floor

Welcome home to casual living with this comfortable tidewater design. Asymmetrical lines celebrate the turn of the new century, and blend a current Gulf Coast style with vintage chic brought forward from its regional past. A glass paneled entry is announced by a hooded pediment and set off by a sunburst transom. The foyer overlooks a decorative half-wall to wide views offered through French doors. The heart of this home is the Great room, where a put-your-feet-up atmosphere prevails. The kitchen is galley styled and has a convenient pass-through. The center vestibule leads to a laundry, full bath and secondary bedroom or study with a large, front facing window. French doors open the master suite to a private area of the covered porch. No materials list is available for this plan.

plan info

Main Floor	1,288 sq. ft.
Bedrooms	two
Baths	2(full)
Foundation	crawl space or post

total living area: 1,583 sq. ft. Home for Today

B price code

plan no. 34043

Traditional Victorian touches in this three-bedroom beauty include a romantic, railed porch and an intriguing breakfast tower just off the kitchen. You will love the step-saving arrangement of the kitchen between the breakfast area and formal dining room. Enjoy the wide-open living room with sliders out to a rear deck, and the handsome master suite with its skylit, compartmentalized bath. Notice the convenient laundry location in the bedroom hall.

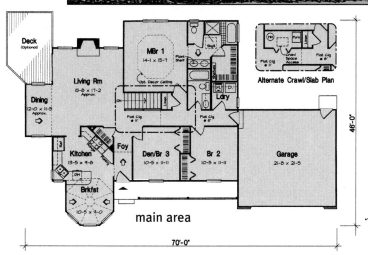

main area

Deck (Optional)

Living Rm 15-8 x 17-2 Approx.

Dining 12-0 x 11-5 Approx.

Kitchen 13-5 x 9-8

Foy

Brkfst 10-5 x 9-0

Den/Br 3 10-5 x 11-11

Br 2 10-5 x 11-11

Garage 21-8 x 21-5

MBr 1 14-1 x 15-7

Ldry

Alternate Crawl/Slab Plan

70'-0"

46'-0"

An EXCLUSIVE DESIGN
By Karl Kreeger

plan info

Main Area	1,583 sq. ft.
Basement	1,573 sq. ft.
Garage	484 sq. ft.
Bedrooms	three
Baths	2(full)
Foundation	bsmt, slab or crawl space

---

total living area: 1,710 sq. ft. Home with Views

B price code

plan no. 24319

The main floor features a living room and dining room split by a fireplace. The kitchen flows into the dining room and is gracefully separated by a bar. There is a bedroom and a full bath on the main floor. The second floor has a bedroom or library loft, with clerestory windows, which opens above the living room. The master bedroom and bath are also on the top floor. The lower floor has a large recreation room with a whirlpool tub and a bar.

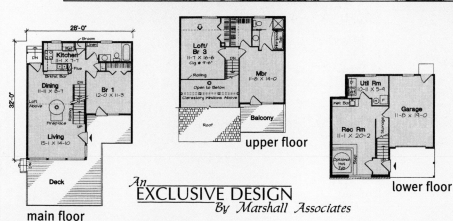

28'-0"

32'-0"

Kitchen 11-4 x 7-7

Brkfst Bar

Dining 11-11 x 8-7

Br 1 12-0 x 11-3

Loft Above

Fireplace

Living 15-1 x 14-10

Deck

main floor

Loft/ Br 3 11-7 x 16-6 Clg @ 9'-6"

Mbr 11-8 x 14-0

Open to Below Clerestory Windows Above

Balcony

Roof

upper floor

Util Rm 10-11 X 5-9

Wet Bar

Rec Rm 11-1 x 20-2

Garage 11-8 x 19-0

Storage

Optional Hot Tub

lower floor

An EXCLUSIVE DESIGN
By Marshall Associates

plan info

Main Flr.	728 sq. ft.
Upper Flr.	573 sq. ft.
Lower Flr.	409 sq. ft.
Garage	244 sq. ft.
Bedrooms	three
Baths	2(full)
Foundation	basement

Easy Living

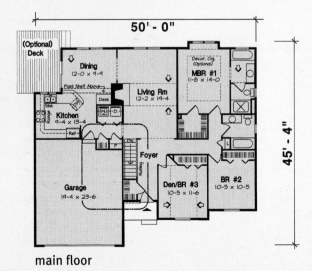

50' - 0"

(Optional) Deck

Dining
12-0 x 9-9

Plant Shelf Above

Kitchen
9-4 x 13-4

Ref.

Decor. Clg. (Optional)

MBR #1
11-8 x 14-0

Living Rm
12-2 x 19-4

Desk

Foyer

Garage
19-4 x 23-6

DN

Den/BR #3
10-5 x 11-6

BR #2
10-5 x 10-5

45' - 4"

main floor

Garage

Furn

Crawl Space Access

slab/crawl
space option

Here's a pretty, one-level home designed for carefree living. The central foyer divides active and quiet areas. Step back to a fireplaced living room with dramatic, towering ceilings and a panoramic view of the backyard. The adjoining dining room features a sloping ceiling crowned by a plant shelf, and sliders to an outdoor deck. Just across the counter, a handy, U-shaped kitchen features abundant cabinets, a window over the sink overlooking the deck, and a walk-in pantry. You'll find three bedrooms tucked off the foyer. The front bedrooms share a handy full bath, but the master suite boasts its own private bath with both shower and tub, a room-sized walk-in closet and a bump-out window that adds light and space.

plan info

Main Floor	1,456 sq. ft.
Basement	1,448 sq. ft.
Garage	452 sq. ft.
Bedrooms	three
Baths	2(full)
Foundation	bsmt, slab, or crawl space

An
EXCLUSIVE DESIGN
By Karl Kreeger

total living area: 1,737 sq. ft. Stacked Windows

An EXCLUSIVE DESIGN
By Karl Kreeger

main floor

B price code

plan no. 20100

S tacked windows fill the wall in the front bedroom of this one-level home, creating an attractive facade and a sunny atmosphere inside. Around the corner, two more bedrooms and two full baths complete the bedroom wing, set apart for bedtime quiet. Notice the elegant vaulted ceiling in the master bedroom. Look at the high, sloping ceilings in the fireplaced living room, the sliders that unite the breakfast room and kitchen with an adjoining deck, and the vaulted ceilings in the formal dining room off the foyer.

plan info	
Main Flr.	1,737 sq. ft.
Basement	1,727 sq. ft.
Garage	484 sq. ft.
Bedrooms	three
Baths	2(full)
Foundation	bsmt, slab, or crawl space

---

total living area: 1,237 sq. ft. Traditional Design

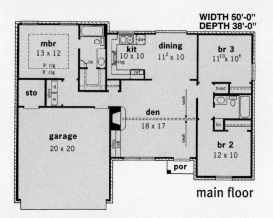

main floor

B price code

plan no. 92502

E ntering the den from the covered front porch, we find a vaulted ceiling with built-in cabinets and a fireplace. The dining room is open to the den creating a Great room feeling for this area. The U-shaped kitchen is adjacent to the dining area and features built-in appliances. The master bedroom is located to the left and rear of the plan and features a large walk-in closet and a private bath. This plan is available with a crawl space or slab foundation. Please specify when ordering.

plan info	
Main Flr.	1,237 sq. ft.
Garage	436 sq. ft.
Bedrooms	three
Baths	2(full)
Foundation	crawl space or slab

10839

Perfect Compact Ranch

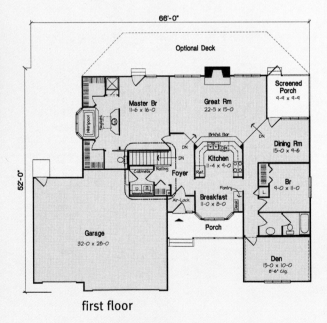

66'-0"

Optional Deck

52'-0"

Master Br
11-6 x 16-0

Great Rm
22-5 x 15-0

Screened Porch
9-9 x 9-9

Brkfst Bar

Kitchen
11-4 x 9-0

Dining Rm
15-0 x 9-6

Foyer

Cabinets Railing

Br
9-0 x 11-0

Pantry

Breakfast
11-0 x 8-0

Air-Lock

Porch

Garage
32-0 x 28-0

Den
15-0 x 10-0
8'-6" Clg.

first floor

crawl/slab option

Crawl Space Access

This Ranch home features a large, sunken Great room, centralized with a cozy fireplace. The master bedroom has an unforgettable bathroom with a super skylight. The huge, three-car plus garage can include a work area for the family carpenter. In the center of this home, a kitchen includes an eating nook for family gatherings. The porch at the rear of the house has easy access from the dining room. One other bedroom and a den, which can easily be converted to a bedroom, are on the opposite side of the house from the master bedroom.

plan info

Main Floor	1,738 sq. ft.
Basement	1,083 sq. ft.
Garage	796 sq. ft.
Bedrooms	two
Baths	2(full)
Foundation	bsmt, slab or crawl space

Country Touch

No. 34601

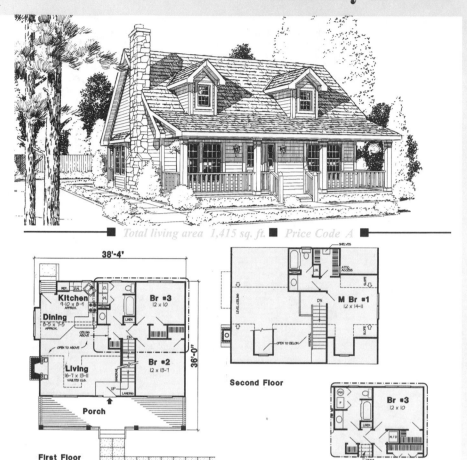

■ **This plan features:**

— Three bedrooms

— Two full baths

■ A large Family Room with a corner fireplace and direct access to the outside

■ Vaulted ceiling in the Living Room which includes a fireplace

■ An efficient Kitchen with double sinks and a peninsula counter that may double as an eating bar

■ Two first floor Bedrooms with ample closet space

■ A second floor Master Suite with sloped ceiling, walk-in closet and private Master Bath

Main floor — 1,007 sq. ft
Second floor — 408 sq. ft.
Basement — 1,007 sq. ft.

■ *Total living area 1,415 sq. ft.* ■ *Price Code A* ■

First Floor

Second Floor

Crawl Space Option

Single Level

No. 24701

■ **This plan features:**

— Three bedrooms

— Two full baths

■ Central Foyer leads to Den/Guest Room with arched window below vaulted ceiling an Living Room accented by two-sided fireplace

■ Efficient, U-shaped Kitchen with peninsula counter/breakfast bar serving Dining Room and adjacent Utility/Pantry

■ Master Suite features large walk-in closet and private Bath with double vanity and whirlpool tub

■ Two additional Bedrooms with ample closet space share a full Bath

Main floor — 408 sq. ft.
Basement — 1,007 sq. ft.
Garage — 455 sq. ft.

■ *Total living area 1,625 sq. ft.* ■ *Price Code B* ■

Main Floor

Alternate Foundation Plan

Skylight Brightens Master Bedroom

■ *Total living area 1,686 sq. ft.* ■ *Price Code B* ■

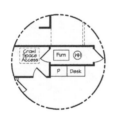

Slab/Crawl Space Option

An
EXCLUSIVE DESIGN
By Karl Kreeger

No. 34029

This plan features:

— Three bedrooms

— Two full baths

- A covered Porch entry

- A Foyer separates the Dining Room from the Breakfast Area and the Kitchen

- The Living Room is enhanced by a vaulted beam ceiling and a fireplace

- The Master Bedroom has a decorative ceiling and a skylight in the Bath

- An optional Deck accessible through sliding doors off the Master Bedroom

Main floor — 1,686 sq. ft.
Basement — 1,676 sq. ft.
Garage — 484 sq. ft.

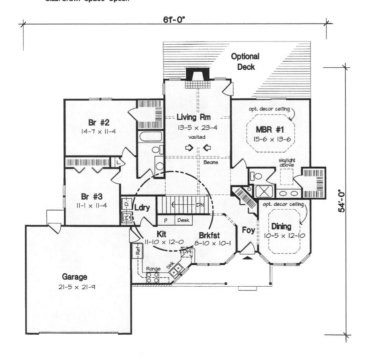

Total living area - 1,560 sq. ft.   ■   Price Code - B

No. 34602

This plan features:

— Three bedrooms

— Two full and one half baths

■ A wrap-around Porch for views and visiting provides access into the Great Room and Dining Area

■ A spacious Great Room with a two-story ceiling and dormer window above a massive fireplace

■ A combination Dining/Kitchen with an island work area and breakfast bar opening to a Great Room

■ The private Master Bedroom has a dormer window, walk-in closet, double vanity Bath and optional Deck with hot tub

First floor — 1,061 sq. ft.
Second floor — 499 sq. ft.
Basement — 1,061 sq. ft.

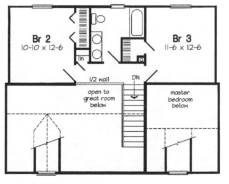

SECOND FLOOR

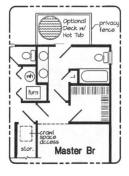

Alternate Foundation Plan

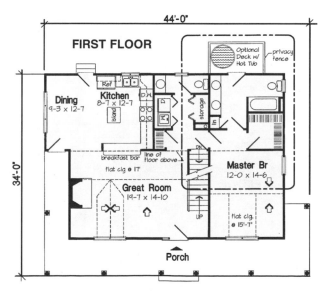

Deck Doubles Outdoor Living Space

■ Total living area 2,352 sq. ft. ■ Price Code E ■

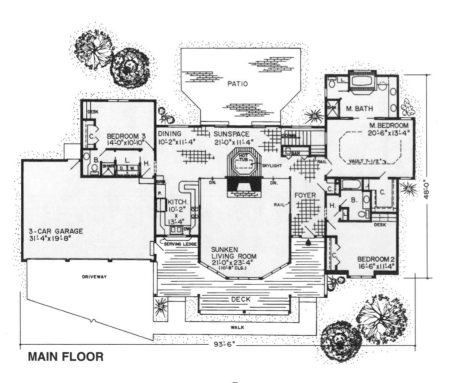

MAIN FLOOR

No. 10619 ✖

■ This plan features:

— Three bedrooms

— Two full and one three-quarter baths

■ A design made for the sun lover with a front Deck and Patio

■ A sunken Living Room with three window walls and a massive fireplace

■ A hot tub with skylight and a vaulted ceiling highlight the Master Suite

Main floor — 2,352 sq. ft.
Basement — 2,352 sq. ft.
Garage — 696 sq. ft.

An EXCLUSIVE DESIGN
By Karl Kreeger

■ *Total living area 1,255 sq. ft.* ■ *Price Code A*

No. 20001

■ **This plan features:**

— Two bedrooms

— One full bath

■ A large Deck with a wood storage bin wraps around the home

■ The Living Room has a sloped ceiling and a corner woodstove

■ The L-shaped Kitchen is fully appointed

■ There are two identically sized Bedrooms on the first floor

■ Upstairs find a Loft with a sloped ceiling

Main Floor — 960 sq. ft.
Upper Floor — 295 sq. ft.
Deck — 422 sq. ft.

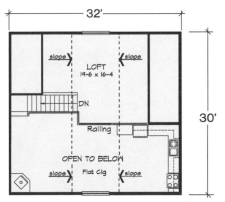

LOFT FLOOR

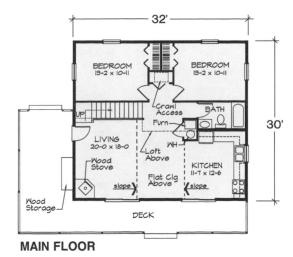

MAIN FLOOR

Convenient Single-Level

No. 84056

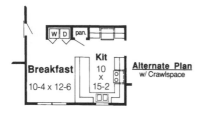

Breakfast
10-4 x 12-6

Kit
10
x
15-2

Alternate Plan
w/ Crawlspace

52'-0"

Optional Garage
24 x 24

Dining/Living
25-8 x 15

Br 1
12 x 15-10

32'-0"

DN

pan.

W D

linen

Breakfast
10 x 12-6

Kit
10
x
12-6

Entry

Br 2
10-8 x 11-8

Br 3
12 x 11-8

MAIN FLOOR

This plan features:

— Three bedrooms

— Two full baths

A well-appointed U-shaped Kitchen that includes a view of the front yard and a built-in Pantry

An expansive Great Room with direct access to the rear yard, expanding the living space

A Master Bedroom equipped with two closets, one a walk-in, and a private Bath

Two additional Bedrooms that share a full hall Bath

A step-saving, centrally located Laundry Center

No materials list is available for this plan

Main floor — 1,644 sq. ft.
Garage — 576 sq. ft.

Home on a Hill

This plan features:

— Two bedrooms

— One full and one three-quarter baths

— Sweeping panels of glass and a wood stove, creating atmosphere for the Great Room

— An open plan that draws the Kitchen into the warmth of the Great Room's wood stove

— A sleeping Loft that has a full bath all to itself

Main floor — 988 sq. ft.
Upper floor — 366 sq. ft.
Basement — 742 sq. ft.
Garage — 283 sq. ft.

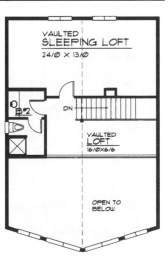

UPPER FLOOR PLAN

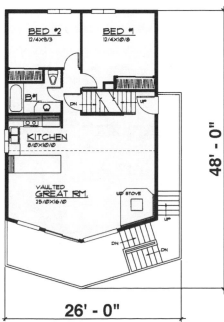

MAIN FLOOR PLAN

L-Shaped Bungalow With Two Porches

■ *Total living area 1,950 sq. ft.* ■ *Price Code C* ■

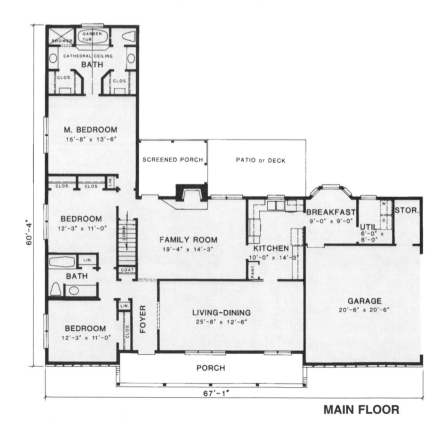

MAIN FLOOR

No. 90407

■ **This plan features:**

— Three bedrooms

— Two full baths

■ A Master Suite with a lavish Master Bath including a garden tub, shower, his-n-her vanities and separate walk-in closets

■ Two additional Bedrooms have ample closet space and share a full hall Bath

■ The large Family Room is accentuated by a fireplace

■ The U-shaped Kitchen has a built-in Pantry, a double sink and ample storage and counter space

■ A sunny, bay Breakfast Nook for informal eating

■ An optional basement, slab or crawl space foundation — please specify when ordering

Main floor — 1,950 sq. ft.

■ *Total living area 2,957 sq. ft.* ■ *Price Code G* ■

No. 94261

■ **This plan features:**

— Three bedrooms

— Three full and one half baths

■ The open Living and Dining Areas are defined by French doors

■ The Kitchen has a center island and a walk-in Pantry

■ The Master Suite is located for the maximum in privacy

■ Upstairs find two luxurious Guest Rooms each with a private Bath and Sun Deck

■ Also upstairs is a Gallery Loft and a Computer Loft, which overlooks the Grand Room

■ The lower floor features a two-car Garage and plenty of storage space

■ No materials list is available for this plan

Main floor — 1,642 sq. ft.
Upper floor — 1,165 sq. ft.
Lower floor — 150 sq. ft.

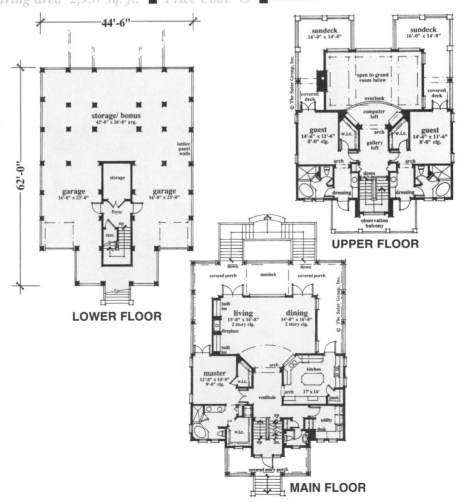

Cathedral Ceiling Enlarges Great Room

© 1996 Donald A Gardner Architects, Inc.

■ Total living area 1,699 sq. ft. ■ Price Code D ■

This plan features:

— Three bedrooms

— Two full baths

— Two dormers add volume to the Foyer

— Great Room, topped by a cathedral ceiling, is open to the Kitchen and Breakfast Area

— Accentuating columns define the Foyer, Great Room, Kitchen and Breakfast Area

— The private Master Suite is crowned by a tray ceiling and highlighted by a skylit Bath

— The front Bedroom is topped by a tray ceiling

Main floor — 1,699 sq. ft.
Bonus — 336 sq. ft.
Garage — 498 sq. ft.

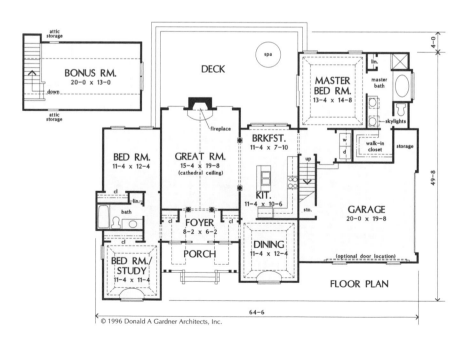

© 1996 Donald A Gardner Architects, Inc.

Inexpensive Ranch Design

■ Total living area 1,500 sq. ft. ■ Price Code A

No. 20062

This plan features:

— Three bedrooms

— Two full baths

■ A large picture window brightening the Breakfast Area

■ A well planned Kitchen

■ The Living Room is accented by an open beam across the sloping ceiling and fireplace

■ The Master Bedroom has an extremely large Bath area

Main floor — 1,500 sq. ft.
Basement — 1,500 sq. ft.
Garage — 482 sq. ft.

An *EXCLUSIVE DESIGN*
By Karl Kreeger

DECK

M. BEDROOM
15'-4" X 13'-4"

LIVING RM.
14'-0" X 20'-0"

DINING
10'-6" X 10'-0"

KIT.
12'-0" X 12'-0"

BRKFST.

DOWN

BEDROOM 2
10'-0" X 11'-0"

BEDROOM 3
10'-0" X 11'-0"

FOYER

GARAGE
19'-4" X 20'-4"

44'-4"

49'-8"

MAIN FLOOR

Ranch Provides Great Kitchen Area

■ *Total living area 1,400 sq. ft.* ■ *Price Code A* ■

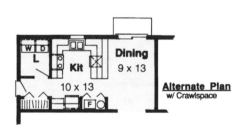

Dining
9 x 13

Kit
10 x 13

W D
L

Alternate Plan
w/ Crawlspace

F

No. 34054

■ **This plan features:**

— Three bedrooms

— Two full baths

■ A Dining Room with sliding glass doors to the backyard

■ Access to the Garage through the Laundry Room

■ The Master Bedroom has a private full Bath

■ Two-car Garage

Main floor — 1,400 sq. ft.
Basement — 1,400 sq. ft.
Garage — 528 sq. ft.

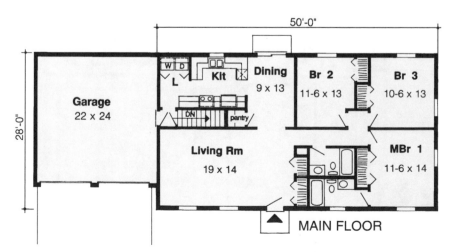

50'-0"

28'-0"

Garage
22 x 24

W D
L

Kit

Dining
9 x 13

Br 2
11-6 x 13

Br 3
10-6 x 13

DN

pantry

Living Rm
19 x 14

MBr 1
11-6 x 14

MAIN FLOOR

Vacation In Style

■ *Total living area 1,600 sq. ft.* ■ *Price Code B* ■

No. 92803

■ **This plan features:**

— Four bedrooms

— Two full baths

■ A long wooden Deck and a Screened Porch provide outdoor living space

■ An expansive Great Room/Dining Area with a fireplace, and windows on three sides

■ An efficient Kitchen with ample storage space and an open counter that separates it from the Dining Area

■ The Master Bedroom has windows on two sides and a walk-in closet adjacent to a full hall Bath

■ An optional post, crawl space, or slab foundation — please specify when ordering

Main floor — 1,600 sq. ft.

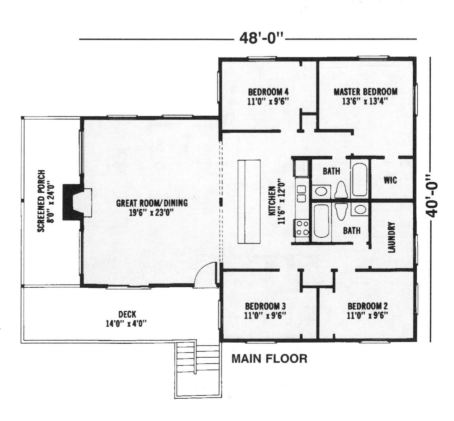

MAIN FLOOR

Multi-Level View

■ *Total living area 1,871 sq. ft.* ■ *Price Code C* ■

An
EXCLUSIVE DESIGN
By Marshall Associates

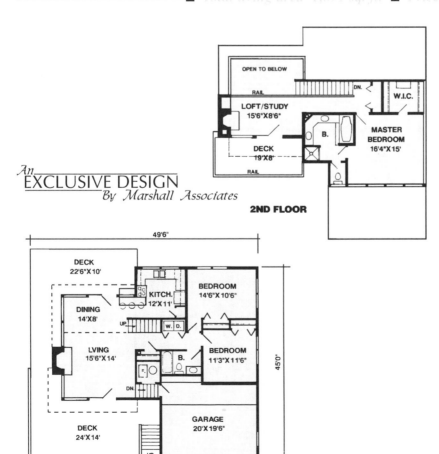

No. 94301

This plan features:

— Three bedrooms

— Two full baths

■ A Deck surrounding three sides to expand living outdoors

■ A cozy fireplace surrounded by windows in Living/Dining Area

■ An efficient, U-shaped Kitchen with an eating bar

■ Two first floor Bedrooms share a full Bath

■ A spacious Master Bedroom on the second floor has a walk-in closet, a plush Bath with raised tub and a double vanity

■ A Loft/Study with a second fireplace and private Deck

■ No materials list is available for this plan

First floor — 1,145 sq. ft.
Second floor — 726 sq. ft.
Garage — 433 sq. ft.

Solar Room More Than Just a Greenhouse

■ *Total living area 1,732 sq. ft.* ■ *Price Code B*

This plan features:

— Three bedrooms

— Two full baths

A passive design that will save on heating costs

A heat-circulating fireplace in the Living Room adds atmosphere and warmth

A Master Suite with lofty views of the living area

Two additional Bedrooms with ample closet space share a full hall Bath

First floor — 1,242 sq. ft.
Second floor — 490 sq. ft.

SECOND FLOOR

FIRST FLOOR

European Flavor

■ *Total living area 1,779 sq. ft.* ■ *Price Code C* ■

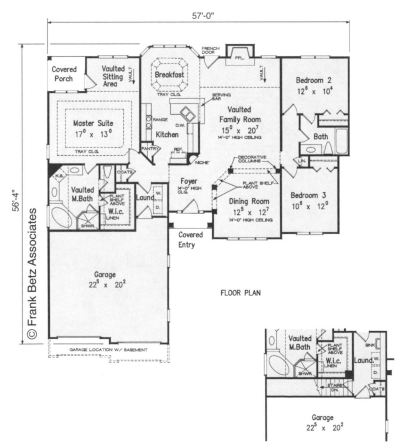

57'-0"

56'-4"

© Frank Betz Associates

Covered Porch

Vaulted Sitting Area

VAULT

Breakfast
TRAY CLG.

FRENCH DOOR

FPL

VAULT

Master Suite
17⁰ x 13⁰
TRAY CLG.

RANGE

D.W.

Kitchen

SERVING BAR

Vaulted Family Room
15⁰ x 20⁷
14'-0" HIGH CEILING

Bedroom 2
12⁶ x 10⁴

PANTRY

REF.

NICHE

DECORATIVE COLUMNS

Bath

K.S.

Vaulted M.Bath

PLANT SHELF ABOVE

W.i.c.

LINEN

SHWR

COATS

Laund.

W.

D.

Foyer
14'-0" HIGH CLG.

PLANT SHELF ABOVE

Dining Room
12⁵ x 12⁷
14'-0" HIGH CEILING

LIN.

Bedroom 3
10⁶ x 12⁰

Covered Entry

Garage
22⁵ x 20²

FLOOR PLAN

GARAGE LOCATION W./ BASEMENT

Vaulted M.Bath

PLANT SHELF ABOVE

SINK

W.i.c.

LINEN

Laund.

W.

D.

SHWR

STAIRS DN.

COATS

Garage
22⁵ x 20²

OPT. BASEMENT STAIR LOCATION

No. 98464

■ This plan features:

— Three bedrooms

— Two full baths

■ A covered entry reveals a Foyer inside with a fourteen-foot ceiling

■ The Family Room has a vaulted ceiling and a fireplace

■ The Kitchen has every imaginable convenience including a walk-in Pantry

■ The Dining Room is defined by columns

■ The Master Suite has a tray ceiling and a private Bath

■ No materials list available for this plan

■ An optional basement or crawl space foundation — please specify when ordering

Main floor — 1,779 sq. ft.
Basement — 1,818 sq. ft.
Garage — 499 sq. ft.

Windows Add Warmth To All Living Areas

■ *Total living area 1,672 sq. ft.* ■ *Price Code B* ■

No. 34011

■ This plan features:

— Three bedrooms

— Two full baths

■ A Master Suite with huge his-n-her walk-in closets and a private Bath

■ A second and third Bedroom with ample closet space

■ A Kitchen equipped with an island counter, and flowing easily into the Dining and Family rooms

■ A Laundry Room conveniently located near all three Bedrooms

■ A two-car Garage

Main area — 1,672 sq. ft.
Garage — 566 sq. ft.

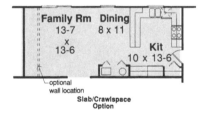

Family Rm
13-7
x
13-6

Dining
8 x 11

Kit
10 x 13-6

optional wall location

Slab/Crawlspace Option

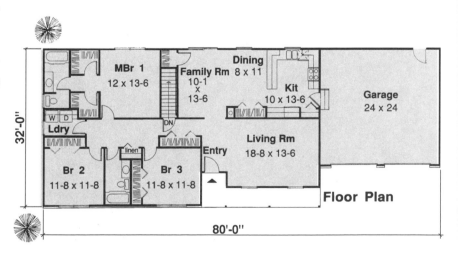

MBr 1
12 x 13-6

Family Rm
10-1
x
13-6

Dining
8 x 11

Kit
10 x 13-6

Garage
24 x 24

W D

Ldry

DN

Living Rm
18-8 x 13-6

linen

Entry

Br 2
11-8 x 11-8

Br 3
11-8 x 11-8

32'-0"

80'-0"

Floor Plan

Angled for Views

■ *Total living area 2,051 sq. ft.* ■ *Price Code C* ■

No. 9107

■ **This plan features:**

— Four bedrooms

— Two full baths

■ A large Foyer leads into the Living Room, the Family Room and the Kitchen

■ The spacious Living Room has large windows and a sliding glass door to the Balcony

■ The efficient, U-shaped Kitchen has a laundry area and eating space

■ The Master Bedroom has an oversized closet and a vanity Bath

■ Two additional bedrooms with ample closets share a full hall Bath

Main Floor — 2,051 sq. ft.
Basement — 1,380 sq. ft.
Garage — 671 sq. ft.

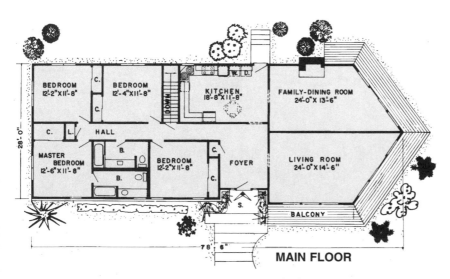

MAIN FLOOR

© 1996 Donald A. Gardner Architects, Inc.

B. NATHAN

■ *Total living area 1,685 sq. ft.* ■ *Price Code D* ■

No. 99810

■ This plan features:

— Three bedrooms

— Two full baths

■ A Foyer open to the dramatic dormer, defined by columns

■ The Dining Room is augmented by a tray ceiling

■ The Great Room expands into the open Kitchen and Breakfast Room

■ A privately located Master Suite is topped by a tray ceiling

■ Two additional Bedrooms are located at the opposite side of the home from the Master Suite

Main floor — 1,685 sq. ft.
Bonus area — 331 sq. ft.
Garage & storage — 536 sq. ft.

FLOOR PLAN

© 1996 Donald A Gardner Architects, Inc.

Family Favorite

■ *Total living area 1,359 sq. ft.* ■ *Price Code A* ■

No. 20156

■ This plan features:

— Three bedrooms

— Two full baths

■ An open arrangement with the Dining Room that combines with ten-foot ceilings to make the Living Room seem more spacious

■ Glass on three sides of the Dining Room, which overlooks the Deck

■ An efficient, compact Kitchen with a built-in Pantry and peninsula counter

■ The Master Suite has a romantic window seat, a compartmentalized private Bath and a walk-in closet

■ Two additional Bedrooms share a full hall Bath

Main floor — 1,359 sq. ft.
Basement — 1,359 sq. ft.
Garage — 501 sq. ft.

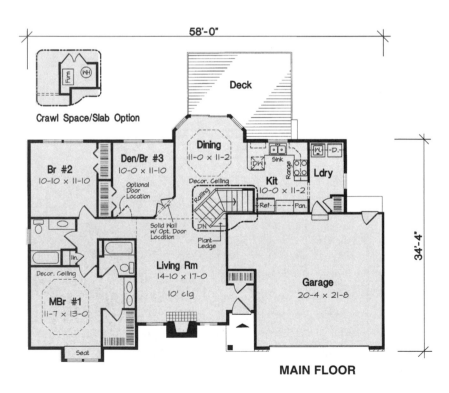

58'-0"

Crawl Space/Slab Option

Deck

Dining
11-0 x 11-2

Br #2
10-10 x 11-10

Den/Br #3
10-0 x 11-10

Optional Door Location

Decor. Ceiling

Sink
DW
Range

Kit
10-0 x 11-2

Ldry
W. D.

Ref.
Pan.

Railing

DN

Plant Ledge

Solid Wall w/ Opt. Door Location

Decor. Ceiling

Lin.

Living Rm
14-10 x 17-0

10' clg

Garage
20-4 x 21-8

MBr #1
11-7 x 13-0

Seat

34'-4"

MAIN FLOOR

An
EXCLUSIVE DESIGN
By Karl Kreeger

© 1997 Donald A. Gardner Architects, Inc.

B. NATHAN

■ *Total living area 1,515 sq. ft.* ■ *Price Code D* ■

No. 99835

■This plan features:

— Three bedrooms

— Two full baths

■ Working at the Kitchen island focuses your view to the Great Room with its vaulted ceiling and a fireplace

■ Clerestory dormers emanate light into the Great Room

■ Both the Dining Room and Master Suite are enhanced by tray ceilings

■ Skylights flood natural light into the Bonus space

■ The private Master Suite has its own Bath and an expansive walk-in closet

Main floor — 1,515 sq. ft.
Bonus — 288 sq. ft.
Garage — 476 sq. ft.

© 1997 Donald A Gardner Architects, Inc.

Ranch with Country Appeal

■ *Total living area 1,539 sq. ft.* ■ *Price Code B* ■

Main area — 1,539 sq. ft.
Basement — 1,530 sq. ft.
Garage — 460 sq. ft.

No. 24721

■ **This plan features:**

— Three bedrooms

— Two full baths

■ A tiled Foyer leads into the Living Room

■ A sloped ceiling tops the Living Room and is further accented by a fireplace

■ There are built-in shelves on either side of the arched opening between the Living Room and the Dining Room

■ An efficient U-shaped Kitchen is highlighted by a breakfast bar

■ A French door accesses the rear Deck from Dining Area

■ The Master Suite is crowned by a decorative ceiling and contains a private whirlpool Bath

■ The roomy secondary Bedrooms share a full hall Bath

■ No materials list is available for this plan

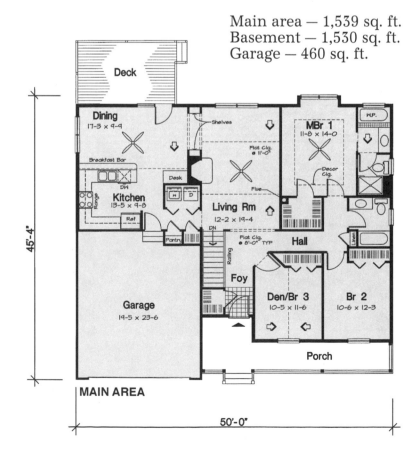

Elegant Window Treatment

■ *Total living area 1,492 sq. ft.* ■ *Price Code A* ■

No. 34150

■ This plan features:

— Two bedrooms (optional third)

— Two full baths

■ An arched window floods the front room with light

■ A homey, well-lit office or Den

■ Compact, efficient use of space

■ The Kitchen has easy access to the Dining Room

■ A fireplaced Living Room with a sloping ceiling and a window wall

■ The Master Bedroom sports a private master bath and a roomy walk-in closet

Main floor — 1,492 sq. ft.
Basement — 1,486 sq. ft.
Garage — 462 sq. ft.

An
EXCLUSIVE DESIGN
By Karl Kreeger

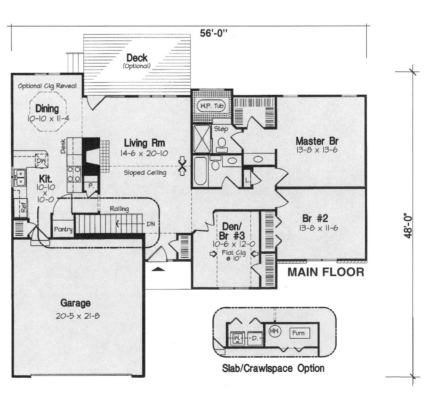

56'-0"

Deck
(Optional)

Optional Clg Reveal

Dining
10-10 x 11-4

W.P. Tub

Step

Master Br
13-8 x 13-6

Desk

Living Rm
14-6 x 20-10

Sloped Ceiling

Kit.
10-10 x 10-0

DW

Ref

P.

Railing

Pantry

DN

Br #2
13-8 x 11-6

Den/
Br #3
10-6 x 12-0

Flat Clg @ 10'

48'-0"

MAIN FLOOR

Garage
20-5 x 21-8

HW

Furn

D.

Slab/Crawlspace Option

A Home For All Seasons

■ *Total living area 2,176 sq. ft.* ■ *Price Code C* ■

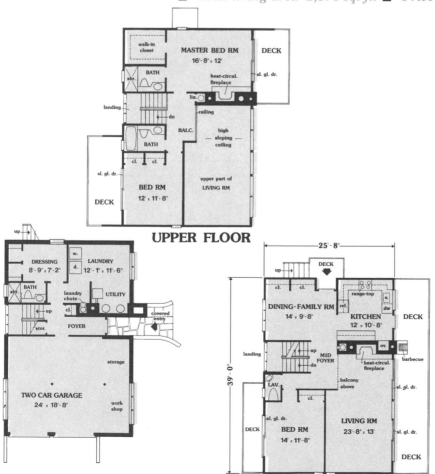

UPPER FLOOR

LOWER FLOOR

MAIN FLOOR

No. 90629

■**This plan features:**

— Three bedrooms

— Three full and one half baths

■All rooms have outdoor Decks

■A Living Room with a heat-circulating fireplace

■A Kitchen with ample counter and cabinet space and easy access to the Dining Room and outdoor dining area

■A Master Bedroom with a heat-circulating fireplace, plush master bath and a walk-in closet

Main floor — 1,001 sq. ft.
Upper floor — 712 sq. ft.
Lower floor — 463 sq. ft.

■ *Total living area 1,575 sq. ft.* ■ *Price Code B* ■

No. 98479

■ **This plan features:**

— Three bedrooms

— Two full and one half baths

■ Foyer, Family Room and Dining Room have 15'8" ceilings

■ Breakfast Room has a vaulted ceiling

■ Arched openings to the Dining Room from the Family Room and Foyer

■ The private Master Suite is enhanced by a tray ceiling and a five-piece Master Bath

■ An optional basement or crawl space — please specify when ordering

■ No materials list is available for this plan

Main floor — 1,575 sq. ft
Basement — 1,612 sq. ft.
Garage — 456 sq. ft.

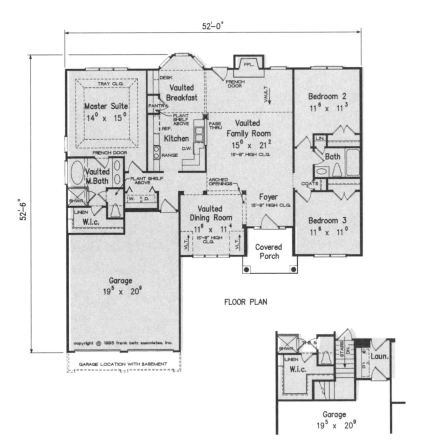

FLOOR PLAN

Opt. Basement Stair Location

Multiple Gables and a Cozy Front Porch

■ *Total living area 1,508 sq. ft.* ■ *Price Code B* ■

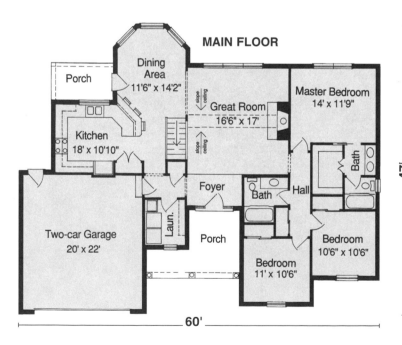

MAIN FLOOR

Porch

Dining Area
11'6" x 14'2"

Kitchen
18' x 10'10"

Great Room
16'6" x 17'

Master Bedroom
14' x 11'9"

Bath

Two-car Garage
20' x 22'

Laun.

Foyer

Bath

Hall

Porch

Bedroom
11' x 10'6"

Bedroom
10'6" x 10'6"

47'

60'

Main floor — 1,508 sq. ft.
Basement — 1,429 sq. ft.
Garage — 440 sq. ft.

No. 92649

■ **This plan features:**

— Three bedrooms

— Two full baths

■ Multiple gables and a cozy front Porch

■ A Foyer Area that leads to a bright and cheery Great Room capped by a sloped ceiling and highlighted by a fireplace

■ The Dining Area includes double hung windows and angles adding light and dimension to the room

■ Kitchen with additional room provided by a breakfast bar

■ The Master Bedroom has a private Bath

■ Two additional Bedrooms share a full Bath in the hall

■ No materials list is available for this plan

Design Features Six Sides

No. 1074

■ This plan features:

— Three bedrooms

— One full and one three-quarter baths

■ Active Living Areas are centrally located between the quiet Bedroom and Bath areas

■ The Living Room can be closed off from the bedroom wings giving privacy to both areas

■ The Kitchen features a breakfast bar for quick meals

■ There is a Bath located behind a third Bedroom

Main floor — 1,040 sq. ft.
Storage — 44 sq. ft.
Deck — 258 sq. ft.
Carport — 230 sq. ft.

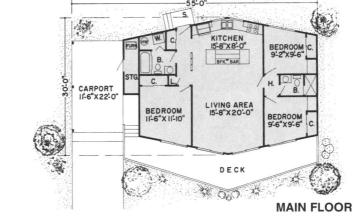

■ Total living area 1,040 sq. ft. ■ Price Code A ■

MAIN FLOOR

Cozy Three-Bedroom

No. 94800

■ This plan features:

— Three bedrooms

— Two full baths

■ Covered entry leads into Activity Room highlighted by a double window and a vaulted ceiling

■ Efficient Kitchen with work island, nearby Laundry and Garage entry, opens to Dining Area with access to Sun Deck

■ Plush Master Bedroom offers a decorative ceiling, walk-in closet and whirlpool tub

■ Two additional Bedrooms, one with a vaulted ceiling, share a full bath

■ Garage with entry into Laundry Room serving as a mud room

■ An optional basement, slab or crawl space foundation — please specify when ordering

Main floor — 1,199 sq. ft.
Basement — 1,199 sq. ft.
Garage — 287 sq. ft.

■ Total living area 1,199 sq. ft. ■ Price Code B ■

ALT. PART FLOOR PLAN
(OMITTING BASEMENT STAIR)

MAIN FLOOR

Cabin in the Woods

■ *Total living area 728 sq. ft.* ■ *Price Code A* ■

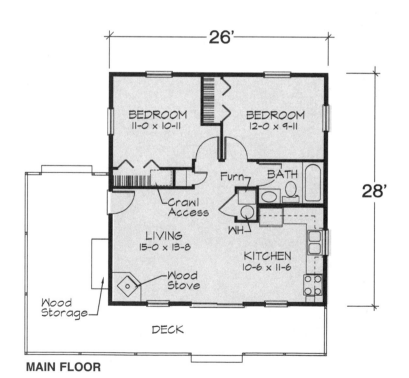

MAIN FLOOR

26'

28'

BEDROOM
11-0 x 10-11

BEDROOM
12-0 x 9-11

Furn.

BATH

Crawl
Access

WH

LIVING
15-0 x 13-8

KITCHEN
10-6 x 11-6

Wood
Stove

Wood
Storage

DECK

No. 20002

■**This plan features:**

— Two bedrooms

— One full bath

■The large Deck has a wood storage bin

■The Living Room is warmed by a woodstove

■The Kitchen is open to the Living Room and is fully appointed

■Two large Bedrooms each have ample closet space

■A full Bath completes this rustic cabin retreat

Main Floor — 728 sq. ft.
Deck — 376 sq. ft.

Open Space Living

■ *Total living area 1,552 sq. ft.* ■ *Price Code B* ■

No. 90844 ⚒

■ This plan features:

— Three bedrooms

— Two full and one half baths

■ A wrap-around Deck provides outdoor living space, ideal for a sloping lot

■ Two-and-a-half story glass wall and two separate atrium doors providing natural light for the Living/Dining Room

■ An efficient galley Kitchen has easy access to the Dining Area

■ The Master Bedroom has a half Bath and ample closet space

■ Another Bedroom on the first floor adjoins a full hall Bath

■ A second floor Bedroom/Studio, with a private Deck, adjacent to a full hall bath and a Loft Area

First floor — 1,086 sq. ft.
Second floor — 466 sq. ft.
Basement — 1,080 sq. ft.

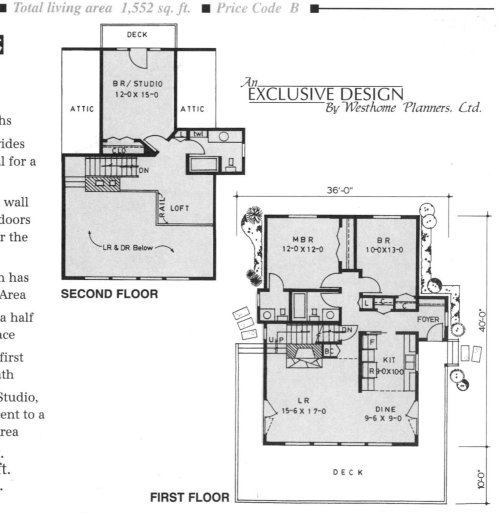

An EXCLUSIVE DESIGN *By Westhome Planners, Ltd.*

SECOND FLOOR

FIRST FLOOR

Country Spirit

■ *Total living area 1,836 sq. ft.* ■ *Price Code C* ■

An
EXCLUSIVE DESIGN
By Marshall Associates

2ND FLOOR

BEDROOM 2
11'X9'6"

W.I.C.

M. BATH

BATH

BEDROOM 3
11'X12'6"

M. BEDROOM
13'6"X15'

OPEN TO BELOW

1ST FLOOR

DINING
12'X11'8"

FAMILY
21'X11'8"

PATIO

KITCHEN
11'X9'8"

FIREPLACE

LIVING RM.
13'6"X15'

UTILITY

PANT.

ENTRY

UP

PORCH

GARAGE
20'6"X21'8"

50'

45'

No. 94313

■ **This plan features:**

— Three bedrooms

— Two full and one half baths

■ An old fashioned wrap-around Porch extending to a large Patio

■ Two-story Entry accented by a curved staircase

■ Formal Living Room enhanced by an open fireplace

■ Expansive Family Area and Dining Area with a glass alcove

■ Efficient Kitchen with a Utility Area and Garage entry

■ Master Bedroom with large walk-in closet, a corner window tub and a double vanity

■ No materials list is available for this plan

First floor — 967 sq. ft.
Second floor — 869 sq. ft.
Basement — 967 sq. ft.
Garage — 462 sq. ft.

Be in Tune with the Elements

No. 24240

■ This plan features:

— Two bedrooms

— Two full baths

■ Cozy front Porch to enjoy three seasons

■ A simple design allowing breezes to flow from front to back, heat to rise to the attic and cool air to settle

■ The Living Room features a fireplace

■ The formal Dining Room is next to the Kitchen

■ The compact Kitchen has a Breakfast Nook and a Pantry

■ The rear entrance has a covered Porch

■ The Master Suite has a private Bath

Main floor — 964 sq. ft.

■ Total living area 964 sq. ft. ■ Price Code A ■

Main Floor

Impressive Two-Sided Fireplace

No. 94972

■ This plan features:

— Three bedrooms

— Two full baths

■ The Foyer directs traffic flow into the Great Room

■ The formal Dining Area offers a view of the fireplace

■ The Kitchen has a large Pantry, a planning desk and a snack bar

■ The Dinette accesses a large screen Porch

■ French doors provide access to the Master Suite topped by a decorative ceiling and highlighted by a pampering Bath

Main floor — 1,580 sq. ft.
Garage — 456 sq. ft.

■ Total living area 1,580 sq. ft. ■ Price Code B ■

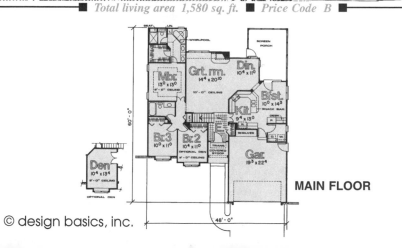

MAIN FLOOR

© design basics, inc.

Three Levels of Living Space

■ *Total living area 2,228 sq. ft.* ■ *Price Code D* ■

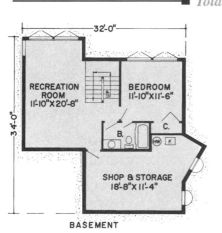

RECREATION ROOM 11'-10"X20'-8"

BEDROOM 11'-10"X11'-6"

B.

C.

HW F.

SHOP & STORAGE 18'-8"X11'-4"

32'-0"

34'-0"

BASEMENT

BALCONY

UPPER LIVING ROOM

LANDING

DN.

MASTER BEDROOM 18'-0" X 11'-6"

DRESSING

B.

WALK-IN CLO.

STOR.

18'-0"

26'-0"

SECOND FLOOR

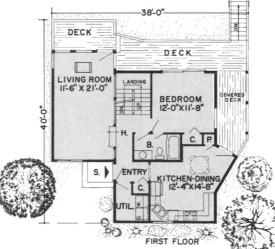

DECK

DECK

LIVING ROOM 11'-6" X 21'-0"

LANDING

DN. UP

BEDROOM 12'-0"X11'-8"

COVERED DECK

H.

B.

C. P.

S.

ENTRY

C.

KITCHEN-DINING 12'-4"X14'-8"

UTIL. W.

38'-0"

40'-0"

DN.

FIRST FLOOR

No. 10396

■ **This plan features:**

— Three bedrooms

— Three baths

■ A passive solar design suitable for vacation or year round living

■ The southern elevation of the home is highlighted by an abundance of Decks

■ The basement level includes a large Shop, Storage and Recreation Area, plus a Bedroom

■ An angled wall lending character to the Kitchen/Dining Area

■ A Master Bedroom occupies the entire second floor and has a private Bath, a walk-in closet and a storage nook

First floor — 886 sq. ft.
Second floor — 456 sq. ft.
Lower level — 886 sq. ft.

Great As A Mountain Retreat

© 1996 Donald A Gardner Architects, Inc.

■ *Total living area 1,912 sq. ft.* ■ *Price Code E* ■

No. 99815

■ This plan features:

— Three bedrooms

— Two full baths

■ Board and batten siding, stone, and stucco combine to give this popular plan a casual feel

■ User friendly Kitchen with huge Pantry for ample storage and island counter

■ Casual family meals in sunny Breakfast Bay; formal gatherings in the columned Dining Area

■ Master Suite is topped by a deep tray ceiling, has a large walk-in closet, an extravagant private Bath and direct access to the back Porch

Main floor — 1,912 sq. ft.
Garage — 580 sq. ft.
Bonus — 398 sq. ft.

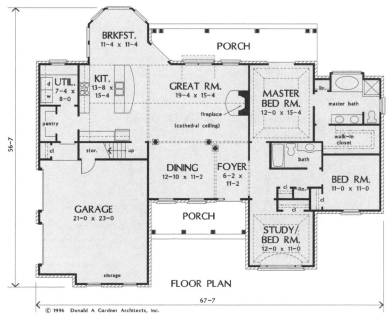

FLOOR PLAN

© 1996 Donald A Gardner Architects, Inc.

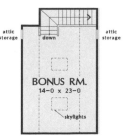

At Home on a Hill

■ *Total living area 1,766 sq. ft.* ■ *Price Code C* ■

An
EXCLUSIVE DESIGN
By Westhome Planners, Ltd.

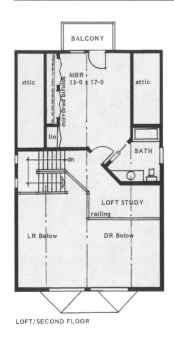

BALCONY

attic

MBR
13-0 x 17-0

attic

mirrored bifolds

lin

BATH

dn

LOFT STUDY
railing

LR Below

DR Below

LOFT/SECOND FLOOR

WIDTH 28'-0"
DEPTH 46'-6"

BR 2
9-6 x 11-0

BR 3
13-6 x 10-0

lin

WIC

D
W

BATH

dn

FOYER

Covered
Entry

dn

up

P

R

F

KITCHEN
13-6 x 10-0

dn

railing

dw

open over

snacks

Heatilator
FP

LIVINGROOM
13-0 x 16-6/19-6

DINING RM
14-0 x 10-0/14-0

SUNDECK

MAIN FLOOR

No. 90869

■ **This plan features:**

— Three bedrooms

— Two full baths

■ A Sun Deck encircles most of the home

■ The Living Room and Dining Room are open to each other and share a bay

■ The Kitchen is well planned and features a snack bar for quick meals

■ The upstairs Master Bedroom has its own Bath and a private balcony

■ Also upstairs, find a loft that overlooks the Living/Dining rooms

■ The basement may be converted to finished space at your leisure

Main Floor — 1,216 sq. ft.
Second Floor — 550 sq. ft.
Basement — 1,228 sq. ft.

Classic Brick with One Floor Living

No. 24709

■ **This plan features:**

— Two bedrooms

— Two full baths

■ The Living Room is enhanced by a triple window and a cozy fireplace

■ The quiet Study, with convenient built-ins and a sloped ceiling, can convert to a third Bedroom

■ The Formal Dining Room is highlighted by a glass alcove and atrium door to the rear yard

■ An efficient, U-shaped Kitchen has a convenient, Garage entry and extended counter/eating bar

■ The corner Master Bedroom has a double vanity Bath

■ The second Bedroom has a large closet and access to a full Bath

■ No materials list is available for this plan

Main area — 1,330 sq. ft.
Garage — 523 sq. ft.

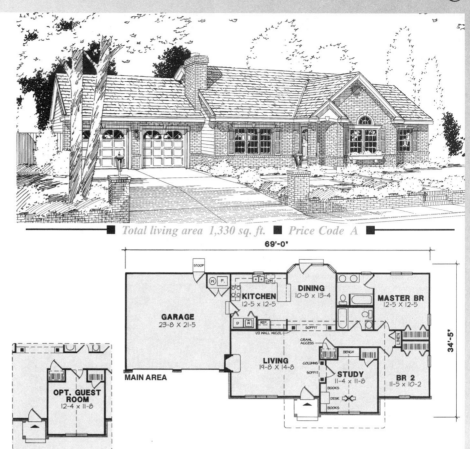

■ *Total living area 1,330 sq. ft.* ■ *Price Code A* ■

Master Retreat Welcomes You Home

No. 34154

■ **This plan features:**

— Three bedrooms

— Two full baths

■ The Foyer opens into a huge Living Room with a fireplace

■ An efficient Kitchen has a Pantry, serving counter, Dining Area, Laundry closet and Garage entry

■ The corner Master Bedroom offers a walk-in closet and a pampering Bath with a raised tub

■ Two more Bedrooms, one with an optional Den, share a full Bath

Main area — 1,486 sq. ft.
Garage — 462 sq. ft.

■ *Total living area 1,486 sq. ft.* ■ *Price Code A* ■

Southwestern Influence

■ *Total living area 1,487 sq. ft.* ■ *Price Code A* ■

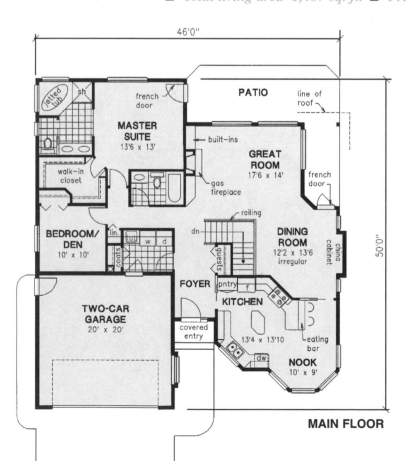

46'0"

50'0"

jetted tub

sh

french door

MASTER SUITE
13'6 x 13'

PATIO

line of roof

built-ins

walk-in closet

GREAT ROOM
17'6 x 14'

french door

gas fireplace

railing

BEDROOM/ DEN
10' x 10'

lin.

dn

guests

DINING ROOM
12'2 x 13'6
irregular

china cabinet

tub

w

d

coats

FOYER

pntry

f

KITCHEN

TWO-CAR GARAGE
20' x 20'

covered entry

13'4 x 13'10

eating bar

dw

NOOK
10' x 9'

MAIN FLOOR

No. 98807

■ This plan features:

— Two bedrooms

— Two full baths

■ A covered entry leads into to a formal Foyer

■ The Great Room is highlighted by a gas fireplace and built-in shelves and flows into the Dining Room

■ The island Kitchen has a built-in Pantry and sunny Eating Nook

■ Master Suite with a French door to the rear Patio and a plush five-piece Bath

Main floor — 1,487 sq. ft.
Basement — 1,480 sq. ft.
Garage — 427 sq. ft.

European Sophistication

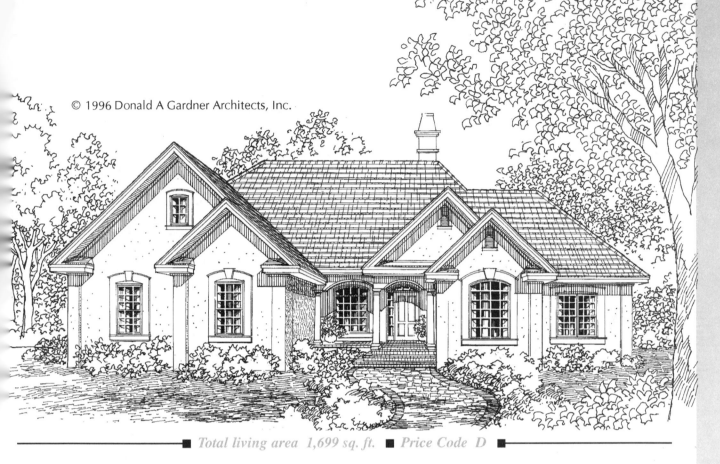

© 1996 Donald A Gardner Architects, Inc.

■ *Total living area 1,699 sq. ft.* ■ *Price Code D* ■

No. 99831

■ **This plan features:**

— Three bedrooms

— Two full baths

■ Keystone arches, gables, and stucco give the exterior European sophistication

■ Large Great Room with fireplace, and U-shaped Kitchen with a large Utility Room nearby

■ Octagonal tray ceiling dresses up the Dining Room

■ Special ceiling treatments include a cathedral ceiling in the Great Room and tray ceilings in the Master and front Bedrooms

■ Indulgent Master Bath with a separate toilet area, a garden tub, a shower and twin vanities

Main floor — 1,699 sq. ft.
Bonus — 386 sq. ft.
Garage — 637 sq. ft.

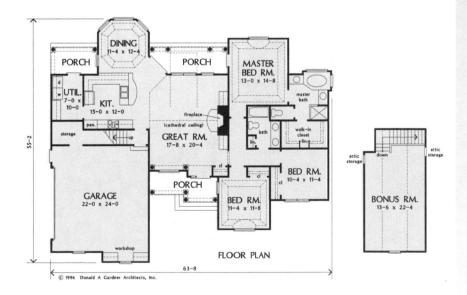

FLOOR PLAN

© 1996 Donald A Gardner Architects, Inc.

Survey the Grand Vista

■ *Total living area 1,951 sq. ft.* ■ *Price Code C* ■

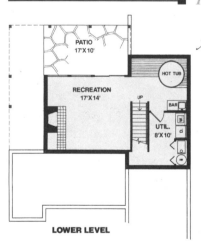

LOWER LEVEL

PATIO
17'X 10'

RECREATION
17'X 14'

HOT TUB

UP

BAR

UTIL.
8'X 10'

W
d

An
EXCLUSIVE DESIGN
By Marshall Associates

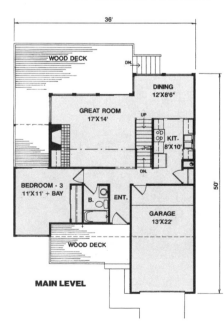

MAIN LEVEL

36'

WOOD DECK

DN.

DINING
12'X8'6"

GREAT ROOM
17'X 14'

UP

KIT.
8'X 10'

DN.

BEDROOM - 3
11'X11' + BAY

B.

ENT.

GARAGE
13'X22'

WOOD DECK

50'

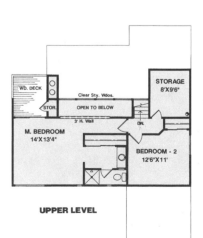

UPPER LEVEL

WD. DECK

STOR.

Clear Sty. Wdos.

OPEN TO BELOW

3' H. Wall

STORAGE
8'X9'6"

DN.

M. BEDROOM
14'X13'4"

BEDROOM - 2
12'6"X11'

No. 94314

■ **This plan features:**

— Three bedrooms

— One full and one three-quarter baths

■ Galley Kitchen serving the Dining Area with ease

■ Great Room enhanced by a fireplace

■ Rear Deck wrapping around the Great Room

■ Master Suite including a private Bath and a private Deck

■ Recreation Room with fireplace and sliding glass doors to Patio

■ The Hot tub and built-in bar add a luxurious flair to the Recreation Room

■ No materials list is available for this plan

Main level — 812 sq. ft.
Upper level — 653 sq. ft.
Lower Level — 486 sq. ft.
Garage — 283 sq. ft.

Perfect for a First Home

No. 92405

■ **This plan features:**

— Three bedrooms

— Two full baths

■ A spacious Master Suite includes a separate Master Bath with a garden tub and shower

■ The Dining Room and Family Room are highlighted by vaulted ceilings

■ An oversized patio is accessible from the Master Suite, Family Room and Breakfast Room

■ The well planned Kitchen measures 12' x 11'

■ No materials list is available for this plan

Main area — 1,564 sq. ft.

Garage & Storage — 476 sq. ft.

■ *Total living area ..... sq. ft.* ■ *Price Code B* ■

MAIN AREA

Appealing Master Suite

No. 92239

■ **This plan features:**

— Three bedrooms

— Two full baths

■ Sheltered Entry into spacious Living Room with a corner fireplace and Patio access

■ Efficient Kitchen with a serving counter for the Dining Area and nearby Utility/Garage entry

■ Private Master Bedroom offers a vaulted ceiling and pampering Bath with two vanities and walk-in closets and a garden window tub

■ Two additional bedrooms with ample closets, share a full Bath

■ No materials list is available for this plan

Main floor — 1,198 sq. ft.

■ *Total living area 1,198 sq. ft.* ■ *Price Code A* ■

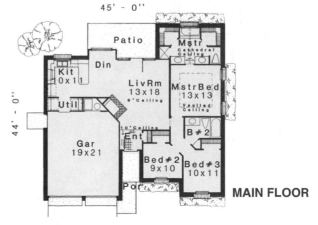

MAIN FLOOR

Clerestory Windows above Window Seat

■ *Total living area 2,624 sq. ft.* ■ *Price Code F* ■

UPPER LEVEL

MAST. BEDRM.
13'-10 X 11'-4"

BEDROOM 2
10'-0" X 11'-4"

LOFT

STUDY
9'-8" X 11'-0"

LIVING ROOM BELOW

JACUZZI

MECHANICAL

LINEN   STOR.

BEDROOM 3
12'-2"X14'-0"

BEDROOM 4
12'-2"X14'-9"

LOWER LEVEL

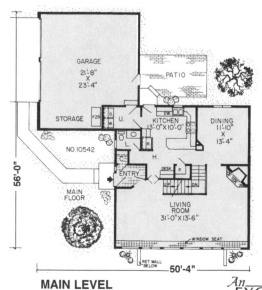

GARAGE
21'-8" X 23'-4"

PATIO

STORAGE

NO. 10542

KITCHEN
13'-0"X10'-0"

DINING
11'-10" X 13'-4"

ENTRY

MAIN FLOOR

LIVING ROOM
31'-0"X13'-6"

WINDOW SEAT

RET. WALL BELOW

56'-0"

50'-4"

MAIN LEVEL

No. 10542

■ **This plan features:**

— Four bedrooms

— Three full and one half baths

■ A tiled Entry leads into a two-story Living Room with a corner fireplace

■ A central Kitchen has a peninsula counter, a double sink, and direct access to the Dining Room

■ The Master Suite has a walk-in closet and a plush Bath with a Jacuzzi

■ On the upper level is a Bedroom, a Study and a Loft

■ Two additional Bedrooms with walk-in closets share a full Bath

Main level — 1,106 sq. ft.
Lower level — 746 sq. ft.
Basement — 296 sq. ft.
Upper level — 772 sq. ft.
Garage — 645 sq. ft.

An
EXCLUSIVE DESIGN
By Karl Kreeger

Cathedral Window Graced by Massive Arch

■ Total living area 1,850 sq. ft. ■ Price Code C ■

No. 20066

■ **This plan features:**

— Three bedrooms

— Two full baths

■ A tiled threshold provides a distinctive entrance

■ The comfortable Living Room has a wood-burning fireplace and tiled hearth

■ The Dining Room has a vaulted ceiling

■ The Kitchen has a central work island, a Pantry, a planning desk and a Breakfast Area

■ The Master Suite has decorative ceilings, a Master Bath and a bow window

Main floor — 1,850 sq. ft.
Basement — 1,850 sq. ft.
Garage — 503 sq. ft.

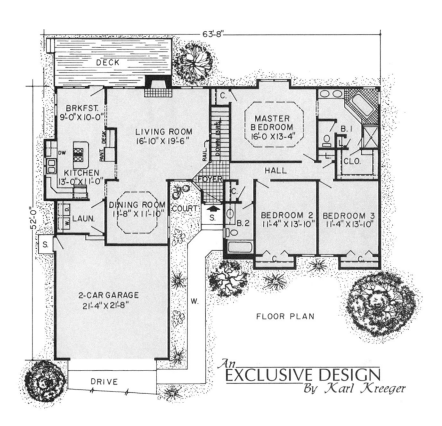

FLOOR PLAN

An EXCLUSIVE DESIGN
By Karl Kreeger

Vaulted Sunken Living Room

■ *Total living area 2,651 sq. ft.* ■ *Price Code F* ■

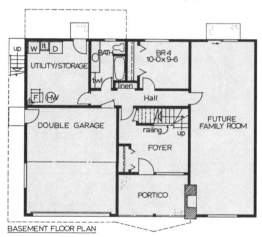

BASEMENT FLOOR PLAN

- UTILITY/STORAGE
- BATH
- BR 4 10-0x9-6
- linen
- DOUBLE GARAGE
- railing
- FUTURE FAMILY ROOM
- FOYER
- PORTICO

MAIN FLOOR PLAN

- Sundeck
- WIDTH=48'-0"
- DEPTH=39'-0"
- KITCHEN 8-6x13-4
- FAMILY ROOM 12-0x13-4
- BR 11-0x9-0
- BR 12-0x9-0
- Hall
- rail
- DR 11-6x10-6
- Sunken LR 14-0x21-0
- vaulted clg.
- MBR 13-6x13-0
- Sundeck

No. 90941

■ This plan features:

— Four bedrooms

— Two full and one three-quarter baths

■ A dramatic, sunken Living Room with a vaulted ceiling, fireplace and glass walls to enjoy the view

■ A well-appointed, Kitchen with a peninsula counter and direct access to the Family Room, Dining Room or the Sun Deck

■ A Master Suite with a walk-in closet and a private full Bath

■ A Family Room with direct access to the rear Sun Deck

Main floor — 1,464 sq. ft.
Basement floor— 1,187 sq. ft.
Garage — 418 sq. ft.

An
EXCLUSIVE DESIGN
By Westhome Planners, Ltd.

Brick Details Add Class

No. 93165

This plan features:

– Three bedrooms

– Two full baths

■ Keystone entrance leads into easy care, tile Entry with plant ledge and convenient closet

■ Expansive Great Room with cathedral ceiling over triple window and a corner gas fireplace

■ Hub Kitchen accented by arches and columns serving Great Room and Dining Area, near Laundry Area and Garage

■ Adjoining Dining Area with large windows, access to rear yard and Screen Porch

■ Private Master Bedroom with a walk-in closet and plush Bath with corner whirlpool tub

■ Two additional Bedrooms share a full Bath

■ No materials list is available for this plan

■ This plan is not to be built within a 20 mile radius of Iowa City, IA

Main floor — 1,472 sq. ft.
Basement — 1,472 sq. ft.
Garage — 424 sq. ft.

■ Total living area 1,472 sq. ft. ■ Price Code A ■

MAIN FLOOR PLAN

Abundance of Closet Space

No. 20204

This plan features:

– Three bedrooms

– Two full baths

■ Roomy walk-in closets in all the Bedrooms

■ The Master Bedroom has a decorative ceiling and a private full Bath

■ The fireplaced Living Room has sloped ceilings and sliders to the Deck

■ The efficient Kitchen has plenty of cupboard space and a Pantry

Main area — 1,532 sq. ft.
Garage — 484 sq. ft.

■ Total living area 1,532 sq. ft. ■ Price Code B ■

An
EXCLUSIVE DESIGN
By Karl Kreeger

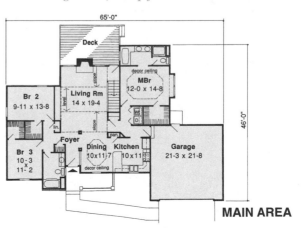

MAIN AREA

For the Young at Heart

■ *Total living area 1,307 sq. ft.* ■ *Price Code A* ■

No. 99324

■ **This plan features:**

— Three bedrooms

— Two full baths

■ Arched transom windows, divided-light windows, bay windows and a covered Porch entry greet you

■ The Great Room has a vaulted ceiling, a fireplace and a transom window

■ The Kitchen has a vaulted ceiling and a Breakfast Area with sliding doors to the Deck

■ The Master Suite has ample closet space and a private full Master Bath

Main floor — 1,307 sq. ft.
Basement — 1,307 sq. ft.
Garage — 374 sq. ft.

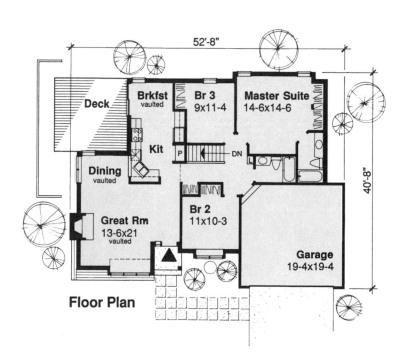

Floor Plan

52'-8"

40'-8"

Deck

Brkfst
vaulted

Br 3
9x11-4

Master Suite
14-6x14-6

Kit

Dining
vaulted

P

DN

Great Rm
13-6x21
vaulted

Br 2
11x10-3

Garage
19-4x19-4

© 1995 Donald A Gardner Architects, Inc.

■ *Total living area 1,417 sq. ft.* ■ *Price Code C* ■

No. 99809

■ This plan features:

— Three bedrooms

— Two full baths

■ Cathedral ceiling expands the Great Room, Dining Room and Kitchen

■ A versatile Bedroom or Study topped by a cathedral ceiling accented by double arched windows

■ Master Suite complete with a cathedral ceiling also includes a Bath with a garden tub, a linen closet and a walk-in closet

Main floor — 1,417 sq. ft.
Garage — 441 sq. ft.

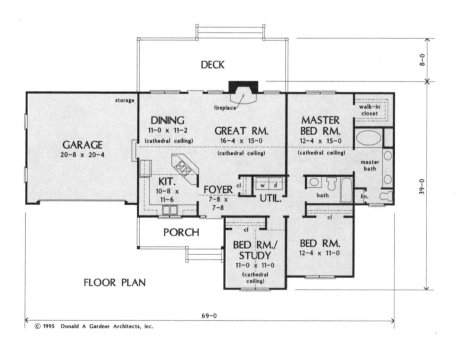

DECK

storage

DINING
11-0 x 11-2
(cathedral ceiling)

GREAT RM.
16-4 x 15-0
(cathedral ceiling)

fireplace

MASTER
BED RM.
12-4 x 15-0
(cathedral ceiling)

walk-in closet

master bath

GARAGE
20-8 x 20-4

KIT.
10-8 x 11-6

FOYER
7-8 x 7-8

UTIL.
w d

cl

bath

lin.

PORCH

cl

BED RM./
STUDY
11-0 x 11-0
(cathedral ceiling)

BED RM.
12-4 x 11-0

cl

8-0

39-0

69-0

FLOOR PLAN

© 1995 Donald A Gardner Architects, Inc.

Country Charm and Convenience

©1995 Donald A. Gardner Architects, Inc.

■ Total living area 1,512 sq. ft. ■ Price Code D ■

No. 96458

■ **This plan features:**

— Three bedrooms

— Two full baths

■ The open design pulls the Great Room, Kitchen and Breakfast Bay into one common area

■ Cathedral ceilings in the Great Room, Master Bedroom and a secondary Bedroom

■ The rear Deck expands the living and entertaining space

■ The Dining Room provides a quiet place for relaxed family dinners

■ Two additional Bedrooms share a full Bath

Main floor — 1,512 sq. ft.
Garage & Storage — 455 sq. ft.

FLOOR PLAN

© 1995 Donald A Gardner Architects, Inc.

Relaxed Style

No. 94985

■ **This plan features:**

— Three bedrooms

— Two full and one half baths

■ A lovely covered Porch fosters the desire to relax and enjoy a cool breeze at the end of the day

■ One Bedroom for an empty nest lifestyle, with an option for two additional Bedrooms in the basement

■ The Kitchen, Breakfast Area and Great Room flow into each other for ease in everyday living

■ A cathedral ceiling tops the Great Room while a fireplace enhances the atmosphere

Main floor — 1,279 sq. ft.
Bonus lower floor — 984 sq. ft.
Garage — 509 sq. ft.

■ *Total living area 1,279 sq. ft.* ■ *Price Code A* ■

MAIN FLOOR

BONUS LOWER FLOOR

© design basics, inc.

Foyer Isolates Bedroom Wing

No. 20087

■ **This plan features:**

— Three bedrooms

— Two full baths

■ A Living Room complete with a window wall that flanks the massive fireplace

■ The Dining Room has recessed ceilings and a pass-through for convenience

■ The Master Suite is tucked behind the two-car garage for maximum noise protection

■ The spacious Kitchen has built-ins and access to the two-car garage

Main floor — 1,568 sq. ft.
Basement — 1,568 sq. ft.
Garage — 484 sq. ft.

■ *Total living area 1,568 sq. ft.* ■ *Price Code B* ■

MAIN FLOOR

An EXCLUSIVE DESIGN *By Karl Kreeger*

Light and Airy

■ *Total living area 1,643 sq. ft.* ■ *Price Code B* ■

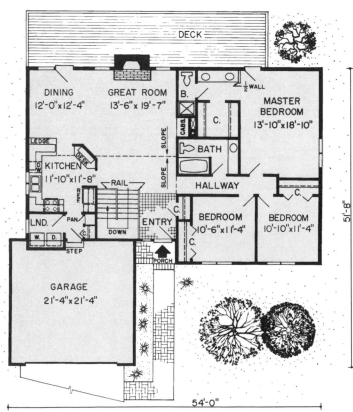

MAIN AREA

No. 10745

■ **This plan features:**

— Three bedrooms

— One full and one three-quarter baths

■ An open plan with cathedral ceilings

■ The fireplaced Great Room flows into the Dining Room

■ The Master Bedroom has a private Master Bath

■ The efficient Kitchen, has a Laundry Area and a Pantry in close proximity

Main area — 1,643 sq. ft.
Basement — 1,643 sq. ft.
Garage — 484 sq. ft.

© design basics inc.

■ *Total living area   1,806 sq. ft.* ■ *Price Code C* ■

No. 99487

■ This plan features:

— Three bedrooms

— Two full baths

■ Ten-foot entry with formal views of the volume Dining Room and Great Room

■ A brick fireplace and arched windows in the Great Room

■ Large island Kitchen with an angled range and a built-in Pantry

■ Master Suite with a whirlpool Bath and a sloped ceiling

■ An optional basement or slab foundation — please specify when ordering

Main floor — 1,806 sq. ft.
Garage — 548 sq. ft.

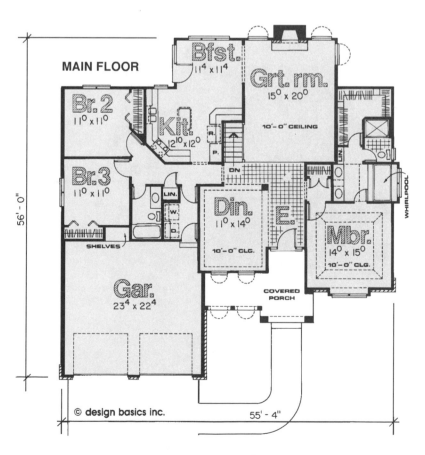

MAIN FLOOR

Bfst.
11⁴ x 11⁴

Grt. rm.
15⁰ x 20⁰
10'- 0" CEILING

Br. 2
11⁰ x 11⁰

Kit.
12¹⁰ x 12⁰

Br. 3
11⁰ x 11⁰

Din.
11⁰ x 14⁰
10'- 0" CLG.

E.

Mbr.
14⁰ x 15⁰
10'- 0" CLG.

WHIRLPOOL

DN

LIN.

SHELVES

Gar.
23⁴ x 22⁴

COVERED PORCH

56' - 0"

55' - 4"

© design basics inc.

Three Bedroom A-Frame

■ *Total living area 1,011 sq. ft.* ■ *Price Code A* ■

An
EXCLUSIVE DESIGN
By Westhome Planners, Ltd.

WIDTH — 32'-0"
DEPTH — 46'-0"

SECOND FLOOR

SUNDECK

french doors

attic MBR
15-0x13-2 attic

← access →

8'-0" clg.

dn railing

LR & DR Below

dn

Bench
Mud Rm
W/D stor.

BR2
10-2x10-0

BR3
9-2x10-2

F

BATH

F R

twl

KITCHEN
8-6x9-0

rail

up

dn

dn

dw

LIVINGROOM
23-0x12-0

DINING

french doors

SUNDECK

FIRST FLOOR

No. 90995

■ **This plan features:**

— Three bedrooms

— One full bath

■ A wrap-around Deck provides panoramic views and access to the Dining/Living Room area through French doors

■ A spacious Living/Dining Area with a glass wall and a vaulted ceiling

■ The well-equipped Kitchen has a serving island and opens to the Dining and Living rooms

■ The Mud Room back entrance has a large closet, a laundry area and a built-in bench

■ The large Master Bedroom has French doors to a private Sun Deck

First floor — 768 sq. ft.
Second floor — 243 sq. ft.

Greek Revival

No. 99610

This plan features:

— Three bedrooms

— Two full baths

■ A large front Porch with pediment and columns

■ A stunning, heat-circulating fireplace is flanked by cabinetry and shelves in the Living Room

■ The formal Dining Room is enhanced by a bay window

■ An efficient, U-shaped Kitchen has a peninsula counter and an informal Dinette Area

■ The Master Suite with a private Master Bath has direct access to the private Terrace

■ Two additional Bedrooms share a full hall Bath

Main floor — 1,528 sq. ft.
Basement — 1,367 sq. ft.
Garage & storage — 494 sq. ft.

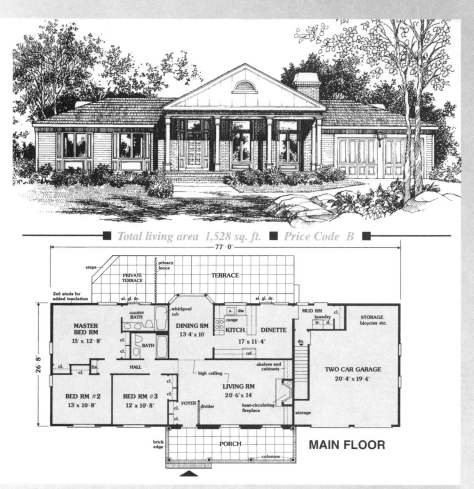

Total living area 1,528 sq. ft. ■ Price Code B

MAIN FLOOR

Two Choices for Courtyard Home

No. 94302

This plan features:

— Three bedrooms

— One full and one three-quarter baths

■ A tiled Entry leads to an open Dining/Living Room area with hearth fireplace and a wall of windows with an atrium door to the Terrace

■ An efficient Kitchen has a corner window and eating bar, and adjoins the Dining Area, Garage and Terrace

■ The Master Bedroom with walk-in closet and private Bath features either a recessed, decorative window or an atrium door to the Terrace

■ No materials list is available for this plan

Main floor — 1,137 sq. ft.
Garage — 390 sq. ft.

Total living area 1,137 sq. ft. ■ Price Code A

An EXCLUSIVE DESIGN
By Marshall Associates

MAIN FLOOR

Enjoy the View

■ *Total living area 2,477 sq. ft.* ■ *Price Code E* ■

PATIO

UP TO DECK

LOWER LEVEL

REC. ROOM
15'-0" x 21'-0"

BEDROOM
11'-0" x 11'-6"

BEDROOM
15'-0" x 11'-0"

C.   C.   C.

BAR

LIN

UP

BATH   UTILITY RM.

BEDROOM
11'-6" x 13'-0"

LOW STORAGE
AREA   E

WH

LOWER FLOOR

An
EXCLUSIVE DESIGN
By Karl Kreeger

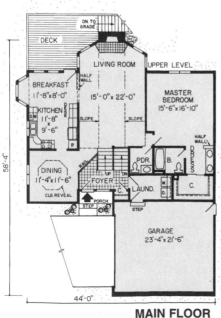

DN. TO GRADE

DECK

LIVING ROOM   UPPER LEVEL

BREAKFAST
11'-8" x 8'-0"   HALF WALL

KITCHEN   15'-0" x 22'-0"
11'-8"
x
9'-6"   SLOPE   SLOPE

P

DINING
11'-4" x 11'-6"

CLG. REVEAL

MASTER BEDROOM
15'-6" x 16'-10"

HALF WALL

PDR.   B.   DRESS.

RAIL   UP   DN
FOYER   LAUND.   W   C.
STEP   D
PORCH
STEP   STEP

GARAGE
23'-4" x 21'-6"

58'-4"

44'-0"

MAIN FLOOR

No. 20095 ⚒

■ This plan features:

— Four bedrooms

— Two full and one half baths

■ A huge, fireplaced Recreation Room has a built-in bar and an adjoining Patio

■ The massive Living Room has sloping ceilings, a tiled fireplace, and a commanding view of the backyard

■ The Breakfast Nook has a sunny bay window and access to an outdoor Deck

■ A convenient Kitchen is just steps away from the formal Dining Room, which features a recessed ceiling

■ The Master Suite has a private Bath and easy access to the living areas of the home

Main floor — 1,448 sq. ft.
Lower floor — 1,029 sq. ft.
Garage — 504 sq. ft.

■ *Total living area 1,247 sq. ft.* ■ *Price Code A* ■

No. 96511

■ This plan features:

— Three bedrooms

— Two full baths

■ A covered front Porch is supported by columns and accented by balusters

■ The Living Room features a cozy fireplace and a ceiling fan

■ The Kitchen is distinguished by an angled serving bar

■ The Dining Room is convenient to the Kitchen and accesses the rear Porch

■ The Master Bedroom has a walk in closet and a private Bath

■ A two car Garage with storage space is located in the rear of the home

Main Floor —1,247 sq. ft.
Garage — 512 sq. ft.

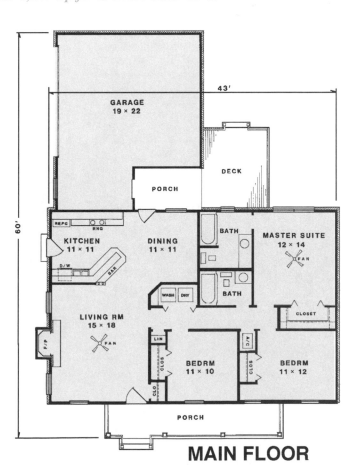

MAIN FLOOR

Central Atrium Highlights Plan

■ *Total living area 2,222 sq. ft.* ■ *Price Code D* ■

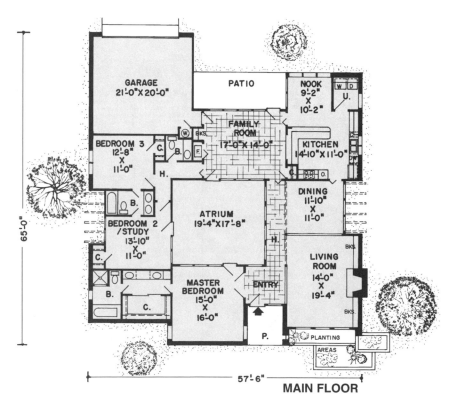

MAIN FLOOR

GARAGE
21'-0"X 20'-0"

PATIO

NOOK
9'-2"
X
10'-2"

W D

U.

BEDROOM 3
12'-8"
X
11'-0"

FAMILY
ROOM
17'-0" X 14'-0"

KITCHEN
14'-10"X11'-0"

BEDROOM 2
/STUDY
13'-10"
X
11'-0"

ATRIUM
19'-4"X17'-8"

DINING
11'-10"
X
11'-0"

MASTER
BEDROOM
15'-0"
X
16'-0"

ENTRY

LIVING
ROOM
14'-0"
X
19'-4"

P.

PLANTING
AREAS

65'-0"

57'-6"

No. 10464

■ **This plan features:**

— Three bedrooms

— Two full and one half baths

■ A tiled entry hall continues into the Family Room

■ A unique Atrium in the center of the home offers outdoor living inside

■ The spacious Living Room has a fireplace flanked by bookcases

■ An efficient Kitchen features a peninsula counter/snackbar dividing the Family Room, Nook and Utility areas

■ The Master Bedroom offers a plush, double vanity Bath

■ Two additional Bedrooms have walk-in closets and private access to a full Bath

Main floor — 2,222 sq. ft.
Garage — 468 sq. ft.

Vacation Retreat or Year Round Living

No. 1078

■ This plan features:

— Two bedrooms

— One full bath

■ A long hallway divides the Bedrooms and living areas assuring privacy

■ A centrally located Utility Room and Bath

■ An open Living/Dining Room area with exposed beams, sloping ceilings and optional fireplace

Main floor — 1,024 sq. ft.
Carport & Storage — 387 sq. ft.
Deck — 411 sq. ft.

■ *Total living area 1,024 sq. ft.* ■ *Price Code A* ■

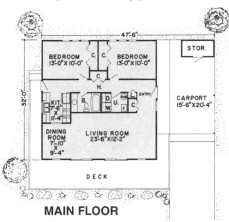

MAIN FLOOR

Well Planned Saltbox

No. 84058

■ This plan features:

— Three bedrooms

— Two full baths

■ An efficient use of living space creates a spacious feeling

■ The Living/Dining Area occupies more than half of the first floor

■ The central chimney accommodates a built-in fireplace

■ An optional Deck

■ No materials list is available for this plan

First floor — 779 sq. ft.
Second floor — 519 sq. ft.

■ *Total living area 1,298* ■ *Price Code A* ■

First Floor

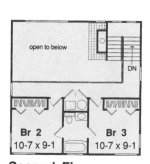

Second Floor

Delightful, Compact Home

■ *Total living area 1,146 sq. ft.* ■ *Price Code A* ■

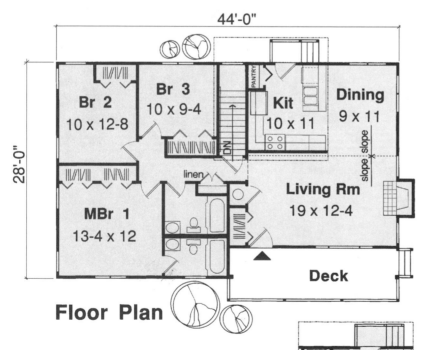

44'-0"

28'-0"

Br 2
10 x 12-8

Br 3
10 x 9-4

Kit
10 x 11

Dining
9 x 11

PANTRY

DN

linen

MBr 1
13-4 x 12

Living Rm
19 x 12-4

slope slope

Deck

Floor Plan

slab/crawlspace option

W

D

No. 34003

■ **This plan features:**

— Three bedrooms

— Two full baths

■ A fireplaced Living Room brightened by a wonderful picture window

■ A counter island featuring double sinks separating the Kitchen and Dining areas

■ The Master Bedroom includes a private Master Bath and double closets

■ Two additional Bedrooms with ample closet space that share a full Bath

Main floor — 1,146 sq. ft.

Carefree Convenience

■ *Total living area 1,600 sq. ft.* ■ *Price Code B* ■

No. 10674

■ This plan features:

— Three bedrooms

— Two full baths

■ A galley Kitchen, centrally-located between the Dining, Breakfast and Living Room areas

■ A huge Family Room which exits onto the Patio

■ A Master Suite with double closets and vanity

Main floor — 1,600 sq. ft.
Garage — 465 sq. ft.

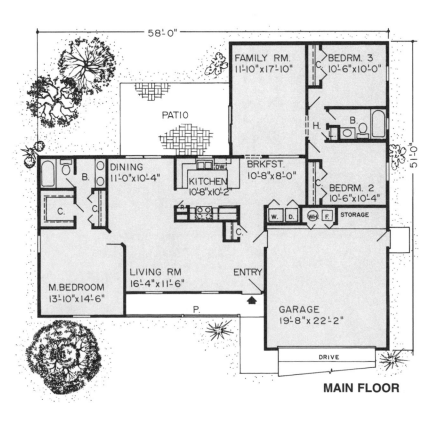

MAIN FLOOR

Delightful Home

■ *Total living area 1,853 sq. ft.* ■ *Price Code C* ■

No. 94248

■ **This plan features:**

— Three bedrooms

— Two full baths

■ Grand Room with a fireplace, vaulted ceiling and double French doors to the rear Deck

■ Kitchen has a large walk-in pantry, island with a sink and dishwasher creating a perfect triangular workspace

■ Dining Room with doors to both decks, has expanses of glass looking out to the rear yard

■ Master Bedroom features a double door entry, private Bath and a morning kitchen

■ No materials list is available for this plan

First floor — 1,342 sq. ft.
Second floor — 511 sq. ft.
Garage — 1,740 sq. ft.

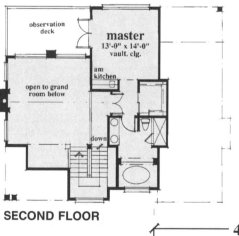

SECOND FLOOR

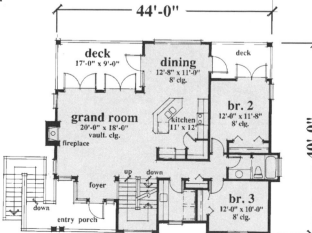

FIRST FLOOR

Compact Design Packs Much In

No. 98804

■ This plan features:

— Three bedrooms

— Two full baths

■ The covered front Porch leads into a Foyer that contains a coat closet

■ The U-shaped Kitchen has it all, including a corner double sink, a Pantry, a desk and a Nook with a bay window

■ Direct access to the formal Dining Room from the Kitchen

■ The Living Room is large and features access to the rear Deck, and an open railed staircase to the Basement

■ The Master Bedroom has double closets, a private Bath, and a French door out to the Deck

■ Two Bedrooms, identical in size, share a Bath in the hall with a skylight above it

■ This home has a Laundry/Utility Room on the way to the two-car Garage

Main floor — 1,372 sq. ft.
Basement — 1,372 sq. ft.
Garage — 484 sq. ft.

An
EXCLUSIVE DESIGN
By Weinmaster Home Design

■ Total living area 1,372 sq. ft. ■ Price Code A ■

MAIN FLOOR

Charming Style

No. 96510

■ This plan features:

— Three bedrooms

— Two full baths

■ A tiled Foyer gives way to a welcoming Living Room highlighted by a cozy fireplace

■ The Living Room and Dining Area adjoin creating the feeling of more space

■ An efficient galley-styled Kitchen has direct access to the Utility Room and the Dining Area

■ A private Master Suite contains a walk-in closet and a private, double vanity Bath

■ Two additional Bedrooms are located in close proximity to a full hall Bath

Main floor — 1,372 sq. ft.
Garage — 465 sq. ft.

■ Total living area 1,372 sq. ft. ■ Price Code A ■

MAIN FLOOR

Deck Surrounds House on Three Sides

■ *Total living area 2,312 sq. ft.* ■ *Price Code E* ■

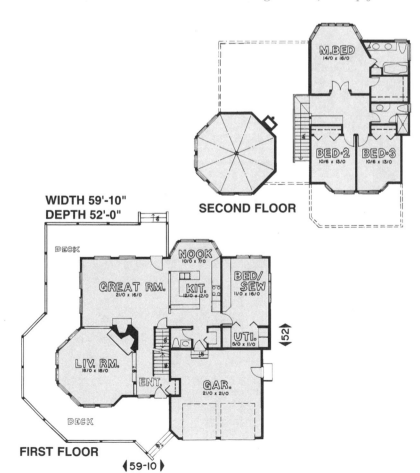

WIDTH 59'-10"
DEPTH 52'-0"

SECOND FLOOR

M.BED
14/0 x 16/0

BED-2
10/6 x 13/0

BED-3
10/6 x 13/0

DECK

NOOK
10/0 x 7/0

GREAT RM.
21/0 x 16/0

KIT.
12/0 x 12/0

BED/
SEW
11/0 x 16/0

LIV. RM.
18/0 x 18/0

ENT.

UTI.
5/0 x 11/0

GAR.
21/0 x 21/0

DECK

52

FIRST FLOOR

59-10

No. 91304

■ This plan features:

— Three bedrooms

— One full bath, one three-quarter and one half bath

■ A sunken, circular Living Room with windows on four sides and a vaulted clerestory for a wide-open feeling

■ Back-to-back fireplaces in the Living Room and the adjoining Great Room

■ A convenient, efficient Kitchen with a sunny Nook

■ A Master Suite with a walk-in closet and a private master Bath

■ Two additional bedrooms that share a full hall Bath

First floor — 1,439 sq. ft.
Second floor — 873 sq. ft.

Versatile Chalet

■ *Total living area 1,360 sq. ft.* ■ *Price Code A* ■

No. 90847 ✄

■ This plan features:

— Two bedrooms

— Two full baths

■ The Sun Deck enters into a spacious Living Room/Dining Room with a fieldstone fireplace, a large window and a sliding glass door

■ A well-appointed Kitchen with extended counter space and easy access to the Dining Room and the Utility Area

■ A first floor Bedroom adjoins a full hall Bath

■ The spacious Master Bedroom has a private Deck, a Bath and plenty of storage

Main floor — 864 sq. ft.
Second floor — 496 sq. ft.
Basement — 864 sq. ft.

An
EXCLUSIVE DESIGN
By Westhome Planners, Ltd.

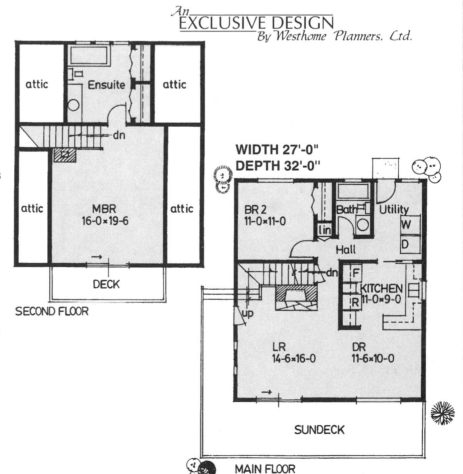

SECOND FLOOR — attic, Ensuite, attic, attic, MBR 16-0×19-6, attic, dn, DECK

WIDTH 27'-0"
DEPTH 32'-0"

MAIN FLOOR — BR 2 11-0×11-0, Bath, Utility, W, D, lin, Hall, dn, F, R, KITCHEN 11-0×9-0, up, LR 14-6×16-0, DR 11-6×10-0, SUNDECK

Classic Ranch

■ *Total living area 1,794 sq. ft.* ■ *Price Code C* ■

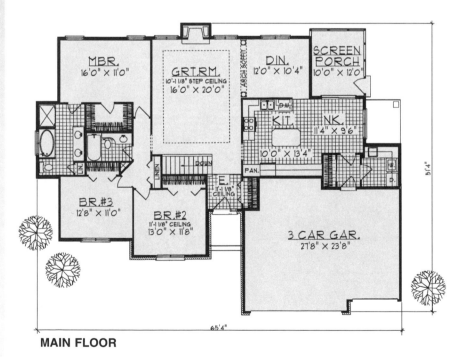

MAIN FLOOR

No. 97108

■ **This plan features:**

— Three bedrooms

— Two full baths

■ A fabulous Great Room with a step ceiling and a cozy fireplace

■ An elegant arched soffit connects the Great Room to the Dining Room

■ The Kitchen has wrap-around counters, a center island and a Nook

■ The Master Bedroom is completed with a walk-in closet, and a private Bath

■ Two additional Bedrooms with ample closet space share a full Bath

■ No materials list is available for this plan

Main floor — 1,794 sq. ft.
Basement — 1,794 sq. ft.

Detailed Ranch Design

No. 90360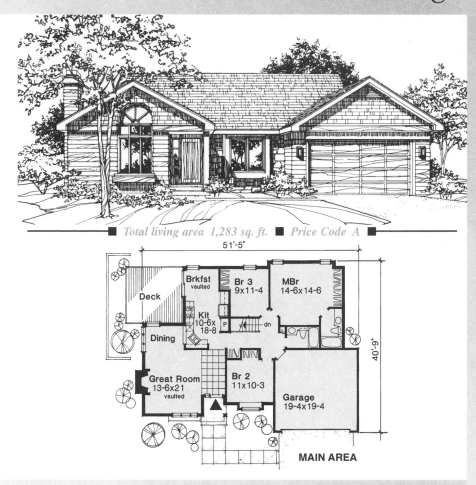

This plan features:

— Three bedrooms

— Two full baths

- The Breakfast Area has a vaulted ceiling and access to the Deck

- An efficient Kitchen has a built-in Pantry and appliances

- The Master Bedroom has a private Bath and ample closet space

- A large Great Room features a vaulted ceiling and cozy fireplace

Main area — 1,283 sq. ft.

■ *Total living area 1,283 sq. ft.* ■ *Price Code A* ■

51'-5"

40'-9"

Deck

Brkfst vaulted

Br 3 9x11-4

MBr 14-6x14-6

Kit 10-6x 18-8

P

dn

Dining

Great Room 13-6x21 vaulted

Br 2 11x10-3

Garage 19-4x19-4

MAIN AREA

Rustic Design Blends into Hillside

No. 10012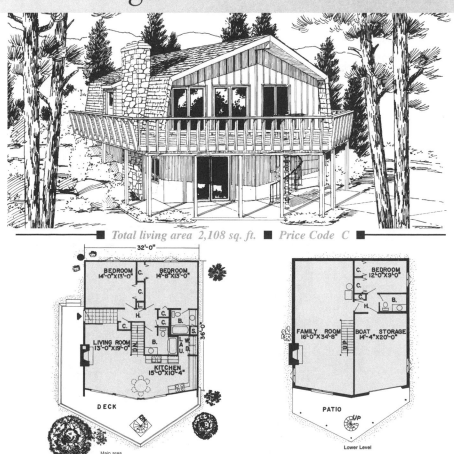

This plan features:

— Three bedrooms

— Two full and one half baths

- A redwood Deck adapts equally to both lake and ocean settings

- The Family Room leads out to a shaded Patio

- Fireplaces in both the Living Room and Family Room

- An open Kitchen with a Laundry Room for maximum convenience

Main area — 1,198 sq. ft.
Lower level — 910 sq. ft.
Garage — 288 sq. ft.

■ *Total living area 2,108 sq. ft.* ■ *Price Code C* ■

32'-0"

BEDROOM 14'-0"X13'-0"

BEDROOM 14'-8"X13'-0"

C.

C.

C.

H.

LIVING ROOM 13'-0"X19'-0"

KITCHEN 15'-0"X10'-4"

L.A.U.

36'

DECK

Main area

BEDROOM 12'-0"X9'-0"

C.

B.

H.

FAMILY ROOM 16'-0"X34'-8"

UP

BOAT STORAGE 14'-4"X20'-0"

PATIO

UP

Lower Level

95

Casual Country Charmer

© 1997 Donald A. Gardner Architects, Inc.   B. NATHAN

■ *Total living area 1,770 sq. ft.* ■ *Price Code D* ■

FLOOR PLAN

© 1997 Donald A Gardner Architects, Inc.

No. 96493

■ This plan features:

— Three bedrooms

— Two full baths

■ Columns and arches frame the front Porch

■ The open floor plan combines the Great Room, Kitchen and Dining Room

■ The Kitchen offers a convenient breakfast bar for meals on the run

■ The Master Suite features a private Bath oasis

■ Secondary Bedrooms share a full Bath with a dual vanity

Main floor — 1,770 sq. ft.
Bonus — 401 sq. ft.
Garage — 630 sq. ft.

Three Porches Offer Outdoor Charm

■ Total living area 1,274 sq. ft. ■ Price Code A ■

No. 90048 ⚒

■ This plan features:

— Three bedrooms

— Two full baths

■ An oversized fireplace in the spacious Living/Dining area which is two stories high with sliding glass doors

■ Three porches offer the maximum in outdoor living space

■ The private Bedroom located on the second floor

■ An efficient Kitchen includes an eating bar and access to the covered Dining Porch

First floor — 974 sq. ft.
Second floor — 300 sq. ft.

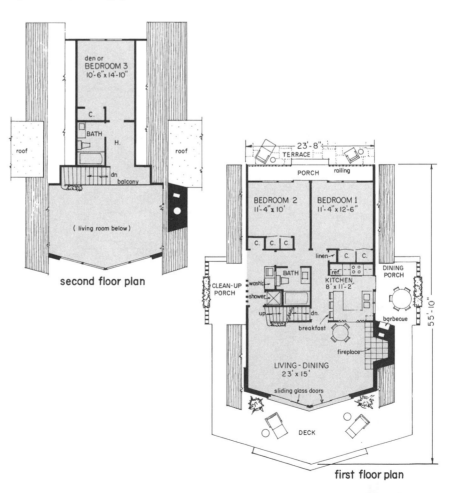

second floor plan

first floor plan

Tandem Garage

■ *Total living area 1,761 sq. ft.* ■ *Price Code C* ■

No. 93133

■ **This plan features:**

— Three bedrooms

— Two full baths

■ Open Foyer leads into the spacious Living Room, which is highlighted by a wall of windows

■ Country-size Kitchen with an efficient, U-shaped counter, a work island and an Eating Nook

■ French doors open to the pampering Master Bedroom with a window alcove, a walk-in closet and a double vanity Bath

■ No materials list is available for this plan

Main floor — 1,761 sq. ft.
Garage — 658 sq. ft.
Basement — 1,761 sq. ft.

MASTER BEDROOM
13'8"x16'4"

LIVING ROOM
15'6"x18'4"

NOOK
10'x11'9"

KITCHEN
10'6"x11'9"

11'x20'

FOYER

DINING ROOM
11'6"x12'4"

3 CAR GARAGE
22'x22'

BEDROOM #2
12'4"x11'9"

BEDROOM #3
13'x10'9"

WIDTH — 67'-8"
DEPTH — 42'-8"

MAIN FLOOR PLAN

Dining in a Greenhouse Bay

No. 90620

■ This plan features:

— Three bedrooms

— Two full baths

■ A covered entrance into the bright Foyer that is highlighted by a skydome

■ The formal Living Room is accented by a heat-circulating fireplace and sliding glass doors to the Terrace

■ The greenhouse Dining Room feels like eating outdoors

■ An efficient Kitchen with a peninsula counter and a bay window Dinette Area is convenient to the Laundry and Garage

■ A comfortable Master Bedroom has a private Bath and walk-in closet

■ Two additional Bedrooms share a full Bath

Main floor — 1,476 sq. ft.
Basement — 1,476 sq. ft.
Garage — 506 sq. ft.
Porch — 70 sq. ft.

Total living area 1,476 sq. ft. ■ *Price Code A*

MAIN FLOOR

Contemporary Living

No. 24305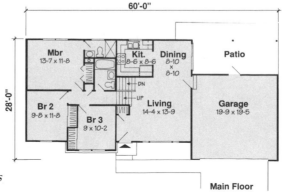

■ This plan features:

— Three bedrooms

— Two full baths

■ This split-level has an open Living Area, so that the Kitchen, Living Room and Dining Room flow into each other

■ A U-shaped Kitchen has a double sink and plenty of storage and counter area

■ The spacious Living Room, has a large multi-paned window offering natural light, and a view of the front yard

■ The Dining Room is convenient to the Kitchen, with direct access to the Patio

■ The Master Suite has a private Bath that includes a step-in shower

■ Two additional Bedrooms share a full hall Bath

Main floor — 984 sq. ft.
Basement — 442 sq. ft.
Garage — 393 sq. ft.

Total living area 984 sq. ft. ■ *Price Code A*

An
EXCLUSIVE DESIGN
By Marshall Associates

99

Sunny Dormer Brightens Foyer

© 1996 Donald A Gardner Architects, Inc.

■ *Total living area 1,386 sq. ft.* ■ *Price Code C* ■

No. 99812

■ This plan features:

— Three bedrooms

— Two full baths

■ Today's comforts with cost effective construction

■ Open Great Room, Dining Room and Kitchen topped by a cathedral ceiling emphasizing spaciousness

■ Adjoining Deck provides extra living or entertaining space

■ The Master Bedroom is crowned by a cathedral ceiling and pampered by a private Bath with a garden tub, a dual vanity and a walk-in closet

■ Skylit Bonus Room above the Garage offers flexibility and opportunity for growth

Main floor — 1,386 sq. ft.
Bonus room — 314 sq. ft.
Garage — 517 sq. ft.

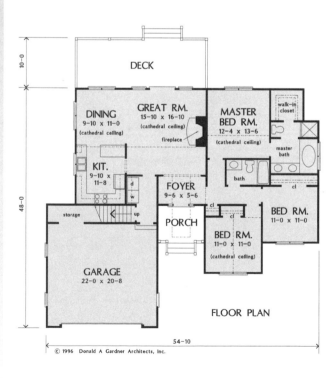

DECK

DINING
9-10 x 11-0
(cathedral ceiling)

GREAT RM.
15-10 x 16-10
(cathedral ceiling)

fireplace

MASTER
BED RM.
12-4 x 13-6
(cathedral ceiling)

walk-in closet

master bath

KIT.
9-10 x 11-8

FOYER
9-6 x 5-6

bath

storage

up

PORCH

BED RM.
11-0 x 11-0

GARAGE
22-0 x 20-8

BED RM.
11-0 x 11-0
(cathedral ceiling)

FLOOR PLAN

54-10

© 1996 Donald A Gardner Architects, Inc.

down

skylights

attic storage

BONUS RM.
12-0 x 20-8
(cathedral ceiling)

Compact Home is Surprisingly Spacious

■ *Total living area 1,314 sq. ft.* ■ *Price Code A* ■

No. 90905 ⚒

■ **This plan features:**

— Three bedrooms

— One full and one three-quarter baths

■ A spacious Living Room warmed by a fireplace

■ The Dining Room flows off the Living Room, with sliding glass doors to the Deck

■ An efficient Kitchen with a snack bar, double sink, and ample cabinet and counter space

■ The Master Suite has a walk-in closet and private full Bath

■ Two additional, roomy Bedrooms have ample closet space

Main area — 1,314 sq. ft.
Basement — 1,488 sq. ft.
Garage — 484 sq. ft.
Width — 50'-0"
Depth — 54'-0"

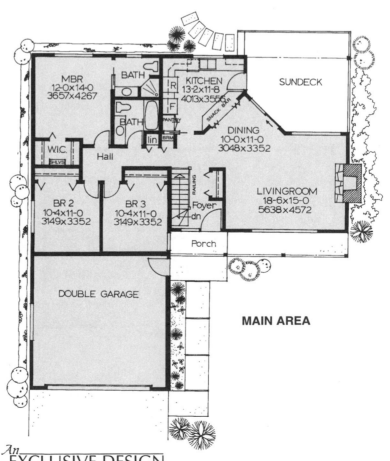

An
EXCLUSIVE DESIGN
By Westhome Planners. Ltd.

Easy Maintenance

■ *Total living area 786 sq. ft.* ■ *Price Code A* ■

No. 94307

■ **This plan features:**

— Two bedrooms

— Two three-quarter baths

■ Abundant glass and a wrap-around Deck to enjoy the outdoors

■ A tiled entrance leads into a large Great Room with a fieldstone fireplace and dining area

■ A compact tiled Kitchen is open to the Great Room and is adjacent to the Utility area

■ Two Bedrooms, one with a private Bath, offer ample closet space

■ No materials list is available for this plan

Main area — 786 sq. ft.

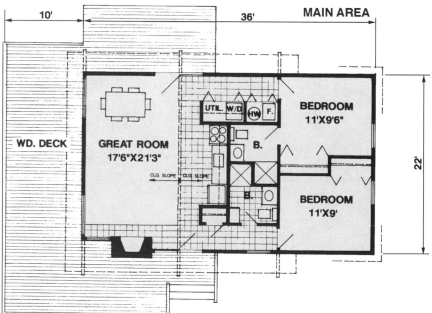

Deck Enlarges and Enhances Cottage

No. 10306

■ **This plan features:**

— One bedroom

— One full bath

■ A large wood Deck for dining, sunbathing or relaxing with friends

■ A one wall Kitchen open to the Living Room, creating simplicity and warmth.

■ A look that is ideal for both beach and mountain enthusiasts

Main floor — 408 sq. ft.

■ Total living area 408 sq. ft. ■ Price Code A ■

An Alpine Retreat

No. 98709

■ **This plan features:**

— Three bedrooms

— One full and one half baths

■ A wrap-around Deck providing views and access to the Living Room and the Dining Area

■ An expansive Living Room with windows on three sides, a hearth fireplace and a Dining Area

■ An efficient Kitchen with ample counter and storage space serving the Dining Area

■ A first level Bedroom with a double closet and private access to the full Bath

■ Two additional bedrooms, one with a private Deck, sharing a half bath

First level — 960 sq. ft.
Second level — 420 sq. ft.

■ Total living area 1,380 sq. ft. ■ Price Code A ■

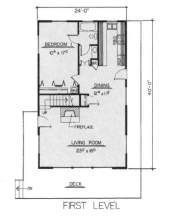

FIRST LEVEL

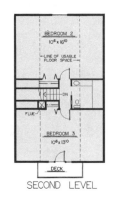

SECOND LEVEL

Clever Design Packs in Plenty of Living Space

■ *Total living area 1,700 sq. ft.* ■ *Price Code B* ■

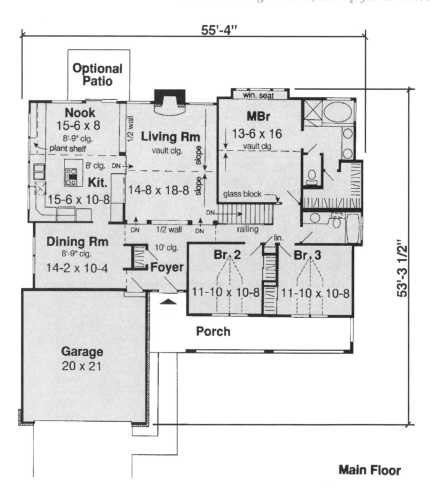

Optional Patio

Nook
15-6 x 8
8'-9" clg.
plant shelf

1/2 wall

Living Rm
vault clg.
slope
slope

8' clg. DN

Kit.
15-6 x 10-8

14-8 x 18-8

win. seat

MBr
13-6 x 16
vault clg

glass block

DN

DN   1/2 wall   DN

railing

Dining Rm
8'-9" clg.
14-2 x 10-4

10' clg.

Foyer

lin.

Br. 2
11-10 x 10-8

Br. 3
11-10 x 10-8

Porch

Garage
20 x 21

55'-4"

53'-3 1/2"

Main Floor

No. 24250

■ **This plan features:**

— Three bedrooms

— Two full baths

■ Custom, volume ceilings

■ A sunken Living Room with a vaulted ceiling, and a fireplace framed by oversized windows

■ A center island and an eating Nook in the Kitchen

■ A formal Dining Room that adjoins the Kitchen, allowing for easy entertaining

■ A spacious Master Suite includes a vaulted ceiling and lavish Bath

■ Secondary Bedrooms with custom ceiling treatments and use of full hall Bath

Main area — 1,700 sq. ft.
Basement — 1,700 sq. ft.
Garage — 462 sq. ft.

An
EXCLUSIVE DESIGN
By Energetic Enterprises

Unique and Desirable

© 1996 Donald A Gardner Architects, Inc.

■ *Total living area 1,977 sq. ft.* ■ *Price Code E* ■

No. 99803

■ This plan features:

— Three bedrooms

— Two full baths

■ Private Master Bedroom has a walk-in closet and a skylit Bath

■ Two additional Bedrooms, one with a possible use as a Study, share a full Bath

■ From the Foyer columns lead into the Great Room with a cathedral ceiling and a fireplace

■ In the rear of the home is a skylit screen Porch and a Deck that features built-in seats and a spa

■ The Kitchen is conveniently located between the Dining Room and the skylit Breakfast Area

■ An optional basement or crawl space foundation — please specify when ordering

Main floor — 1,977 sq. ft.
Bonus room — 430 sq. ft.
Garage & storage — 610 sq. ft.

© 1996 Donald A Gardner Architects, Inc.

Brick Design has Striking Exterior

■ *Total living area 2,280 sq. ft.* ■ *Price Code E* ■

MAIN FLOOR

An
EXCLUSIVE DESIGN
By Karl Kreeger

No. 10549

■ **This plan features:**

— Three bedrooms

— Three full and one half baths

■ A circle-head window that sets off a striking exterior

■ A Master Bedroom including a sloping ceiling, large closet space, and a private Bath with both a tub and shower

■ A Great Room with impressive open-crossed beams and a wood-burning fireplace

■ A Kitchen with access to the Dining Room and Breakfast Room

Main floor — 2,280 sq. ft.
Basement — 2,280 sq. ft.
Garage — 528 sq. ft.

Contemporary Styling

No. 94311

■ This plan features:

— Three bedrooms

— Two full baths

■ Perfect plan for a mountain side or lot with a view

■ Front Deck gives far reaching view of surrounding vistas

■ Cozy fireplace in the Living Room, illuminated by sunlight during the day through a wall of windows

■ Galley Kitchen with access to the rear Deck

■ Two first floor Bedrooms share a full hall Bath

■ Loft overlooks the Living Room

■ The Master Suite has a private Deck, a private Master Bath and a walk-in closet

■ No materials list is available for this plan

First floor — 810 sq. ft.

Second floor — 560 sq. ft.

An EXCLUSIVE DESIGN
By Marshall Associates

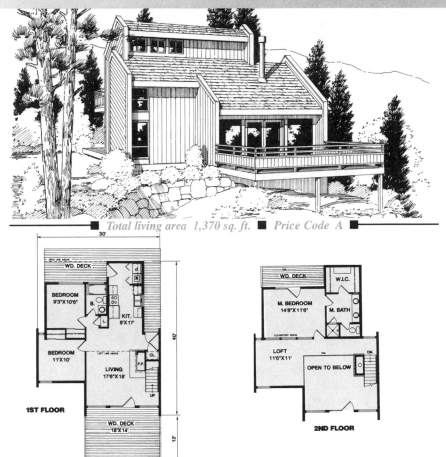

■ Total living area 1,370 sq. ft. ■ Price Code A ■

Brick Abounds

No. 98522

■ This plan features:

— Three bedrooms

— Two full baths

■ The covered front Porch opens into the entry that has a 10-foot ceiling and a coat closet

■ The large Living Room is distinguished by a fireplace and a front window wall

■ The Dining Room features a 10-foot ceiling and access to the rear covered Patio

■ The Kitchen is angled and has a Pantry, and a cooktop island

■ The Master Bedroom is located in the rear for privacy and boasts a triangular walk-in closet, plus a private Bath

■ Two more Bedrooms each have large closets and share a hallway Bath

■ This home has a two-car Garage that is accessed through the Utility Room

■ No materials list is available for this plan

Main floor — 1,528 sq. ft.

Garage — 440 sq. ft.

■ Total living area 1,830 sq. ft. ■ Price Code C ■

Floor Plan

Quaint Starter Home

■ *Total living area 1,050 sq. ft.* ■ *Price Code A* ■

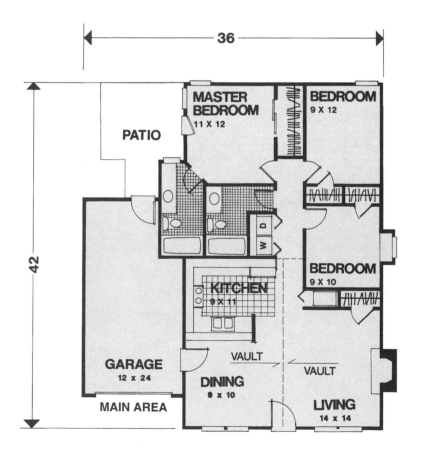

No. 92400

■ **This plan features:**

— Three bedrooms

— Two full baths

■ A vaulted ceiling gives an airy feeling to the Dining and Living rooms

■ A streamlined Kitchen with a comfortable work area, a double sink and ample cabinet space

■ A cozy fireplace in the Living Room

■ A Master Suite with a large closet, French doors leading to the Patio and a private Bath

■ Two additional Bedrooms share a full Bath

■ No materials list is available for this plan

Main area — 1,050 sq. ft.
Garage — 261 sq. ft.

■ *Total living area 1,346 sq. ft.* ■ *Price Code A* ■

No. 98434

■ This plan features:

— Three bedrooms

— Two full baths

■ Vaulted ceiling crowns spacious Living Room highlighted by a fireplace

■ Built-in Pantry and direct access from the Garage add to the conveniences of the Kitchen

■ Walk-in closet and a private five piece bath topped by a vaulted ceiling in the Master Bedroom

■ Proximity to the full Bath in the hall from the secondary Bedrooms

■ An optional basement, slab or crawl space foundation available — please specify when ordering

Main floor — 1,346 sq. ft.
Basement — 1,358 sq. ft.
Garage — 395 sq. ft.

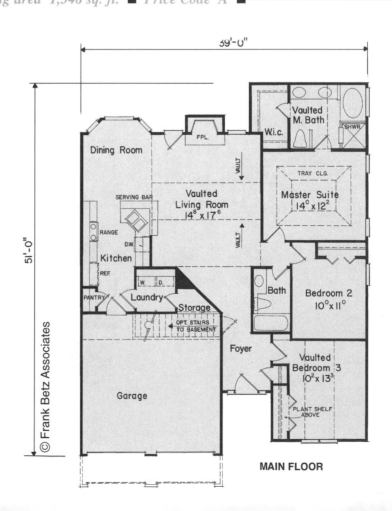

MAIN FLOOR

109

Classic and Convenient

■ Total living area 1,786 sq. ft. ■ Price Code C ■

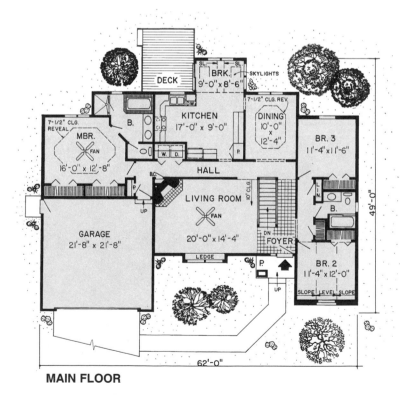

MAIN FLOOR

An
EXCLUSIVE DESIGN
By Karl Kreeger

No. 20110

■ **This plan features:**

— Three bedrooms

— Two full baths

■ Clapboard and brick add curbside appeal

■ A spacious Living Room is dominated by a corner fireplace

■ A hallway off the Foyer leads to the two additional Bedrooms

■ A formal Dining Room and a skylit Breakfast Nook adjoin the Kitchen

■ A rear Deck is perfect for summer barbecues

■ The Master Suite has a double vanity, a raised Bath and a walk-in shower

Main area — 1,786 sq. ft.
Basement — 1,786 sq. ft.
Garage — 484 sq. ft.

Contemporary   Energy-Saver

No. 90669

■ **This plan features:**

— Three bedrooms

— Two full baths plus shower

■ An enormous Deck, expands living outdoors

■ A spacious Living Room with a sloped ceiling and a wood stove is flanked by windows with built-in seats

■ An efficient, eat-in Kitchen has ample work space and easy access to all living areas

■ The first floor Bedroom has a double closet and a private Deck adjoins a full hall Bath

■ Two additional Bedrooms have double closets and share a full hall Bath

First floor — 877 sq. ft.
Second floor — 455 sq. ft.

Total living area 1,332 sq. ft. ■ *Price Code A*

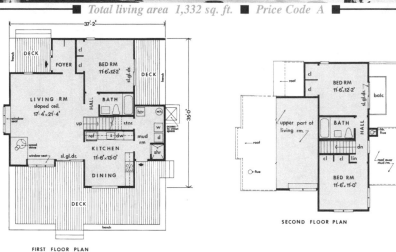

FIRST FLOOR PLAN

SECOND FLOOR PLAN

Cabin with a Gambrel

No. 99701

■ **This plan features:**

— Three bedrooms

— Two full baths

■ An open-beam ceiling and six huge windows in the Living Room/Dining Room that includes a vaulted ceiling

■ A private Master Suite has a full bath and two closets

■ The compact Kitchen has plenty of cupboard and counter space

■ Two additional small bedrooms have the use of a full hall bath

■ An average sized Utility Room with a laundry center

First floor — 864 sq. ft.
Second floor — 396 sq. ft.
Width — 24'-0"
Depth — 36'-0"

Total living area 1,260 sq. ft. ■ *Price Code A*

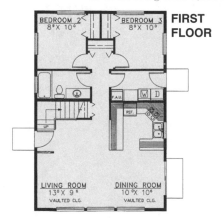

FIRST FLOOR

BEDROOM 2
8'⁹ X 10'⁰

BEDROOM 3
8'⁹ X 10'⁰

LIVING ROOM
13'⁹ X 9'⁶
VAULTED CLG.

DINING ROOM
10'⁹ X 10'⁰
VAULTED CLG.

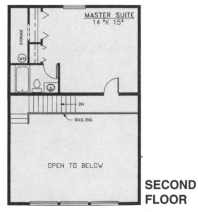

SECOND FLOOR

MASTER SUITE
14'⁰ X 15'⁶

OPEN TO BELOW

Charming Southern Traditional

■ Total living area 1,271 sq. ft. ■ Price Code B ■

No. 92503

■ **This plan features:**

— Three bedrooms

— Two full baths

■ A covered front Porch with striking columns, brick quoins and dentil molding

■ A spacious Great Room with vaulted ceilings, a fireplace and built-in cabinets

■ A Utility Room adjacent to the Kitchen which leads to the two-car Garage and Storage Rooms

■ The Master Bedroom includes a large walk-in closet and a compartmentalized Bath

■ An optional crawl space or slab foundation — please specify when ordering

Main area — 1,271 sq. ft.
Garage — 506 sq. ft.

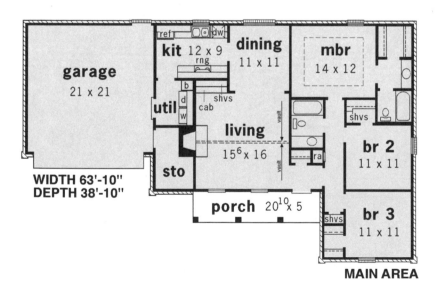

garage 21 x 21

kit 12 x 9

dining 11 x 11

mbr 14 x 12

util

sto

living 15⁶ x 16

br 2 11 x 11

br 3 11 x 11

porch 20¹⁰ x 5

WIDTH 63'-10"
DEPTH 38'-10"

MAIN AREA

Great Room With Columns

© 1995 Donald A Gardner Architects, Inc.

■ *Total living area 1,879 sq. ft.* ■ *Price Code E* ■

No. 99807

■ This plan features:

— Three bedrooms

— Two full baths

■ Great Room crowned with a cathedral ceiling and accented by columns and a fireplace

■ Tray ceilings and arched picture windows accent the front Bedroom and the Dining Room

■ Secluded Master Suite highlighted by a tray ceiling and contains a Bath with a skylight, a garden tub and a spacious walk-in closet

■ Two additional Bedrooms share a full Bath

■ An optional crawl space or basement foundation — please specify when ordering

Main floor — 1,879 sq. ft.
Bonus — 360 sq. ft.
Garage — 485 sq. ft.

Floor Plan w/Basement Option

© 1995 Donald A Gardner Architects, Inc.

Floor Plan

© 1995 Donald A Gardner Architects, Inc.

Easy, Economical Building

© 1996 Donald A Gardner Architects, Inc.

■ *Total living area 1,959 sq. ft.* ■ *Price Code E* ■

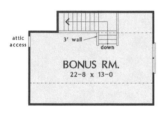

attic access

3' wall

down

BONUS RM.
22-8 x 13-0

Main floor — 1,959 sq. ft.
Bonus room — 385 sq. ft.
Garage & storage — 484 sq. ft.

No. 99813

■ **This plan features:**

— Three bedrooms

— Two full baths

■ Many architectural elements offer an efficient and economical design

■ Great Room with vaulted ceiling that gracefully arches to include an arched window dormer

■ Open Kitchen with angled counter easily serves Breakfast Area

■ Tray ceilings enhance Dining Room, front Bedroom and Master Bedroom

■ Private Master Bath includes a garden tub, a double vanity and a skylight

■ An optional basement or crawl space foundation — please specify when ordering

DECK

MASTER BED RM.
14-0 x 16-0

skylight

master bath

lin.

UTILITY
7-0 x 6-4

down

walk-in closet

BED RM.
12-0 x 13-0

GREAT RM.
16-8 x 19-6

(cathedral ceiling)

fireplace

BRKFST.
12-0 x 9-8

up

storage

cl

bath

lin.

KIT.
12-0 x 12-2

GARAGE
22-8 x 19-8

cl

FOYER
8-2 x 6-8

cl

BED RM./ STUDY
12-0 x 11-4

PORCH

DINING
12-0 x 12-4

(optional door location)

FLOOR PLAN

55-2

65-8

© 1996 Donald A Gardner Architects, Inc.

When There's a Hill

No. 90633

This plan features:

— Three bedrooms

— Three full baths

■ A design for a site that slopes down

■ A sky-lit Dining Room with a high sloping ceiling and heat-circulating fireplace

■ An efficient Kitchen with a peninsula counter and all the amenities

■ A second floor Master Suite with a private balcony, Deck and Bath

Main level — 790 sq. ft.
Upper level — 453 sq. ft.
Lower level — 340 sq. ft.

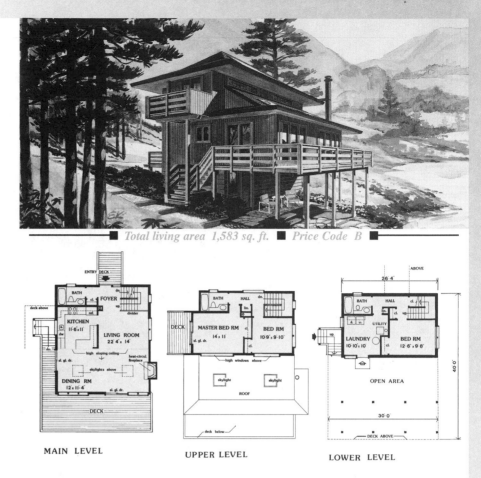

■ *Total living area 1,583 sq. ft.* ■ *Price Code B* ■

MAIN LEVEL   UPPER LEVEL   LOWER LEVEL

Compact Three Bedroom

No. 96418

This plan features:

— Three bedrooms

— Two full baths

■ Contemporary interior punctuated by elegant columns

■ Dormers above the covered Porch light the foyer leading to the dramatic Great Room crowned in a cathedral ceiling and enhanced by a fireplace

■ Great Room opens to the island Kitchen with Breakfast Area and access to a spacious rear Deck

■ Tray ceilings adding interest to the Bedroom/Study, Dining Room and the Master Suite

■ Luxurious Master Suite highlighted by a walk-in closet and a Bath with dual vanity, separate shower and a whirlpool tub

Main floor — 1,452 sq. ft.
Garage and Storage — 427 sq. ft.

■ *Total living area 1,452 sq. ft.* ■ *Price Code C* ■

FLOOR PLAN

115

Attractive Ceiling Treatments and Open Layout

■ *Total living area 1,654 sq. ft.* ■ *Price Code B* ■

No. 96506

■ **This plan features:**

— Three bedrooms

— Two full and one half baths

■ Great Room and Master Suite with step-up ceiling treatments

■ A cozy fireplace provides a warm focal point in the Great Room

■ Open layout between Kitchen, Dining Room and Great Room lends a more spacious feeling

■ Five-piece, private Bath and walk-in closet pamper the Master Suite

■ Two additional Bedrooms located at opposite end of home from Master Suite

Main floor — 1,654 sq. ft.
Garage — 480 sq. ft.

MAIN FLOOR

68'

46'

SHOWER

BATH

MASTER SUITE
15 × 16
FAN
STEP UP CEIL
11'-0"

CLOSET

1/2 BATH

GARAGE
21 × 22

A/C

UTIL

DRY · WASH

PORCH
10 × 30

DINING
12 × 12

F/P

GREAT RM
16 × 24
FAN

STEP UP CEIL
11'-6"

KITCHEN
12 × 12

REFG

D/W

9' CEILINGS

PORCH

BEDRM
12 × 12

LIN · CLOS

BATH

CLO · CLOS

BEDRM
11 × 12

■ *Total living area 1,715 sq. ft.* ■ *Price Code B* ■

No. 98456

■ This plan features:

— Three bedrooms

— Two full baths

■ A covered entry gives way to a 14-foot high ceiling in the Foyer

■ An arched opening greets you in the Great Room that also has a vaulted ceiling and a fireplace

■ The Dining Room is brightened by triple windows with transoms above

■ The Kitchen is a gourmet's delight and is open to the Breakfast Nook

■ The Master Suite is sweet with a tray ceiling, vaulted Sitting Area and private Bath

■ Two Bedrooms on the opposite side of the home share a hall Bath

■ An optional basement, slab or crawl space foundation — please specify when ordering

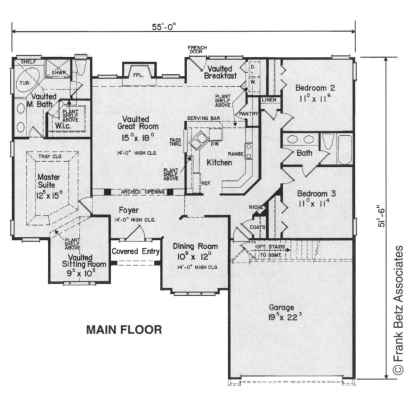

MAIN FLOOR

Main floor — 1,715 sq. ft.
Basement — 1,715 sq. ft.
Garage — 450 sq. ft.

Comfortable and Charming

■ *Total living area 1,964 sq. ft.* ■ *Price Code C* ■

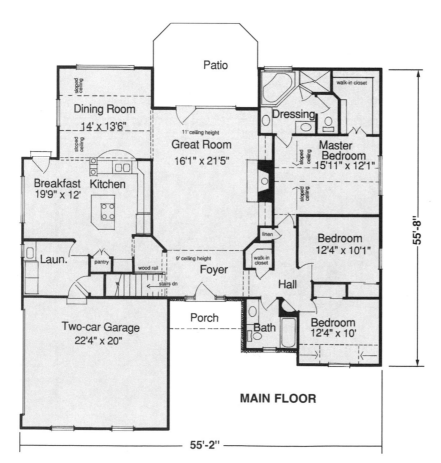

MAIN FLOOR

No. 92660

■ **This plan features:**

— Three bedrooms

— Two full baths

■ Great Room with massive fireplace and lots of windows with Patio access

■ Formal Dining Room with sloped ceiling and expansive view of backyard

■ Cooktop island and Pantry in Kitchen efficiently serve Breakfast Area and Dining Room

■ Corner Master Bedroom offers a sloped ceiling, walk-in closet and pampering Bath with whirlpool tub and two vanities

■ No materials list is available for this plan

Main floor — 1,964 sq. ft.
Basement — 1,809 sq. ft.
Garage — 447 sq. ft.

No. 94310

■ This plan features:

— Three bedrooms

— One full, one three-quarter and one half baths

■ Interesting angles create a unique look to this home

■ A large Deck is located off of the Living Room

■ A fireplace warms the Living and Dining rooms

■ The U-shaped Kitchen also features an eating bar

■ The Master Bedroom on the upper level includes a walk-in closet

■ There is a Deck off of each of the secondary Bedrooms

■ In bad weather enter the home through the Garage to stay dry

■ No materials list is available for this plan

Lower Level — 629 sq. ft.
Upper Level — 884 sq. ft.
Garage — 320 sq. ft.

An
EXCLUSIVE DESIGN
By Marshall Associates

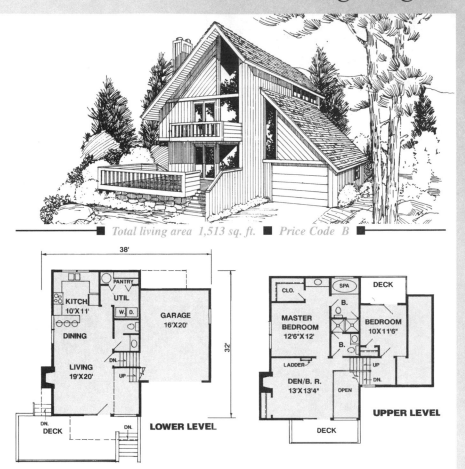

Total living area 1,513 sq. ft. ■ *Price Code B*

No. 97124

■ This plan features:

— Three bedrooms

— Two full baths

■ A column supported covered entry greets you

■ Inside a tiled Foyer with a vaulted ceiling leads to the Great Room

■ A corner fireplace and a wall of windows distinguishes the Great Room

■ The Dining Room has a cathedral ceiling and an access door to the rear yard

■ Wrap-around counters provide working convenience in the Kitchen

■ The Master Bedroom is secluded and has an enormous walk-in closet

■ The secondary Bedrooms are located on the opposite side of the home

■ A two-car Garage completes this home

■ No material list is available for this plan

Main Floor — 1,416 sq. ft.
Basement — 1,430 sq. ft.

Total living area 1,416 sq. ft. ■ *Price Code A*

MAIN FLOOR

Attractive Sloped Ceiling

■ Total living area 1,688 sq. ft. ■ Price Code B ■

No. 10548

■ **This plan features:**

— Three bedrooms

— Two full and one half baths

■ A fireplace and sloped ceiling in the Living Room

■ A Master Bedroom complete with a full Bath, shower and dressing area

■ A decorative ceiling in the Dining Room

Main floor — 1,688 sq. ft.
Basement — 1,688 sq. ft.
Screened porch — 120 sq. ft.
Garage — 489 sq. ft.

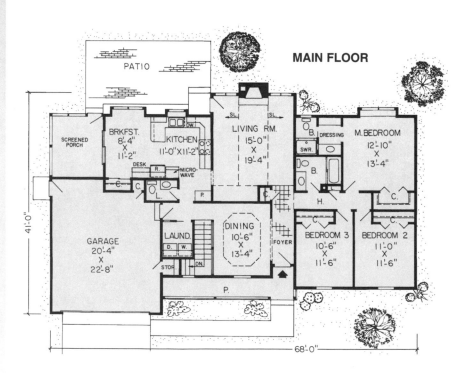

MAIN FLOOR

PATIO

SCREENED PORCH

BRKFST.
8'-4"
X
11'-2"

KITCHEN
11'-0"X11'-2"

DESK

MICROWAVE

LIVING RM.
15'-0"
X
19'-4"

DRESSING

SWR.

B.

M. BEDROOM
12'-10"
X
13'-4"

GARAGE
20'-4"
X
22'-8"

LAUND.
D. W.

STOR

DINING
10'-6"
X
13'-4"

DN.

FOYER

H.

BEDROOM 3
10'-6"
X
11'-6"

BEDROOM 2
11'-0"
X
11'-6"

41'-0"

68'-0"

An
EXCLUSIVE DESIGN
By Karl Kreeger

A Comfortable, Informal Design

■ *Total living area 1,300 sq. ft.* ■ *Price Code B* ■

No. 94801 ✕

■ **This plan features:**

— Three bedrooms

— Two full baths

■ Warm, Country style front Porch with wood details

■ Spacious Activity Room is enhanced by a pre-fab fireplace

■ Open and efficient Kitchen/ Dining area is highlighted by bay window

■ Corner Master Bedroom offers a pampering Bath with a garden tub and double vanity topped by a vaulted ceiling

■ Two additional Bedrooms with ample closets, share a full Bath

■ An optional crawl space or slab foundation available — please specify when ordering

Main floor — 1,300 sq. ft.
Garage — 576 sq. ft.

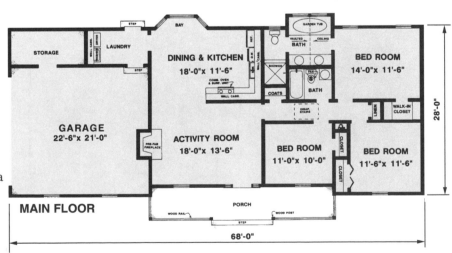

Classic Arches

■ *Total living area 1,592 sq. ft.* ■ *Price Code B* ■

No. 20180

■ **This plan features:**

— Three bedrooms

— Two full baths

■ Twin arched windows and a friendly covered Porch

■ An angled entry adds intrigue to the sunny, soaring Kitchen-Breakfast Room combination

■ Living and Dining rooms at rear of the house flow together

Main area — 1,592 sq. ft.
Garage — 487 sq. ft.
Basement — 1,579 sq. ft.

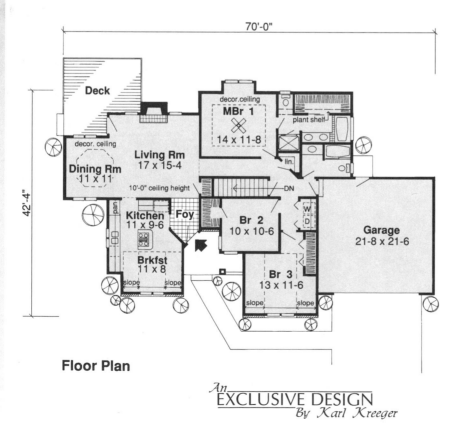

Floor Plan

An EXCLUSIVE DESIGN *By Karl Kreeger*

Bedrooms Sliders Open Onto Wooden Deck

No. 10220

■ **This plan features:**

— Two bedrooms

— One full bath

■ A fifty-foot Deck sets the stage for a relaxing lifestyle encouraged by this home

■ A simple, yet complete floor plan centers around the large Family Area, warmed by a prefab fireplace

■ An efficient L-shaped Kitchen includes a double sink with a window above, and direct access to the rear yard and the Laundry Room

■ Two Bedrooms privately located, each outfitted with sliding doors to the Deck and a large window for plenty of light

Main floor — 888 sq. ft.

■ *Total living area 888 sq. ft.* ■ *Price Code A* ■

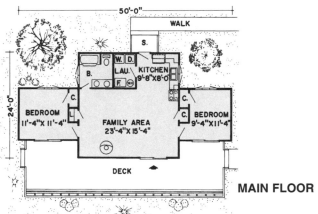

MAIN FLOOR

Sophisticated European Stucco

No. 92562

■ **This plan features:**

— Three bedrooms

— Two full baths

■ A raised ceiling in Master Suite and in the Den add architectural interest to the plan

■ A spacious Kitchen serves the Breakfast Area and Dining Room with efficiency and ease

■ A Breakfast Bar for snacks or meals on the go

■ The vaulted ceiling in the Dining Room adds elegance to the room

■ The luxurious Master Bath with a separate tub and shower pampers you in the Master Suite

■ Secondary Bedrooms are in close proximity to the full Bath in the hall

■ An optional slab or crawl space foundation — please specify when ordering

Main floor — 1,856 sq. ft.
Garage & storage — 521 sq. ft.

■ *Total living area 1,856 sq. ft.* ■ *Price Code C* ■

WIDTH 68'-10"
DEPTH 48'-10"

MAIN FLOOR

Outdoor-Lovers' Delight

■ *Total living area 1,540 sq. ft.* ■ *Price Code B* ■

No. 10748 ⚒

■ **This plan features:**

— Three bedrooms

— Two full baths

■ A roomy Kitchen and Dining Room

■ A massive Living Room with a fireplace and access to the wraparound porch via double French doors

■ An elegant Master Suite and two additional spacious bedrooms closely located to the laundry area

Main Area — 1,540 sq. ft.
Porches — 530 sq. ft.

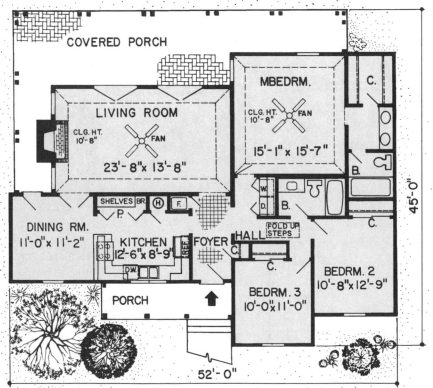

MAIN AREA

A-Frame for Year-Round Living

■ *Total living area 1,702 sq. ft.* ■ *Price Code B* ■

No. 90930

■ **This plan features:**

— Three bedrooms

— One full and one three-quarter baths

■ A vaulted ceiling in the Living Room and a massive fireplace

■ A wrap-around Sun Deck that gives you a lot of outdoor living space

■ A luxurious Master Suite complete with a walk-in closet, full Bath and private Deck

■ Two additional Bedrooms share a full hall Bath

Main floor — 1,238 sq. ft.
Loft — 464 sq. ft.
Basement — 1,175 sq. ft.

An
EXCLUSIVE DESIGN
By Westhome Planners, Ltd.

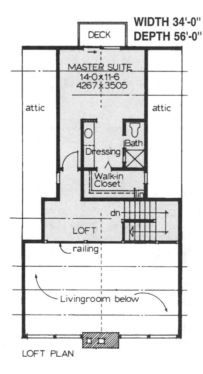

WIDTH 34'-0"
DEPTH 56'-0"

DECK

MASTER SUITE
14-0 x 11-6
4267 x 3505

attic   attic

Bath

Dressing

Walk-in Closet

dn

LOFT

railing

Livingroom below

LOFT PLAN

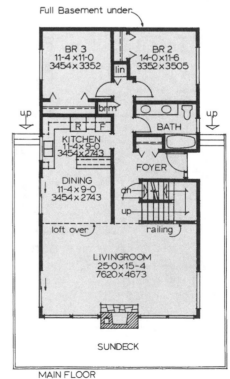

Full Basement under

BR 3
11-4 x 11-0
3454 x 3352

BR 2
14-0 x 11-6
3352 x 3505

lin

up   up

BATH

KITCHEN
11-4 x 9-0
3454 x 2743

FOYER

DINING
11-4 x 9-0
3454 x 2743

dn
up
railing

loft over

LIVINGROOM
25-0 x 15-4
7620 x 4673

SUNDECK

MAIN FLOOR

Distinctive European Design

■ *Total living area 1,887 sq. ft.* ■ *Price Code D* ■

No. 92516

■ **This plan features:**

— Three bedrooms

— Two full baths

■ The Living Room is topped by a vaulted ceiling

■ The gourmet Kitchen has a peninsula counter/snackbar and a built-in Pantry

■ The Master Bedroom is crowned by a raised ceiling, and has French doors leading to a covered Porch

■ Two additional Bedrooms have decorative windows and over-sized closets and share a full hall Bath

■ An optional crawl space or slab foundation — please specify when ordering

Main floor — 1,887 sq. ft.
Garage & Storage — 524 sq. ft.

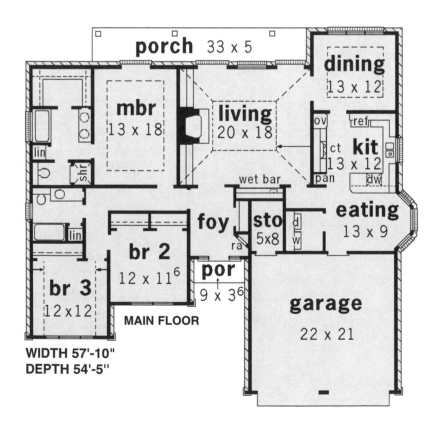

porch 33 x 5

dining 13 x 12

mbr 13 x 18

living 20 x 18

ov

ref

ct

kit 13 x 12

pan

dw

lin

shr

wet bar

foy

sto 5x8

d w

eating 13 x 9

ra

br 2 12 x 11⁶

por 9 x 3⁶

lin

br 3 12x12

MAIN FLOOR

garage 22 x 21

WIDTH 57'-10"
DEPTH 54'-5"

Living Room Focus of Spacious Home

No. 10328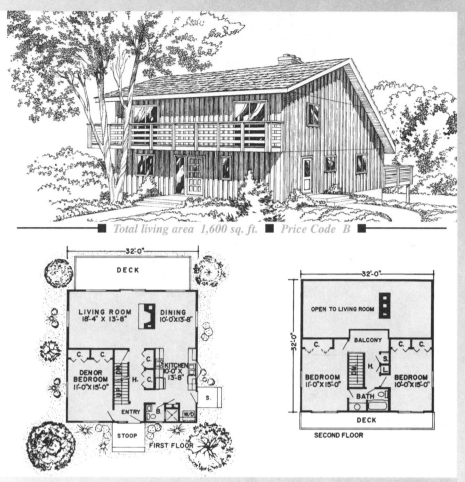

■ This plan features:

— Three bedrooms

— One full and one three-quarter baths

■ A well planned traffic pattern connects the Dining Area, the Kitchen, the laundry niche and the Bath

■ A balcony overlooks the open Living Room

■ Sliding glass doors open to the Deck

■ There is fireplace in the sizable Living Room

First floor — 1,024 sq. ft.
Second floor — 576 sq. ft.
Basement — 1,024 sq. ft.

■ Total living area 1,600 sq. ft. ■ Price Code B ■

Build In Stages

No. 90638

■ This plan features:

— Three bedrooms

— One full and one three-quarter baths

■ A covered entrance into spacious Living/Dining Area with a 13-foot cathedral ceiling, fireplace and two sliding glass doors to a huge Deck

■ An efficient L-shaped Kitchen with separate counter space for dining is adjacent to Deck and Laundry/Utility room

■ The Master Bedroom has a private Bath

■ Two additional Bedrooms share a full hall Bath

■ An option to build in stages

Main floor — 1,042 sq. ft.

REAR ELEVATION

■ Total living area 1,042 sq. ft. ■ Price Code A ■

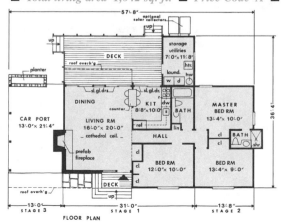

FLOOR PLAN

Great Starter or Empty Nester

■ *Total living area 1,420 sq. ft.* ■ *Price Code A* ■

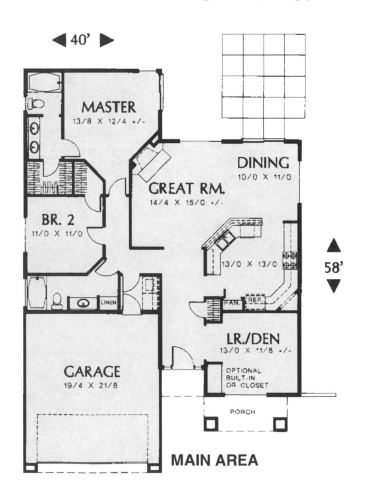

◀ 40' ▶

MASTER
13/8 X 12/4 +/-

BR. 2
11/0 X 11/0

GREAT RM.
14/4 X 15/0 +/-

DINING
10/0 X 11/0

13/0 X 13/0

LINEN

PAN. REF.

LR./DEN
13/0 X 11/8 +/-

GARAGE
19/4 X 21/8

OPTIONAL
BUILT-IN
OR CLOSET

PORCH

▲
58'
▼

MAIN AREA

No. 91545

■ **This plan features:**

— Two bedrooms

— Two full baths

■ A formal Living Room or a cozy Den to the right of the Entry Hall

■ An efficient Kitchen with ample counter and storage space

■ A formal Dining Room situated next to the Kitchen and flowing from the Great Room

■ A corner fireplace highlights the Great Room

■ A walk-in closet and a private double vanity Bath in the Master Suite

■ An additional Bedroom that easily accesses the full hall Bath

■ This plan cannot be built in Clark County, WA

Main area — 1,420 sq. ft.

■ *Total living area 1,782 sq. ft.* ■ *Price Code C* ■

No. 94917 ✕

■ **This plan features:**

— Three bedrooms

— Two full baths

■ Entry opens to formal Dining Room with arched window

■ Angles and transom windows add interest to the Great Room

■ Bright Hearth area expands Breakfast/Kitchen area and shares three-sided fireplace

■ Efficient Kitchen offers an angled snack bar, a large Pantry and nearby Laundry/Garage entry

■ Secluded Master Suite crowned by decorative ceiling, a large walk-in closet and a plush Bath with a whirlpool tub

■ Two secondary Bedrooms in separate wing from Master Suite for added privacy

Main floor — 1,782 sq. ft.
Basement — 1,782 sq. ft.
Garage — 466 sq. ft.

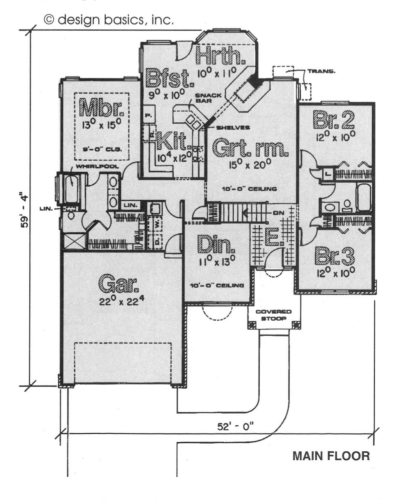

© design basics, inc.

MAIN FLOOR

Distinctive Ranch

■ *Total living area 1,802 sq. ft.* ■ *Price Code C* ■

No. 93143

■ **This plan features:**

— Three bedrooms

— Two full baths

■ This hipped roofed ranch has an exterior that mixes brick and siding

■ The cozy front Porch leads into a recessed Entry with sidelights and transoms

■ The Great Room has a cathedral ceiling, and a rear wall fireplace

■ The Kitchen has a center island and opens into the Nook

■ The Dining Room features a high ceiling and a bright front window

■ The Bedroom wing has three large Bedrooms and two full Baths

■ The two-car Garage could easily be expanded to three with a door placed in the rear storage area

■ No materials list is available for this plan

Main floor — 1,802 sq. ft.
Basement — 1,802 sq. ft.

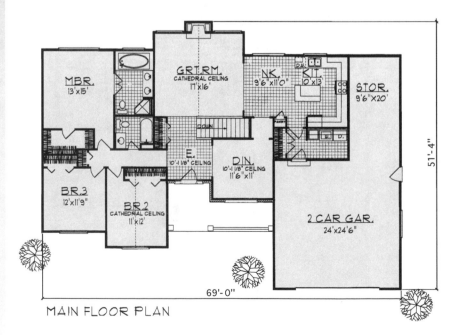

MAIN FLOOR PLAN

A Cozy Cabin

No. 34075

This plan features:

— Two bedrooms

— One full bath

■ A compact design that can accommodate four to six people comfortably

■ The Living Room is connected to the Kitchen and Dining Area giving an open feeling

■ A perfect design for a weekend get-away

Main floor — 576 sq. ft.

■ Total living area 576 sq. ft. ■ Price Code A ■

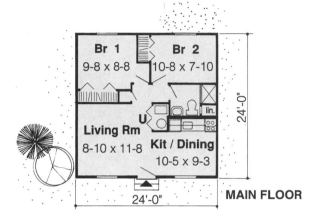

Br 1 9-8 x 8-8

Br 2 10-8 x 7-10

Living Rm 8-10 x 11-8

Kit / Dining 10-5 x 9-3

24'-0"

24'-0"

MAIN FLOOR

Vacation Cottage

No. 90821

This plan features:

— Two bedrooms

— One full bath

■ An economical, neat and simple design

■ Two picture windows in the Living/Dining Room

■ An efficient Kitchen design

■ A large, cozy Loft bedroom flanked by big storage rooms

■ An optional basement or crawl space foundation — please specify when ordering

Main floor — 616 sq. ft.
Loft — 180 sq. ft.
Width — 22'-0"
Depth — 28'-0"

■ Total living area 796 sq. ft. ■ Price Code A ■

BR 10-0x10-0 3048x3048

Bath

KITCHEN 10-6x9-0 3200x2743

LR **DR**
21-0x11-0
6400x3352

up

MAIN FLOOR

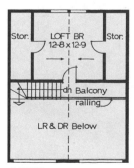

Stor. **LOFT BR** 12-8 x 12-9 **Stor.**

dn Balcony railing

LR & DR Below

LOFT

An EXCLUSIVE DESIGN
By Westhome Planners, Ltd.

131

From Times Gone By

■ *Total living area 1,957 sq. ft.* ■ *Price Code C* ■

An
EXCLUSIVE DESIGN
By Marshall Associates

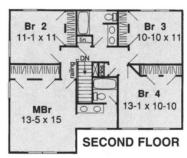

Br 2
11-1 x 11

Br 3
10-10 x 11

Br 4
13-1 x 10-10

MBr
13-5 x 15

DN

lin.

railing

SECOND FLOOR

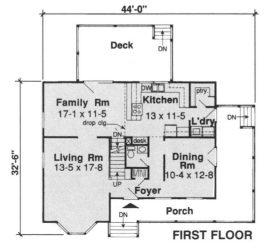

44'-0"

Deck

DN

Family Rm
17-1 x 11-5

drop clg.

Kitchen
13 x 11-5

DW

ptry.

L'dry

DN

DN

desk

Living Rm
13-5 x 17-8

UP

DN

Dining Rm
10-4 x 12-8

Foyer

DN

Porch

32'-6"

FIRST FLOOR

No. 24301

■ **This plan features:**

— Four bedrooms

— Two full and one half baths

■ The Family Room opens to a large Deck in the rear

■ The Master Bedroom has a private Bath and ample closet space

■ A large Living Room has a bay window

■ A modern Kitchen with many amenities

First floor — 987 sq. ft.
Second floor — 970 sq. ft.
Basement — 985 sq. ft.

■ *Total living area 1,670 sq. ft.* ■ ● *Price Code B* ■

No. 90409

■ This plan features:

— Three bedrooms

— Two full baths

■ A massive fireplace separates the Living and Dining rooms

■ An isolated Master Suite has a walk-in closet and handy compartmentalized Bath

■ The galley-type Kitchen is between the Breakfast Room and the Dining Room

■ An optional basement, slab or crawl space foundation — please specify when ordering

Main area — 1,670 sq. ft.
Basement — 1,670 sq. ft.
Garage — 427 sq. ft.

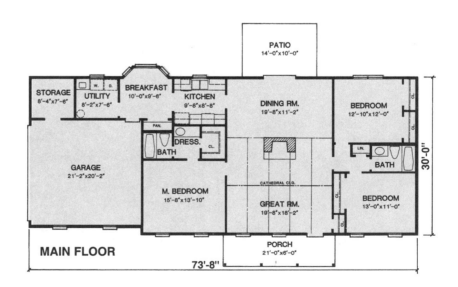

PATIO
14'-0"x10'-0"

STORAGE
8'-4"x7'-6"

UTILITY
8'-2"x7'-6"

BREAKFAST
10'-0"x9'-6"

KITCHEN
9'-8"x8'-8"

DINING RM.
19'-8"x11'-2"

BEDROOM
12'-10"x12'-0"

PAN.

BATH

DRESS.

CL.

LIN.

BATH

GARAGE
21'-2"x20'-2"

M. BEDROOM
15'-8"x13'-10"

CATHEDRAL CLG.

GREAT RM.
19'-8"x18'-2"

BEDROOM
13'-0"x11'-0"

30'-0"

MAIN FLOOR

PORCH
21'-0"x6'-0"

73'-8"

Country Charmer

■ *Total living area 1,438 sq. ft.* ■ *Price Code A* ■

No. 96509

■ This plan features:

— Three bedrooms

— Two full baths

■ Quaint front Porch is perfect for sitting and relaxing

■ Great Room opens into the Dining Area and Kitchen

■ Corner Deck in rear of home accessed from Kitchen and Master Suite

■ Master Suite with a private Bath, walk-in closet and built-in shelves

■ Two large secondary Bedrooms in the front of the home share a hall Bath

■ Two-car Garage located in the rear of the home

Main floor — 1,438 sq. ft.
Garage — 486 sq. ft.

MAIN FLOOR

Deck Defies Gravity

No. 24306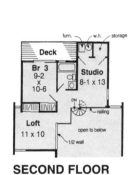

■ This plan features:

- Three bedrooms
- Two full baths

■ Perfect layout for a mountain side with a far reaching view

■ Fireplace in a large and sunny Living Room

■ Spiral staircase to the second floor adding style

■ Galley Kitchen with access to rear Deck

■ Loft area, with closet, overlooking the Living Room

■ Third Bedroom with a private Deck and Bathroom

First floor — 841 sq. ft.
Second floor — 489 sq. ft.

An
EXCLUSIVE DESIGN
By Marshall Associates

■ Total living area 1,330 sq. ft. ■ Price Code A ■

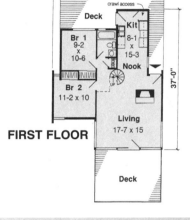

SECOND FLOOR

FIRST FLOOR

Roof Garden Delight

No. 94304

■ This plan features:

- Three bedrooms
- Two full baths

■ A tiled Entry Court leads into the Foyer and sets a southwestern theme

■ The Living/Dining area has a corner fireplace, window walls and access to a Patio

■ An efficient, U-shaped Kitchen with an eating bar and Laundry area

■ Two first floor Bedrooms share a full Bath

■ The second floor Master Bedroom has a double closet, built-in shelves, a private Bath and direct access to the Roof Garden

■ No materials list is available for this plan

First floor — 981 sq. ft.
Second floor — 396 sq. ft.

An
EXCLUSIVE DESIGN
By Marshall Associates

■ Total living area 1,377 sq. ft. ■ Price Code A ■

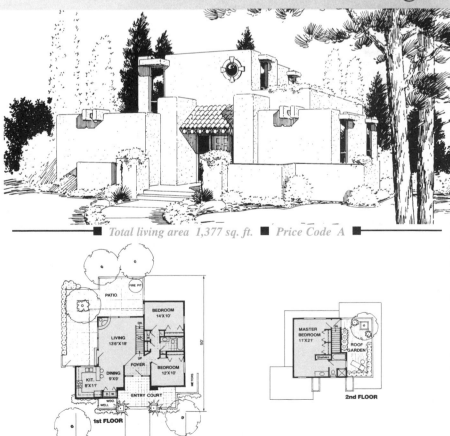

1st FLOOR

2nd FLOOR

Perfect for Family Gatherings

© 1994 Donald A. Gardner Architects, Inc.

■ *Total living area 1,346 sq. ft.* ■ *Price Code C* ■

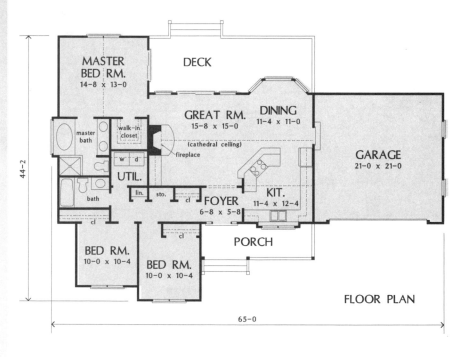

FLOOR PLAN

No. 99826

■ This plan features:

— Three bedrooms

— Two full baths

■ An open layout between the Great Room, Kitchen and Dining Area, sharing a cathedral ceiling and a fireplace

■ Master Bedroom has a soaring cathedral ceiling, direct access to the Deck and a well appointed Bath with a large walk-in closet

■ Additional Bedrooms share a full Bath in the hall

■ Centrally located Utility and storage spaces

Main floor — 1,346 sq. ft.
Garage & storage — 462 sq. ft.

Private Master Suite

■ *Total living area 1,293 sq. ft.* ■ • *Price Code B* ■

No. 92523 ✖

■ This plan features:

— Three bedrooms

— Two full baths

■ A spacious Den is enhanced by a vaulted ceiling and fireplace

■ A well-equipped Kitchen has a double sink

■ A secluded Master Suite has a decorative ceiling, private Master Bath and walk-in closet

■ Two additional Bedrooms share a hall Bath

■ An optional crawl space or slab foundation — please specify when ordering

Main floor — 1,293 sq. ft.
Garage — 433 sq. ft.

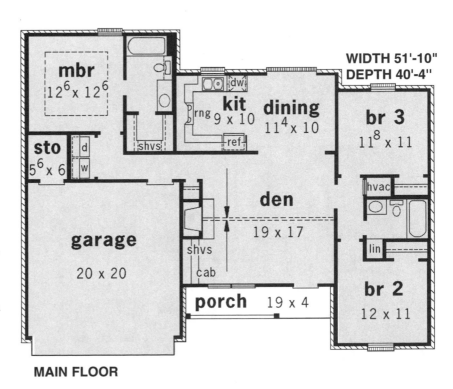

WIDTH 51'-10"
DEPTH 40'-4"

mbr
12^6 x 12^6

sto
5^6 x 6

kit
9 x 10

rng

dining
11^4 x 10

br 3
11^8 x 11

garage
20 x 20

den
19 x 17

hvac

lin

porch   19 x 4

br 2
12 x 11

MAIN FLOOR

Carefree Living on One Level

■ *Total living area 1,588 sq. ft.* ■ *Price Code B* ■

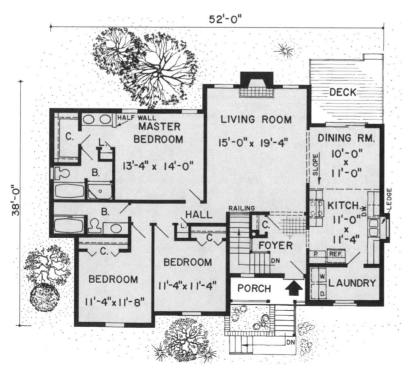

An
EXCLUSIVE DESIGN
By Karl Kreeger

52'-0"

38'-0"

HALF WALL

MASTER BEDROOM
13'-4" x 14'-0"

C.
L.
B.
B.

LIVING ROOM
15'-0" x 19'-4"

DECK

SLOPE

DINING RM.
10'-0" x 11'-0"

LEDGE

HALL
RAILING

L.
C.

BEDROOM
11'-4" x 11'-8"

BEDROOM
11'-4" x 11'-4"

C.

FOYER
DN

KITCH.
11'-0" x 11'-4"

DW

PORCH
DN

P.
REF.

W.
LAUNDRY
D.

MAIN FLOOR

No. 20089

■ **This plan features:**

— Three bedrooms

— Two full baths

■ A full basement and an oversized two-car Garage

■ The spacious Master Suite has a walk-in closet

■ A fireplaced Living Room, and an open Dining Room and Kitchen for convenience

Main floor — 1,588 sq. ft.
Basement — 780 sq. ft.
Garage — 808 sq. ft.

Expansive, Not Expensive

No. 90623

■ This plan features:

— Three bedrooms

— Two full baths

■ The Master Suite has his-n-her closets and a private Master Bath

■ Two additional Bedrooms share a full hall closet

■ A pleasant Dining Room overlooks the rear garden

■ A well-equipped Kitchen has a built-in planning corner and eat-in space

Main floor — 1,474 sq. ft.
Basement — 1,370 sq. ft.
Garage — 563 sq. ft.

■ *Total living area 1,474 sq. ft.* ■ *Price Code A* ■

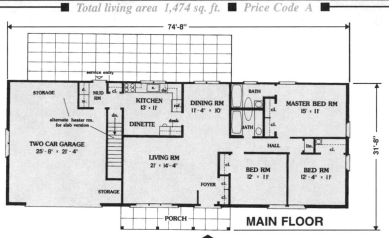

MAIN FLOOR

Unusual A-Frame

No. 10228

■ This plan features:

— Two bedrooms

— One full and one half baths

■ A covered Entry leading down to a large Living Room with a cheerful, metal fireplace

■ An L-shaped Kitchen opens into the Family Room with sliding glass doors to the Patio

■ The second floor has two spacious Bedrooms and private Decks

First floor — 768 sq. ft.
Second floor — 521 sq. ft.

■ *Total living area 1,289 sq. ft.* ■ *Price Code A* ■

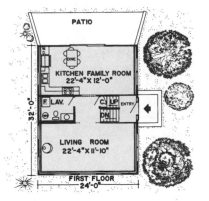

FIRST FLOOR

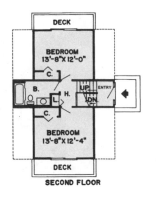

SECOND FLOOR

Rambling Ranch

■ *Total living area 1,850 sq. ft.* ■ *Price Code C* ■

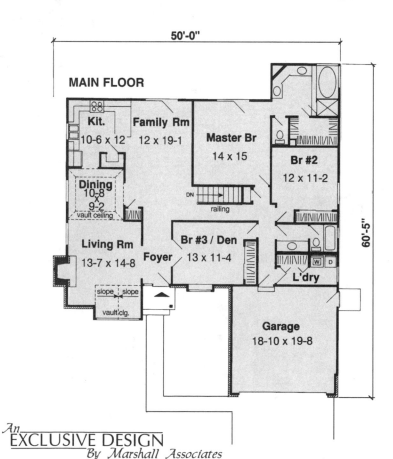

MAIN FLOOR

50'-0"

60'-5"

Kit.
10-6 x 12

Family Rm
12 x 19-1

Master Br
14 x 15

Br #2
12 x 11-2

Dining
10-8 x 9-2
vault ceiling

DN
railing

Living Rm
13-7 x 14-8

Foyer

Br #3 / Den
13 x 11-4

L'dry

slope   slope
vault clg.

Garage
18-10 x 19-8

An EXCLUSIVE DESIGN
By Marshall Associates

No. 24314 ✖

■ **This plan features:**

— Three bedrooms

— Two full baths

■ A cozy Living Room that flows into an elegant Dining Room with a vaulted ceiling

■ A well-appointed Kitchen conveniently serves the Dining Room and contains a double sink and a walk-in Pantry

■ A Family Room with direct access to the rear yard

■ A Master Suite with a lavish private Bath and a walk-in closet

■ Two additional Bedrooms share a full hall Bath

Main floor — 1,850 sq. ft.

A Nest for Empty-Nesters

■ *Total living area 884 sq. ft.* ■ *Price Code A* ■

No. 90934 ✘

■ This plan features:

— Two bedrooms

— One full bath

■ An economical design

■ A covered Sun Deck adds outdoor living space

■ A Mudroom/Laundry Area inside the side door, trapping dirt before it enters the house

■ An open layout between the Living Room with fireplace, Dining Room and Kitchen

Main floor — 884 sq. ft.
Width — 34'-0"
Depth — 28'-0"

An
EXCLUSIVE DESIGN
By Westhome Planners, Ltd.

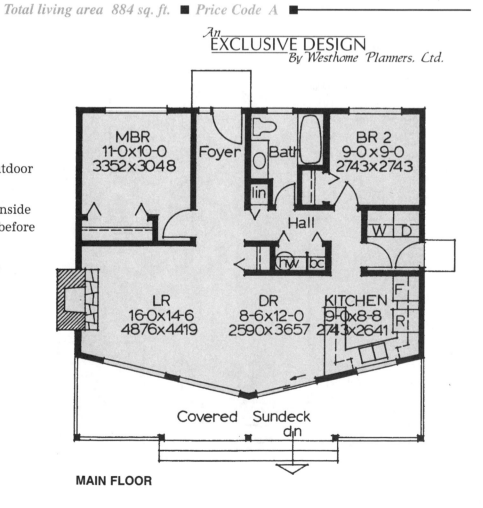

MAIN FLOOR

European Flair

© Frank Betz Associates

■ *Total living area 1,544 sq. ft.* ■ *Price Code B* ■

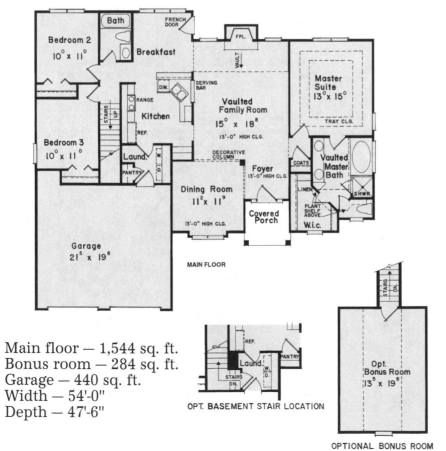

Bath
Bedroom 2
10⁰ x 11⁰
Breakfast
FRENCH DOOR

FPL.
VAULT

D.W.
SERVING BAR
RANGE
Kitchen
REF.
STAIRS UP

Vaulted Family Room
15⁰ x 18⁸
13'-0" HIGH CLG.

Master Suite
13⁰ x 15⁰
TRAY CLG.

Bedroom 3
10⁰ x 11⁰
Laund.
PANTRY

DECORATIVE COLUMN

Foyer
13'-0" HIGH CLG.

COATS

Vaulted Master Bath
SHWR.

Dining Room
11² x 11⁹
13'-0" HIGH CLG.

Covered Porch

LINEN
PLANT SHELF ABOVE
W.i.c.

Garage
21⁵ x 19⁸

MAIN FLOOR

Main floor — 1,544 sq. ft.
Bonus room — 284 sq. ft.
Garage — 440 sq. ft.
Width — 54'-0"
Depth — 47'-6"

REF.
Laund.
PANTRY
STAIRS DN.
W D

OPT. BASEMENT STAIR LOCATION

STAIRS DN.

Opt. Bonus Room
13⁵ x 19⁸

OPTIONAL BONUS ROOM

No. 98460

■ **This plan features:**

— Three bedrooms

— Two full baths

■ Large fireplace serving as an attractive focal point for the vaulted Family Room

■ A decorative column defines the elegant Dining Room

■ Kitchen includes a serving bar for the Family Room and a Breakfast Area

■ Master Suite topped by a tray ceiling over the Bedroom and a vaulted ceiling over the five-piece Master Bath

■ Optional Bonus Room for future expansion

■ An optional basement or crawl space foundation — please specify when ordering

■ No materials list is available for this plan

Nostalgia Returns

No. 99321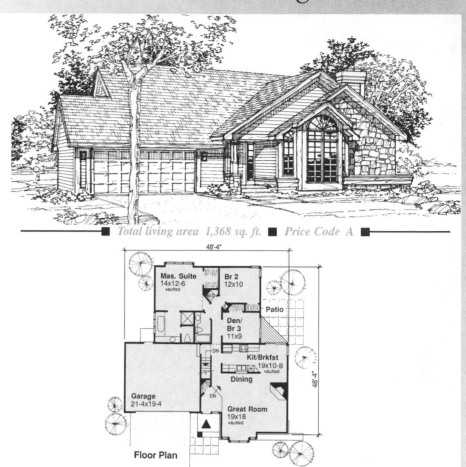

■ **This plan features:**

– Three bedrooms

– Two full baths

■ There is an arched transom window with quarter-round detail and a vaulted ceiling in the Great Room

■ A cozy corner fireplace adds warmth to the Great Room

■ There is a vaulted ceiling in the Kitchen/Breakfast Area

■ The Master Suite has a walk-in closet and a private Master Bath

■ Two additional Bedrooms share a full hall Bath

Main area — 1,368 sq. ft.
Garage — 412 sq. ft.

■ Total living area 1,368 sq. ft. ■ Price Code A ■

48'-4"

Mas. Suite 14x12-6 vaulted

Br 2 12x10

Patio

Den/ Br 3 11x9

Kit/Brkfst 19x10-8 vaulted

Dining

Garage 21-4x19-4

Great Room 19x18 vaulted

48'-4"

Floor Plan

Lots of Room in Ranch Design

No. 10594

■ **This plan features:**

– Two bedrooms with optional third bedroom

– Two full baths

■ A sloping, open-beamed ceiling and a wood-burning fireplace are in the Great Room

■ The Dining Room with sliding glass doors leads onto a large wooden Deck

■ A Laundry Room is located near the Kitchen and Dining Room

Main floor — 1,565 sq. ft.
Basement — 1,576 sq. ft.
Garage — 430 sq. ft.

■ Total living area 1,565 sq. ft. ■ Price Code B ■

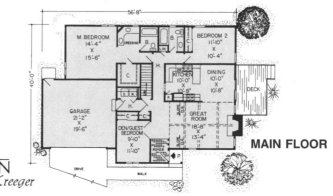

56'-8"

M. BEDROOM 14'-4" X 15'-6"

BEDROOM 2 11'-10" X 10'-4"

KITCHEN 10'-0" X 10'-8"

DINING 10'-0" X 10'-8"

GARAGE 21'-2" X 19'-6"

DEN/GUEST BEDROOM 9'-10" X 11'-10"

GREAT ROOM 18'-8" X 13'-4"

DECK

40'-0"

DRIVE   WALK

MAIN FLOOR

An EXCLUSIVE DESIGN *By Karl Kreeger*

Secluded Vacation Retreat

■ *Total living area 1,837 sq. ft.* ■ *Price Code C* ■

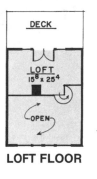

LOFT FLOOR

No. 91704

■ **This plan features:**

— Two bedrooms

— One full and two three-quarter baths

■ A high vaulted ceiling in the Living Area with a large masonry fireplace and circular stairway

■ A wall of windows along the full cathedral height of the Living Area

■ A Kitchen with ample storage and counter space including a sink and a chopping block island

■ Private full Baths and ten-foot closets for each of the Bedrooms

■ A Loft with windowed doors opening to a Deck

Main floor — 1,448 sq. ft.
Loft — 389 sq. ft.
Carport — 312 sq. ft.

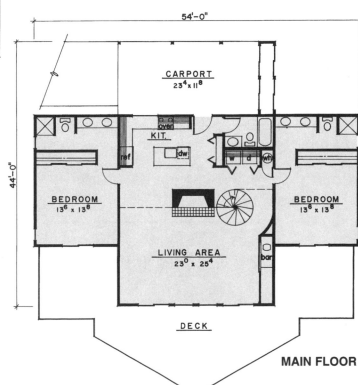

MAIN FLOOR

Plush Master Bedroom Wing

■ *Total living area 1,849 sq. ft.* ■ *Price Code C* ■

No. 92705

■ **This plan features:**

— Three bedrooms

— Two full baths

■ A raised, tile Foyer with a decorative window leads into an expansive Living Room, accented by a tiled fireplace and framed by French doors

■ An efficient Kitchen has a walk-in Pantry and serving bar adjoining the Breakfast and Utility areas

■ A private Master Bedroom is crowned by a stepped ceiling

■ Two additional Bedrooms with walk-in closets, share a full hall Bath

■ No materials list is available for this plan

Main floor — 1,849 sq. ft.
Garage — 437 sq. ft.

MAIN FLOOR

Ranch Offers Attractive Window Facade

■ *Total living area 1,840 sq. ft.* ■ *Price Code C* ■

No. 10569

■ **This plan features:**

— Four bedrooms

— One full and two three-quarter baths

■ The Living Room has a sloping, open-beamed ceiling and a fireplace

■ The Dining Room has a vaulted ceiling, which adds a feeling of spaciousness

■ The Master Bedroom has ample closet space and a private Bath

■ A two-car Garage

Main floor — 1,840 sq. ft.
Basement — 1,803 sq. ft.
Garage — 445 sq. ft.

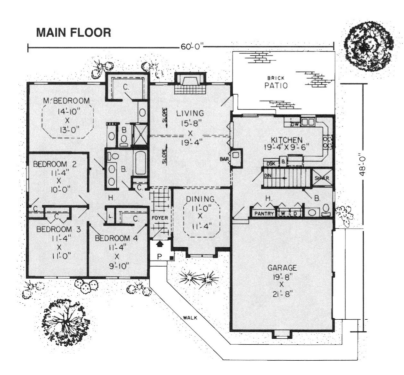

MAIN FLOOR

An
EXCLUSIVE DESIGN
By Karl Kreeger

146

Sunken Living Room

No. 26112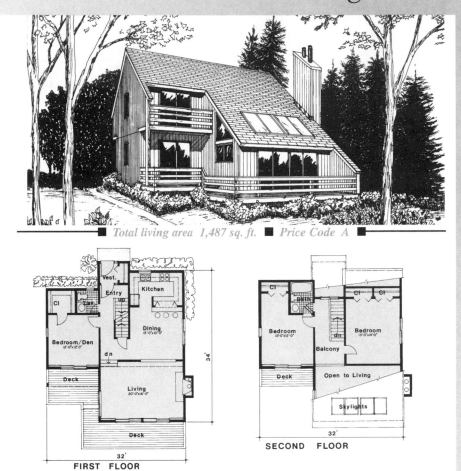

■ **This plan features:**

— Three bedrooms

— One full and one half baths

■ A design with southern glass doors, windows, and an air-lock Entry

■ R-26 insulation used for floors and sloping ceilings

■ A Deck rimming the front of the home

■ A Dining Room separated from the Living Room by a half wall

■ An efficient Kitchen with an eating bar

First floor — 911 sq. ft.
Second floor — 576 sq. ft.
Basement — 911 sq. ft.

■ Total living area 1,487 sq. ft. ■ Price Code A ■

FIRST FLOOR

SECOND FLOOR

Carefree Comfort

No. 90692

■ **This plan features:**

— Three bedrooms

— Two full baths

■ Cedar shingle siding and flowerboxes

■ A heat-circulating fireplace

■ A central Foyer separating active areas from the bedroom wing

■ A sunny Living Room with an arched window, fireplace and soaring cathedral ceilings

■ A formal Dining Room adjoining the Living Room

Main floor — 1,492 sq. ft.

■ Total living area 1,492 sq. ft. ■ Price Code A ■

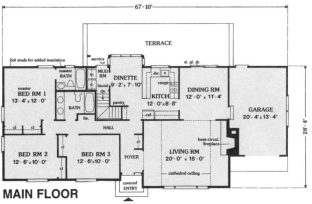

MAIN FLOOR

147

Amenity-Packed Affordability

■ *Total living area 1,484 sq. ft.* ■ *Price Code B* ■

No. 92525

■ **This plan features:**

— Three bedrooms

— Two full baths

■ A sheltered entrance inviting your guests onward

■ A fireplace in the Den offers a focal point, while the decorative ceiling adds definition to the room

■ A well-equipped Kitchen flows with ease into the Breakfast Bay or Dining Room

■ The Master Bedroom, has two closets and a private Master Bath

■ An optional crawl space or slab foundation — please specify when ordering

Main area — 1,484 sq. ft.
Garage — 544 sq. ft.

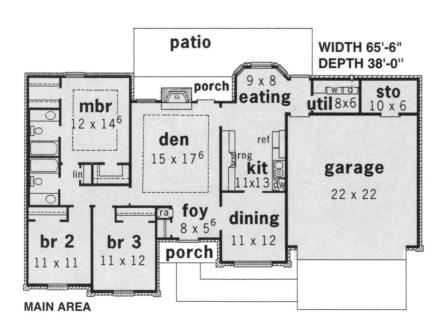

WIDTH 65'-6"
DEPTH 38'-0"

MAIN AREA

© 1995 Donald A Gardner Architects, Inc.

■ *Total living area 1,832 sq. ft.* ■ *Price Code E* ■

No. 99808

■ This plan features:

— Three bedrooms

— Two full baths

■ Dormers, arched windows and multiple columns give this home country charm

■ Foyer, expanded by vaulted ceiling, accesses Dining Room, Bedroom/Study and Great Room

■ Expansive Great Room, with hearth fireplace topped by cathedral ceiling, opens to rear Porch and efficient Kitchen

■ Tray ceiling adds volume to the private Master Bedroom with a plush Bath and a walk-in closet

■ Extra room for growth offered by the Bonus Room with skylight

Main floor — 1,832 sq. ft.
Bonus room — 425 sq. ft.
Garage & storage — 562 sq. ft.

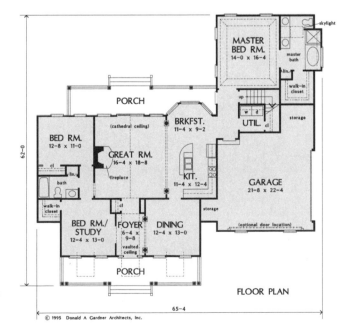

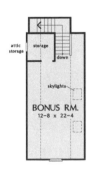

FLOOR PLAN

© 1995 Donald A Gardner Architects, Inc.

Compact Plan

© 1996 Donald A. Gardner Architects, Inc.

■ *Total living area 1,372 sq. ft.* ■ *Price Code C* ■

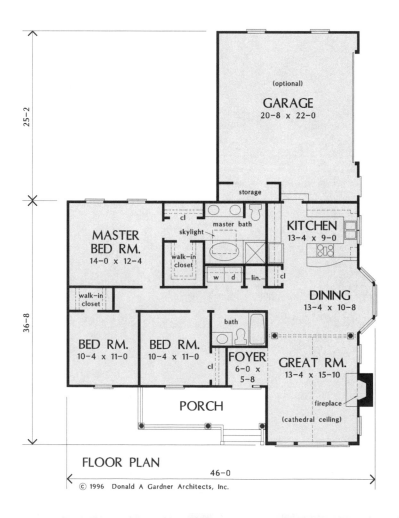

FLOOR PLAN

© 1996 Donald A Gardner Architects, Inc.

No. 99830

■ **This plan features:**

— Three bedrooms

— Two full baths

■ A Great Room topped by a cathedral ceiling, combining with the openness of the adjoining Dining Room and Kitchen, to create a spacious living area

■ A bay window enlarges the Dining Room and a palladian window allows ample light into the Great Room

■ An efficient U-shaped Kitchen leads directly to the Garage, convenient for unloading groceries

■ The Master Suite is highlighted by ample closet space and a private skylit Bath

Main floor — 1,372 sq. ft.
Garage & Storage — 537 sq. ft.

Economical Three-Bedroom

No. 99849

■ **This plan features:**

— Three bedrooms

— Two full baths

■ Dormers above the covered Porch casts light into the Foyer

■ Columns punctuate the entrance to the Great Room/Dining Room area with a shared cathedral ceiling and a bank of operable skylights

■ The Kitchen with its breakfast counter is open to the Dining Area

■ The private Master Suite with a tray ceiling and luxurious Bath features a double vanity, separate shower and skylights over the whirlpool tub

Main floor — 1,322 sq. ft.
Garage & Storage — 413 sq. ft.

■ *Total living area 1,322 sq. ft.* ■ *Price Code C* ■

© 1993 Donald A. Gardner Architects, Inc.

Sunshine Special

No. 20150

■ **This plan features:**

— Three bedrooms

— Two full baths

■ The Living Room has a large fireplace and a sloped ceiling

■ There are walk-in closets in each Bedroom

■ The Master Suite includes a luxury Bath and a decorative ceiling

Main floor — 1,638 sq. ft.
Basement — 1,320 sq. ft.
Garage — 462 sq. ft.

■ *Total living area 1,638 sq. ft.* ■ *Price Code B* ■

An **EXCLUSIVE DESIGN** *By Karl Kreeger*

Slab/Crawl Space Option

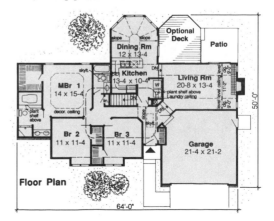

Floor Plan

Living Room Features Exposed Beams

■ *Total living area 1,876 sq. ft.* ■ *Price Code C* ■

Main floor — 1,876 sq. ft.
Garage — 619 sq. ft.

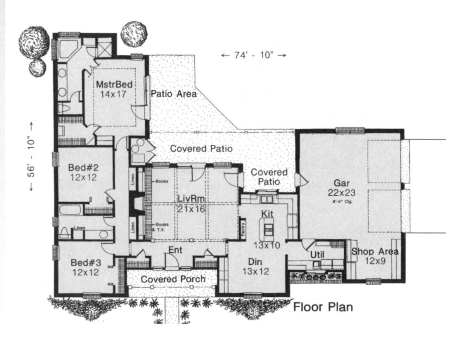

Floor Plan

No. 98503

■ **This plan features:**

– Three bedrooms

– Two full baths

■ A covered Porch shelters the entry to this home

■ The large Living Room with exposed beams includes a fireplace and built-ins

■ The bright Dining Room is located next to the Kitchen which features a center island

■ The Bedroom wing features three spacious Bedrooms and two full Baths

■ The two-car Garage has a handy workshop area

■ An optional crawl space or slab foundation available — please specify when ordering

■ No materials list is available for this plan

Country Style Home With Corner Porch

© 1997 Donald A Gardner Architects, Inc.

Total living area 1,815 sq. ft. ■ *Price Code D*

No. 99804

■ This plan features:

— Three bedrooms

— Two full baths

■ Dining Room has four floor-to-ceiling windows that overlook front Porch

■ Great Room topped by a cathedral ceiling, enhanced by a fireplace, and sliding doors to the back Porch

■ Utility Room located near Kitchen and Breakfast Nook

■ Master Bedroom has a walk in closet and private Bath

■ Two additional Bedrooms with ample closet space share a full Bath

■ A skylight Bonus Room over the two-car Garage

Main floor — 1,815 sq. ft.
Garage — 522 sq. ft.
Bonus — 336 sq. ft.

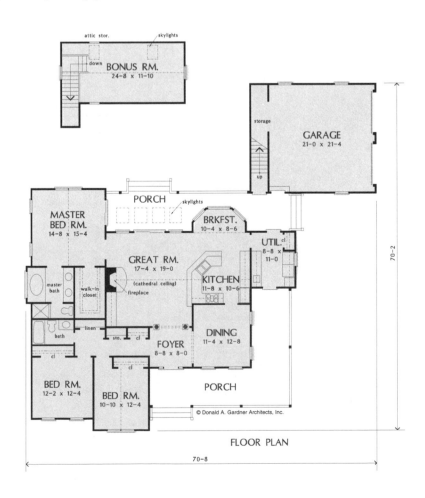

Attractive Roof Lines

■ *Total living area 1,396 sq. ft.* ■ *Price Code A* ■

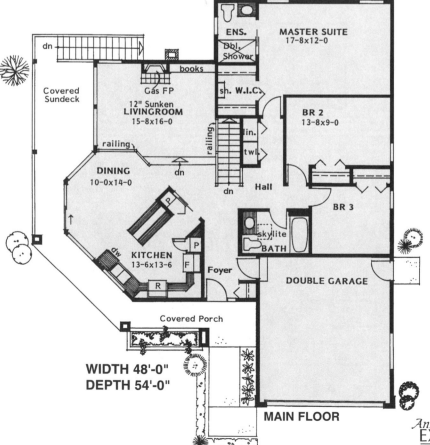

dn

Covered Sundeck

Gas FP

12" Sunken
LIVINGROOM
15-8x16-0

railing

railing

DINING
10-0x14-0

dn

KITCHEN
13-6x13-6

dw

P

F

R

Covered Porch

WIDTH 48'-0"
DEPTH 54'-0"

ENS.

Dbl. Shower

books

sh. W.I.C.

MASTER SUITE
17-8x12-0

lin.

twl.

Hall

dn

BR 2
13-8x9-0

BR 3

skylite

BATH

Foyer

DOUBLE GARAGE

MAIN FLOOR

No. 90983

■ **This plan features:**

— Three bedrooms

— One full and one three-quarter baths

■ An open floor plan shared by the sunken Living Room, Dining and Kitchen areas

■ An unfinished daylight Basement will provide future Bedrooms, a Bathroom and Laundry facilities

■ The Master Suite has a big walk-in closet and a private Bath featuring a double shower

Main floor — 1,396 sq. ft.
Basement — 1,396 sq. ft.
Garage — 389 sq. ft.

An
EXCLUSIVE DESIGN
By Westhome Planners. Ltd.

No. 24303

■ **This plan features:**

— Three bedrooms

— Two full baths

■ A simple, yet gracefully designed exterior

■ A sheltered entrance leads into the Living Room that is graced with a large front window

■ A formal Dining Room flows from the Living Room, allowing for ease in entertaining

■ A well-appointed U-shaped Kitchen has double sinks and adequate storage space

■ The Master Bedroom is equipped with a full Bath

■ Two additional bedrooms share a full hall bath complete with a convenient laundry center

■ A covered Patio tucked behind the garage is perfect for a cook out

Main floor — 984 sq. ft.
Basement — 960 sq. ft.
Garage — 280 sq. ft.
Opt. 2-car Garage — 400 sq. ft.

■ *Total living area 984 sq. ft.* ■ *Price Code A* ■

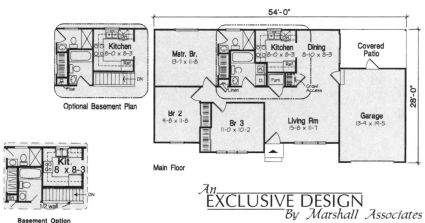

An
EXCLUSIVE DESIGN
By Marshall Associates

Large Family Living Area

No. 35005

■ **This plan features:**

— Three bedrooms

— One full and one three-quarter baths

■ A sheltered front entrance

■ The formal Living Room is located at the front of this home

■ An efficient U-shaped Kitchen is situated between the formal Dining Room and the Family Room

■ A double sink, a built-in Pantry and a peninsula counter/eating bar highlight the Kitchen

■ A large fireplace in the Family Room serves as a focal point for the room

■ The Master Suite is equipped with a full Bath and a double closet

■ Two additional Bedrooms share a full hall Bath

Main floor — 1,484 sq. ft.
Garage — 480 sq. ft.

■ *Total living area 1,484 sq. ft.* ■ *Price Code A* ■

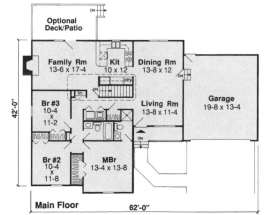

155

Champagne Style on a Soda-Pop Budget

■ *Total living area 988 sq. ft.* ■ *Price Code A* ■

No. 24302

■ This plan features:

— Three bedrooms

— One full and one three-quarter baths

■ Multiple gables, arched windows, and a unique exterior set this delightful Ranch apart in any neighborhood

■ Living and Dining Rooms flow together to create a very roomy feeling

■ Sliding doors lead from the Dining Room to a Covered Patio

■ The Master Bedroom has a private Bath

Main floor — 988 sq. ft.
Basement — 988 sq. ft.
Garage — 280 sq. ft

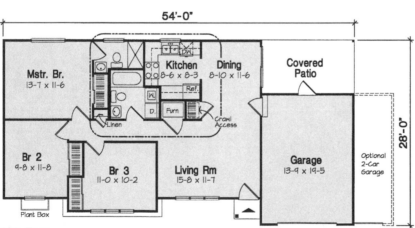

Main Floor

54'-0"
28'-0"

Mstr. Br.
13-7 x 11-6

Kitchen
8-6 x 8-3

Dining
8-10 x 11-6

Covered Patio

Br 2
9-8 x 11-8

Br 3
11-0 x 10-2

Living Rm
15-8 x 11-7

Garage
13-9 x 19-5

Optional 2-Car Garage

Linen

Furn

Crawl Access

Plant Box

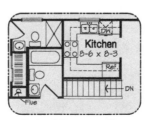

Optional Basement Plan

Kitchen
8-6 x 8-3

An EXCLUSIVE DESIGN *By Marshall Associates*

■ *Total living area 1,540 sq. ft.* ■ *Price Code B* ■

No. 93161

■ This plan features:

— Three bedrooms

— Two full baths

■ Cozy front Porch leads into Entry with vaulted ceiling and sidelights

■ Open Living Room enhanced by a cathedral ceiling, a wall of windows and corner fireplace

■ Large and efficient Kitchen with an extended counter and a bright Dining Area with access to Screen Porch

■ Convenient Utility area with access to Garage and Storage area

■ Spacious Master Bedroom with a walk-in closet and private Bath

■ Two additional Bedrooms with ample closets share a full Bath

■ No materials list is available for this plan

Main floor — 1,540 sq. ft.
Basement — 1,540 sq. ft.

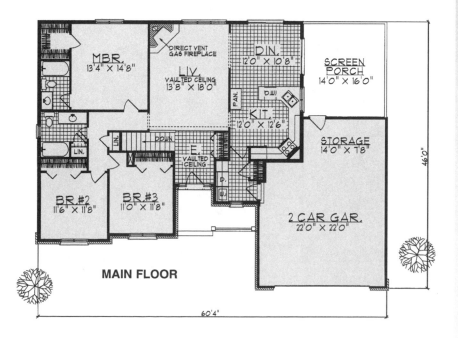

MAIN FLOOR

MBR.
13'4" X 14'8"

DIRECT VENT GAS FIREPLACE

LIV.
VAULTED CEILING
13'8" X 18'0"

DIN.
12'0" X 10'8"

SCREEN PORCH
14'0" X 16'0"

PAN.

DW

KIT.
12'0" X 12'6"

STORAGE
14'0" X 7'8"

LIN.

DOWN

E.
VAULTED CEILING

BR. #2
11'6" X 11'8"

BR. #3
11'0" X 11'8"

2 CAR GAR.
22'0" X 22'0"

46'0"

60'4"

A Modern Slant On A Country Theme

■ *Total living area 1,648 sq. ft.* ■ *Price Code B* ■

No. 96513

■ **This plan features:**

— Three bedrooms

— Two full and one half baths

■ Country style front Porch highlights exterior which is further enhanced by dormers

■ Modern open floor plan for a more spacious feeling

■ Great Room is accented by a quaint, corner fireplace and a ceiling fan

■ Dining Room flows from the Great Room for easy entertaining

■ The Kitchen is graced with natural light from an attractive bay window

■ Master Suite secluded in separate wing for total privacy

■ Two additional Bedrooms share a full Bath in the hall

Main floor — 1,648 sq. ft.
Garage — 479 sq. ft.

MAIN FLOOR

Turret Dining Views

No. 93061

■ This plan features:

— Three bedrooms

— Two full baths

■ The Front Porch and Entry lead into the Dining and Great rooms

■ An expansive Great Room has a focal point fireplace and access to the rear yard

■ The unique Dining Room has an alcove of windows and adjoins the Kitchen

■ An angled counter has an eating bar and a built-in Pantry in the Kitchen easily serves the Breakfast Area and Great Room

■ The comfortable Master Bedroom and Bath with a corner whirlpool tub, a double vanity and a huge walk-in closet

■ Two additional Bedrooms have oversized closets share a full Bath

■ An optional slab or crawl space foundation — please specify when ordering

■ No materials list is available for this plan

Main floor — 1,742 sq. ft.
Garage — 566 sq. ft.

■ Total living area 1,742 sq. ft. ■ Price Code B ■

© Larry E. Belk

Exciting Ceilings

No. 20191 ✖

■ This plan features:

— Three bedrooms

— Two full baths

■ A brick hearth fireplace in the Living Room

■ An efficient Kitchen, with an island and double sinks, that flows into the Dining Room, which features a decorative ceiling

■ A private Master Suite with a decorative ceiling and a Master Bath

■ Two additional Bedrooms that share a full Bath

Main area — 1,606 sq. ft.
Basement — 1,575 sq. ft.
Garage — 545 sq. ft.

■ Total living area 1,606 sq. ft. ■ Price Code B ■

An
EXCLUSIVE DESIGN
By Karl Kreeger

MAIN AREA

159

Comfortable Vacation Living

■ *Total living area 2,017 sq. ft.* ■ *Price Code C* ■

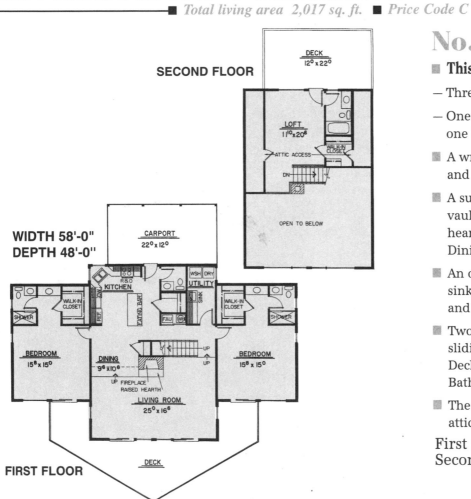

SECOND FLOOR

DECK
12⁰ x 22⁰

LOFT
11¹⁰ x 20⁶

WALK-IN CLOSET

ATTIC ACCESS

DN

OPEN TO BELOW

WIDTH 58'-0"
DEPTH 48'-0"

CARPORT
22⁰ x 12⁰

KITCHEN

WSH DRY

UTILITY

SINK

R&O

WALK-IN CLOSET

EATING BAR

FAU

WALK-IN CLOSET

SHOWER

REF

SHOWER

BEDROOM
15⁸ x 15⁰

DINING
9⁶ x 10⁶

UP
UP

BEDROOM
15⁸ x 15⁰

UP FIREPLACE
RAISED HEARTH

LIVING ROOM
25⁰ x 16⁶

DECK

FIRST FLOOR

No. 98714

■ **This plan features:**

— Three bedrooms

— One full, two three-quarter and one half baths

■ A wrap-around Deck offers views and access into the Living Room

■ A sunken Living Room with a vaulted ceiling, and a raised-hearth fireplace adjoins the Dining area

■ An open Kitchen with a corner sink and windows, an eating bar and a walk-in storage/pantry

■ Two private Bedroom Suites have sliding glass doors leading to a Deck, walk-in closets and plush Baths

■ The Loft area has a walk-in closet, attic access, and a private Bath

First floor — 1,704 sq ft
Second floor — 313 sq. ft.

Traditional Ranch

■ *Total living area 1,568 sq. ft.* ■ *Price Code B* ■

No. 20220

■ This plan features:

— Three bedrooms

— Two full baths

■ A large front palladian window provides great curb appeal, and allows a view of the front yard from the Living Room

■ A vaulted ceiling in the Living Room adds to the architectural interest and the spacious feel of the room

■ Sliding glass doors in the Dining Room that lead to a wood Deck

■ A built-in Pantry, double sink, and breakfast bar in the efficient Kitchen

■ The Master Suite includes a walk-in closet and a private Bath with a double vanity

Main floor — 1,568 sq. ft.
Basement — 1,568 sq. ft.
Garage — 509 sq. ft.

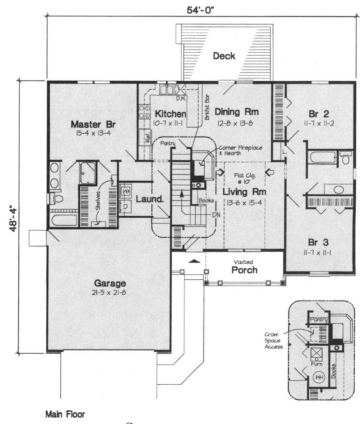

An
EXCLUSIVE DESIGN
By Karl Kreeger

Luxury Bath In Master Suite

■ Total living area 2,545 sq. ft. ■ Price Code F ■

SECOND FLOOR

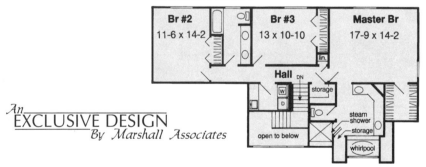

Br #2
11-6 x 14-2

Br #3
13 x 10-10

Master Br
17-9 x 14-2

Hall

storage

steam shower

storage

whirlpool

open to below

An
EXCLUSIVE DESIGN
By Marshall Associates

No. 24315

■ **This plan features:**

— Three bedrooms

— Two full and one half baths

■ Sloped ceiling and angled fireplace in spacious Living Room

■ Formal Dining Room in proximity to Kitchen

■ Family Room with second fireplace

■ Master Suite with lavish, private, whirlpool bath

■ Two good-sized secondary Bedrooms and a full, dual vanity Bath

First floor — 1,322 sq. ft.
Second floor — 1,223 sq. ft.

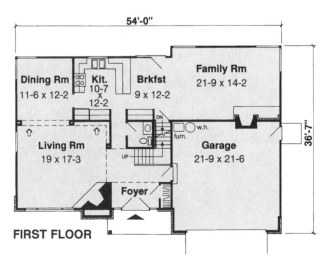

54'-0"

Dining Rm
11-6 x 12-2

Kit.
10-7 x 12-2

Brkfst
9 x 12-2

Family Rm
21-9 x 14-2

Living Rm
19 x 17-3

w.h.
furn.

UP
DN

Garage
21-9 x 21-6

36'-7"

Foyer

FIRST FLOOR

Compact Four-Bedroom

No. 94315

■ **This plan features:**

— Four bedrooms

— Two full and one half baths

■ Open living space between Living Room and Kitchen

■ Convenient Pantry and laundry room easily accessible from the Kitchen

■ Family Room enhanced by a fireplace and has direct access to rear Patio

■ Master Bedroom includes full Bath and walk-in closet

■ Welcoming front Porch achieves curb appeal

■ No materials list is available for this plan

First floor — 736 sq. ft.
Second floor — 814 sq. ft.
Basement — 746 sq. ft.
Garage — 400 sq. ft.

An EXCLUSIVE DESIGN
By Marshall Associates

■ Total living area 1,550 sq. ft. ■ Price Code B ■

Easy-Living Ranch

No. 99081

■ **This plan features:**

— Three bedrooms

— Two full baths

■ Distinct exterior features, including vinyl siding, a series of gables, an arched window and a protected front door with sidelights

■ Dining Room with a 14-foot ceiling

■ Directly behind the Dining Room is the Kitchen with a serving bar

■ Breakfast area with easy access to the Great Room

■ Master Bedroom crowned in a tray ceiling

■ Master Bath includes a large walk-in closet and separate shower and garden tub

■ No material list is available for this plan

Main floor — 1,590 sq. ft.
Basement — 1,590 sq. ft.
Garage — 560 sq. ft.

■ Total living area 1,590 sq. ft. ■ Price Code B ■

Secluded Master Suite

■ *Total living area 1,680 sq. ft.* ■ *Price Code C* ■

No. 92527

■ This plan features:

— Three bedrooms

— Two full baths

■ A convenient one-level design with an open floor plan between the Kitchen, Breakfast Area and Great Room

■ A vaulted ceiling and a cozy fireplace in the spacious Great Room

■ A well-equipped Kitchen uses a peninsula counter as an eating bar

■ The Master Suite has a luxurious Master Bath

■ Two additional Bedrooms have use of a full hall Bath

■ An optional crawl space or slab foundation — please specify when ordering

Main area — 1,680 sq. ft.
Garage — 538 sq. ft.

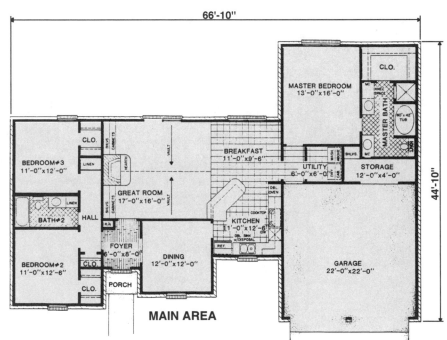

MAIN AREA

© 1994 Donald A Gardner Architects, Inc.

■ *Total living area 1,787 sq. ft.* ■ *Price Code E* ■

No. 99805

■ This plan features:

— Three bedrooms

— Two full baths

■ A Great Room enhanced by a fireplace, cathedral ceiling and built-in bookshelves

■ A Kitchen designed for efficiency with a food preparation island and a Pantry

■ A Master Suite topped by a cathedral ceiling and pampered by a luxurious Bath and a walk-in closet

■ Two additional Bedrooms, one with a cathedral ceiling and a walk-in closet, sharing a skylit Bath

■ A second floor Bonus Room, perfect for a study or a play area

■ An optional basement or crawl space foundation — please specify when ordering

Main floor — 1,787 sq. ft.
Garage & storage — 521 sq. ft.
Bonus room — 326 sq. ft.

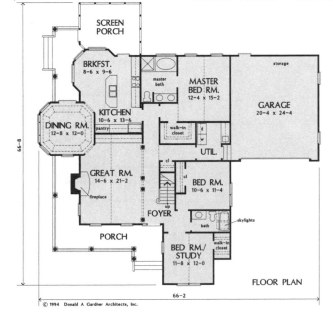

Mixture of Traditional and Country Charm

© 1994 Donald A. Gardner Architects, Inc.

■ *Total living area 1,954 sq. ft.* ■ *Price Code E* ■

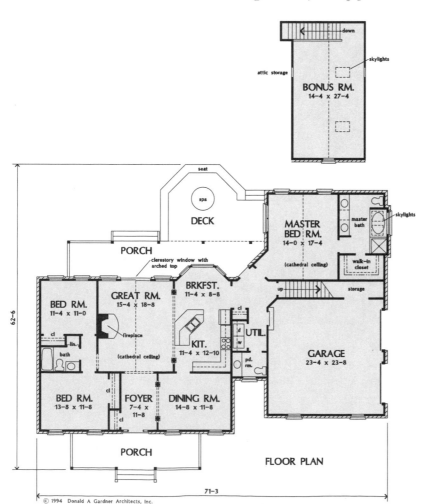

FLOOR PLAN

No. 99845

■ **This plan features:**

— Three bedrooms

— Two full and one half baths

■ Stairs to the skylit Bonus Room located near the Kitchen and Master Suite

■ Master Suite is crowned by a cathedral ceiling and has a skylit Bath that contains a whirlpool tub and a dual vanity

■ Great Room, topped by a cathedral ceiling and highlighted by a fireplace, is adjacent to the Country Kitchen

■ Two additional Bedrooms share a hall Bath

Main floor — 1,954 sq. ft.
Bonus area — 436 sq. ft.
Garage — 649 sq. ft.

Inviting Entrance Welcomes All

No. 92026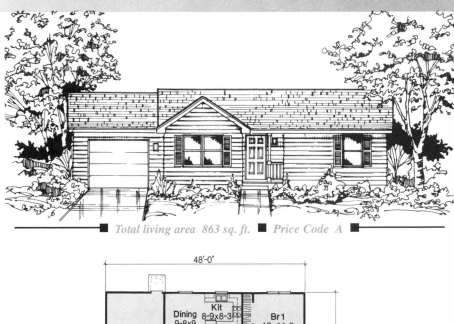

This plan features:

— Two bedrooms

— One full bath

■ A covered front Porch

■ A large Living Room/Dining Room combination

■ An efficient U-shaped Kitchen has a double sink and ample cabinet and counter space

■ Two Bedrooms share the full hall Bath and have ample storage space

Main area — 863 sq. ft.

Total living area 863 sq. ft. ■ *Price Code A*

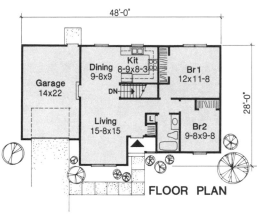

48'-0"

28'-0"

Garage
14x22

Dining
9-8x9

Kit
8-9x8-3

Br 1
12x11-8

DN

Living
15-8x15

Br2
9-8x9-8

FLOOR PLAN

Relaxing Retreat

No. 94306

This plan features:

— Three bedrooms

— Two full baths

■ A wood Deck, expands living space and leads into a tiled Entry, the Living/Dining area and Kitchen

■ A central fireplace warms both temperature and atmosphere in the Living/Dining area

■ An efficient Kitchen has a side entry and a convenient closet

■ The roomy Master Bedroom has a private Bath and second floor Deck

■ The first floor Bedroom is next to a full Bath

■ The Loft Bedroom has clerestory windows and an oversized closet

■ No materials list is available for this plan

First floor — 598 sq. ft.

Second floor — 414 sq. ft.

Total living area 1,012 sq. ft. ■ *Price Code A*

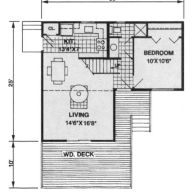

30'

25'

10'

CL.

KIT.
13'8"X7'

BEDROOM
10'X10'6"

LIVING
14'6"X16'8"

WD. DECK

1ST FLOOR

LOFT
BEDROOM
11'X13'8"

HW

M. BEDROOM
10'X10'8"

DN

W/D

CLEARSTORY WDO.

WD. DECK

2ND FLOOR

Steep Pitched Roof with Quoins

■ *Total living area 1,556 sq. ft.* ■ *Price Code C* ■

No. 92556

Main floor — 1,556 sq. ft.
Bonus — 282 sq. ft.
Garage — 565 sq. ft.

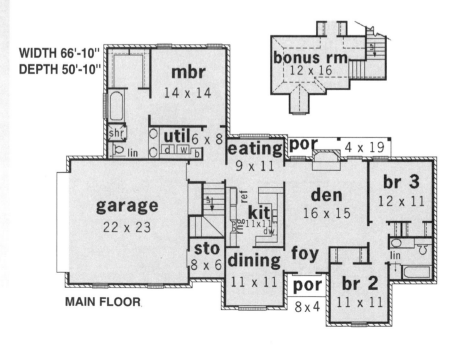

WIDTH 66'-10"
DEPTH 50'-10"

mbr
14 x 14

bonus rm
12 x 16

util 6 x 8

eating
9 x 11

por
4 x 19

den
16 x 15

br 3
12 x 11

garage
22 x 23

kit
11x11

sto
8 x 6

dining
11 x 11

foy

por
8 x 4

br 2
11 x 11

MAIN FLOOR

■ **This plan features:**

— Three bedrooms

— Two full baths

■ Classic brick exterior features a steep pitched roof, and decorative quoins

■ The Foyer leads into the Den which is highlighted by a fireplace

■ The Kitchen is centered between the Dining Room and the Eating Nook

■ Two secondary Bedrooms each have walk-in closets and share a full hall Bath

■ The isolated Master Bedroom has a walk-in closet and a full Bath

■ There is a Bonus Room over the two-car Garage for future expansion

■ An optional slab or crawl space foundation — please specify when ordering

■ *Total living area 1,454 sq. ft.* ■ *Price Code A* ■

No. 90412 ⚒

■ This plan features:

— Three bedrooms

— Two full baths

■ The centrally located Great Room with a cathedral ceiling, exposed wood beams, and large areas of fixed glass

■ The Living and Dining areas are separated by a massive stone fireplace

■ The secluded Master Suite has a walk-in closet and private Master Bath

■ An efficient Kitchen

■ An optional basement, slab or crawl space foundation — please specify when ordering

Main area — 1,454 sq. ft.

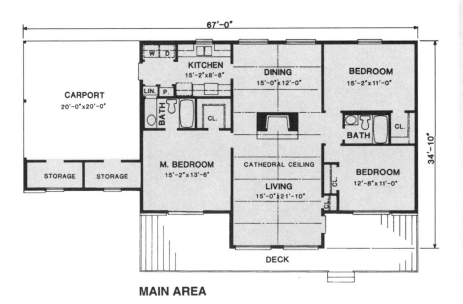

MAIN AREA

Cozy Traditional

■ *Total living area 1,862 sq. ft.* ■ *Price Code C* ■

No. 93000

■ **This plan features:**

— Three bedrooms

— Two full baths

■ An angled eating bar separating the Kitchen, Breakfast Room and Great Room, leaving these areas open for easy entertaining

■ An efficient, well-appointed Kitchen that is convenient to both the formal Dining Room and the sunny Breakfast Room

■ A spacious Master Suite with an oval tub, a step-in shower, a double vanity and a walk-in closet

■ Two additional Bedrooms with ample closet space share a full hall Bath

■ No materials list is available for this plan

Main floor — 1,862 sq. ft.
Garage — 520 sq. ft.

© Larry E. Belk

WIDTH 65-0

MAIN FLOOR

DEPTH 46-2

MASTER BATH

MASTER BEDROOM
14-6 X 15-6

BEDROOM 2
12-4 X 13-2

BEDROOM 3
11-4 X 12-0

BATH 2

ENTRY

PORCH

GREAT ROOM
16-10 X 15-6

BRKFST RM
11-4 X 11-6

KITCHEN
11-4 X 13-6

PAN

UTIL

STORAGE

GARAGE

DINING ROOM
11-6 X 12-0

NOTE: ALL CEILINGS 10 FT

No. 20104

■ This plan features:

— Three bedrooms

— Two full baths

■ There is a skylight in the Kitchen

■ Ample closet space in all of the Bedrooms

■ There are built-in storage areas in the Kitchen

■ The Master Bath has twin vanities, a raised tub and a walk-in shower

■ The Living Room has a fireplace with a bookshelf to one side

Main area — 1,686 sq. ft.
Basement — 1,677 sq. ft.
Garage — 475 sq. ft.

■ Total living area 1,686 sq. ft. ■ Price Code B ■

MAIN AREA

An
EXCLUSIVE DESIGN
By Karl Kreeger

No. 97702

■ This plan features:

— Three bedrooms

— Two full baths

■ Brick, stone and siding combine to create an exciting facade

■ A covered Porch shelters the Entry through the front door

■ The sloping ceiling and a fireplace make the Great Room impressive

■ Skylights brighten the Dining Area

■ The large Kitchen is well planned for meal preparation

■ The Master Bedroom is located for privacy and has a large Bath and closet

■ Both secondary Bedrooms have front wall windows to maximize illumination

■ A plan for the lower floor is included that calls for future for recreation space

■ No materials list is available for this plan

Main Floor — 1,601 sq. ft.
Basement — 1,601 sq. ft.
Garage — 426 sq. ft.

■ Total living area 1,601 sq. ft. ■ Price Code B ■

MAIN FLOOR

LOWER FLOOR

Easy Living

■ Total living area 1,743 sq. ft. ■ Price Code B ■

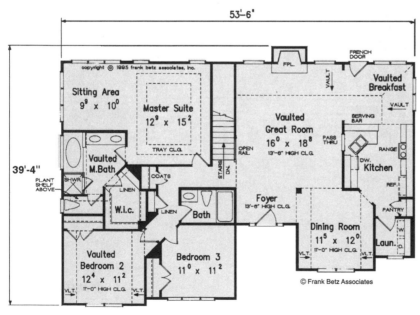

MAIN FLOOR

No. 97233

■ **This plan features:**

— Three bedrooms

— Two full baths

■ Arched windows, keystones, and shutters highlight the exterior

■ The Great Room and the Breakfast Nook feature vaulted ceilings

■ The Kitchen has a Pantry and plenty of counter space

■ Both secondary Bedrooms have spectacular front wall windows

■ The Master Suite is enormous and features a glass walled Sitting Area

■ A walk-in closet, a dual vanity and a whirlpool tub highlight the Master Bath

■ No materials list is available for this plan

Main Floor — 1,743 sq. ft.
Basement — 998 sq. ft.
Garage — 763 sq. ft.

Surrounded with Sunshine

■ Total living area 1,731 sq. ft. ■ Price Code B ■

No. 90986

■ This plan features:

— Three bedrooms

— Two full and one half baths

■ An Italianate style, featuring columns and tile originally designed to sit on the edge of a golf course

■ An open design has pananoramic vistas in every direction

■ A whirlpool tub in the elaborate and spacious Master Bedroom

■ The Great Room has a corner gas fireplace

■ A turreted Breakfast Nook and an efficient Kitchen with peninsula counter

■ Two family Bedrooms share a full hall Bath

■ An optional basement or crawl space foundation — please specify when ordering

Main floor — 1,731 sq. ft.
Garage — 888 sq. ft.
Basement — 1,715 sq. ft.

GREAT ROOM
BATH
railing
down
STUDY/BR3
10-0x11-6
ALTERNATE STAIRCASE LOCATION

An EXCLUSIVE DESIGN
By Westhome Planners, Ltd.

WIDTH 74'-0"
DEPTH 45'-0"

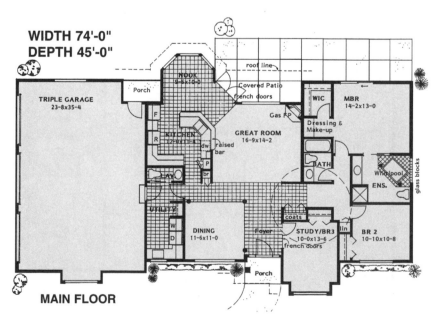

MAIN FLOOR

173

Split Bedroom Floor Plan

■ *Total living area 1,243 sq. ft.* ■ *Price Code A* ■

No. 96519

■ **This plan features:**

— Three bedrooms

— Two full baths

■ A split bedroom floor plan gives the Master Bedroom ultimate privacy

■ The Great Room is highlighted by a fireplace and a vaulted ten-foot ceiling

■ A snack bar peninsula counter is one of the many conveniences of the Kitchen

■ The Patio is accessed from the Dining Room and expands dining to the outdoors

■ Two additional Bedrooms share the full Bath in the hall

■ No materials list is available for this plan

Main floor — 1,243 sq. ft.
Garage — 523 sq. ft.

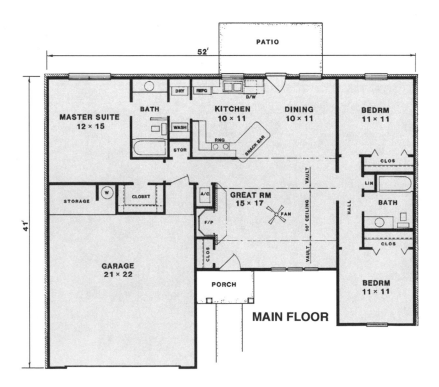

Unusual Angles Add Style

No. 92804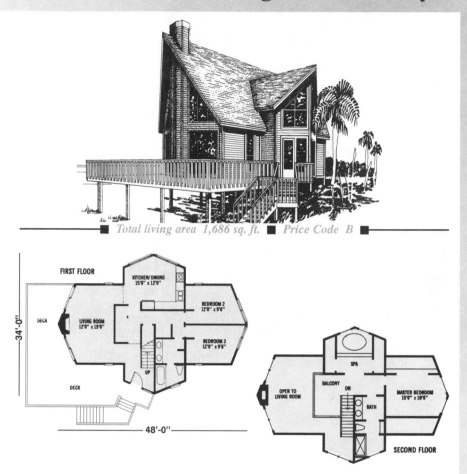

■ **This plan features:**

— Three bedrooms

— Two full baths

■ A wooden Deck provides an entrance and expands living space

■ A fireplace surrounded by windows in the two-story Living Room

■ An efficient Kitchen/Dining Area with angled windows

■ Two first floor Bedrooms sharing a full hall Bath

■ A unique Master Suite has a spa area, a balcony and a private Bath

■ An optional basement, slab, post or crawl space foundation — please specify when ordering

First floor — 1,051 sq. ft.
Second floor — 635 sq. ft.

Total living area 1,686 sq. ft. ■ Price Code B

A Special Kind of Coziness

No. 98805

■ **This plan features:**

— Three bedrooms

— One full and one half baths

■ An open rail staircase compliments the central Foyer

■ The Living Room has a warm fireplace and combines with the Dining Area

■ The Kitchen is highlighted by a desk, a pantry, and a serving bar

■ Laundry conveniently located near the Bedrooms

■ The Master Suite includes a private half Bath

■ Two secondary Bedrooms have ample closet space

Main floor — 1,089 sq. ft.
Basement — 1,089 sq. ft.
Garage — 462 sq. ft.

Total living area 1,089 sq. ft. ■ Price Code A

Coastal Style Design

■ *Total living area 1,440 sq. ft.* ■ *Price Code A* ■

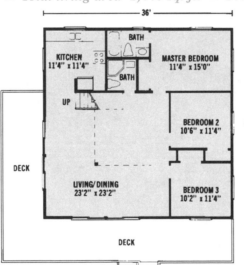

LOFT

ROOF

ROOF

DN

LOFT
12'0" x 12'0"

ROOF

ROOF

ROOF

36'

KITCHEN
11'4" x 11'4"

BATH

BATH

MASTER BEDROOM
11'4" x 15'0"

UP

BEDROOM 2
10'6" x 11'4"

36'

DECK

LIVING/DINING
23'2" x 23'2"

BEDROOM 3
10'2" x 11'4"

DECK

MAIN FLOOR

No. 92801

■ **This plan features:**

— Three bedrooms

— Two full baths

■ A wrap-around Deck, sliding glass doors and many windows to enjoy the view

■ An expansive Living/Dining Area

■ An efficient Kitchen with windows on two sides

■ A Master Bedroom with a private full Bath

■ A second floor Loft Area with windows all around

■ An optional basement, pole, slab or crawl space foundation — please specify when ordering

Main floor — 1,296 sq. ft.
Loft — 144 sq. ft.

Inviting Porch Has Dual Function

■ *Total living area 1,295 sq. ft.* ■ *Price Code A* ■

No. 91021 ✕

■ This plan features:

— Three bedrooms

— One full and one three-quarter baths

■ An inviting, wrap-around Porch Entry with sliding glass doors leading right into a bayed Dining Room

■ A Living Room with a cozy feeling, enhanced by the fireplace

■ An efficient Kitchen opening to both Dining and Living rooms

■ A Master Suite with a walk-in closet and private Master Bath

■ An optional basement, slab or crawl space foundation — please specify when ordering

Main floor — 1,295 sq. ft.
Garage — 400 sq. ft.

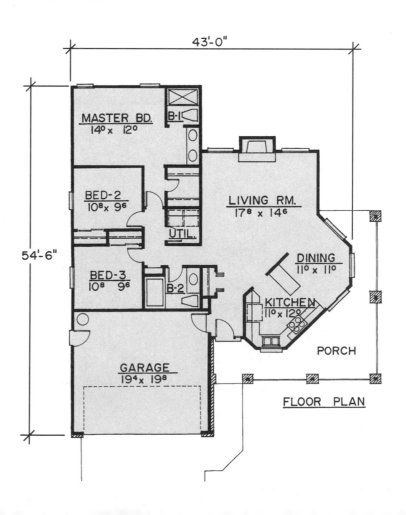

Natural Light Gives Bright Living Spaces

■ *Total living area 1,620 sq. ft.* ■ *Price Code B* ■

An
EXCLUSIVE DESIGN
By Marshall Associates

No. 24317

■ **This plan features:**

— Three bedrooms

— One full and one three-quarter baths

■ The generous use of windows throughout the home creates a bright living space

■ There are a center work island and a built-in Pantry in the Kitchen

■ A sunny Eating Nook for informal eating and a formal Dining Room for entertaining

■ The cozy fireplace in the large Living Room adds atmosphere to the room as well as warmth

■ The Master Bedroom has a private Bath and double closets

■ Two additional Bedrooms share a full, compartmented hall Bath

Main floor — 1,620 sq. ft.

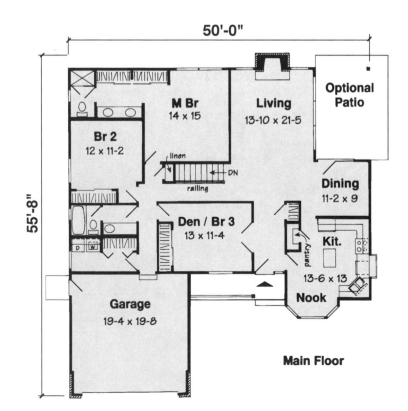

50'-0"

55'-8"

M Br
14 x 15

Living
13-10 x 21-5

Optional Patio

Br 2
12 x 11-2

linen

DN

railing

Dining
11-2 x 9

Den / Br 3
13 x 11-4

pantry

Kit.

13-6 x 13

Garage
19-4 x 19-8

Nook

Main Floor

Warm and Inviting

No. 92528 ✂

This plan features:

— Three bedrooms

— Two full baths

■ The Den has a cozy fireplace and vaulted ceiling

■ The well-equipped Kitchen has a windowed double sink and built-in Pantry

■ The spacious Master Bedroom has a private Master Bath and walk-in closet

■ Additional bedrooms share full hall bath

■ An optional crawl space or slab foundation — please specify when ordering

Main floor — 1,363 sq. ft.
Garage — 434 sq. ft.

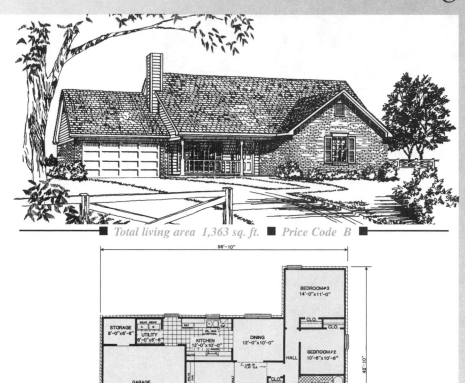

■ *Total living area 1,363 sq. ft.* ■ *Price Code B* ■

MAIN FLOOR

Eye-Catching Elevation

No. 94305

This plan features:

— Two bedrooms

— Two full baths

■ Entrance leads to Deck with hot tub and a few steps down to an open Living area with a cozy fireplace, a vaulted ceiling and atrium door to the side Deck

■ An efficient Kitchen with a peninsula counter/eating bar opens to Living area

■ A first floor Bedroom is next to a full Bath and the Utility area

■ The second floor Master Bedroom has an over-sized, private Bath

■ No materials list is available for this plan

Lower level — 680 sq. ft.
Upper level — 345 sq. ft.
Garage — 357 sq. ft.

■ *Total living area 1,025 sq. ft.* ■ *Price Code A* ■

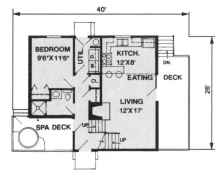

LOWER/MID LEVELS

UPPER LEVEL

An
EXCLUSIVE DESIGN
By Marshall Associates

Victorian Accents the Exterior

© 1991 Donald A. Gardner Architects, Inc.

■ *Total living area 1,865 sq. ft.* ■ *Price Code E* ■

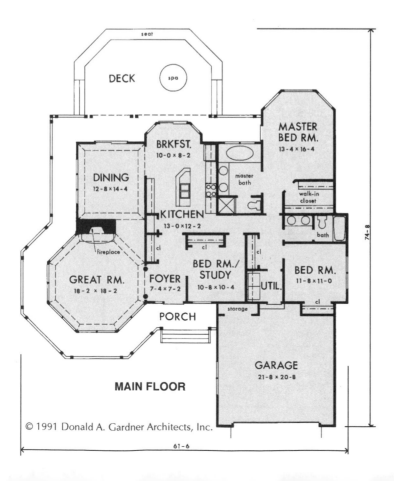

MAIN FLOOR

© 1991 Donald A. Gardner Architects, Inc.

No. 99857

■ This plan features:

— Three bedrooms

— Two full baths

■ The covered wrap-around Porch connects to the rear Deck

■ The Foyer opens into the octagonal Great Room that is warmed by a fireplace

■ The Dining Room has a tray ceiling and convenient access to the Kitchen

■ The galley Kitchen opens into the Breakfast bay

■ The Master Bedroom has a bay area in the rear, a walk in closet, and a fully appointed Bath

■ Two more Bedrooms complete this plan as does another full Bath

Main floor — 1,865 sq. ft.
Garage — 505 sq. ft.

Enhanced by a Columned Porch

■ *Total living area 1,754 sq. ft.* ■ *Price Code C* ■

No. 92531

■ This plan features:

— Three bedrooms

— Two full baths

■ The Great Room has a fireplace and decorative ceiling

■ The large efficient Kitchen has a Breakfast Area

■ The Master Bedroom has a private Master Bath and walk-in closet

■ A formal Dining Room is conveniently located near the Kitchen

■ Two additional Bedrooms have walk-in closets and use of full hall Bath

■ An optional crawl space or slab foundation available — please specify when ordering

Main floor — 1,754 sq. ft.
Garage — 552 sq. ft.

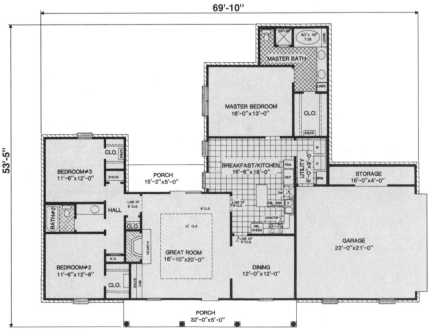

MAIN FLOOR

Surprisingly Spacious for a Smaller Home

■ *Total living area 1,958 sq. ft.* ■ *Price Code C* ■

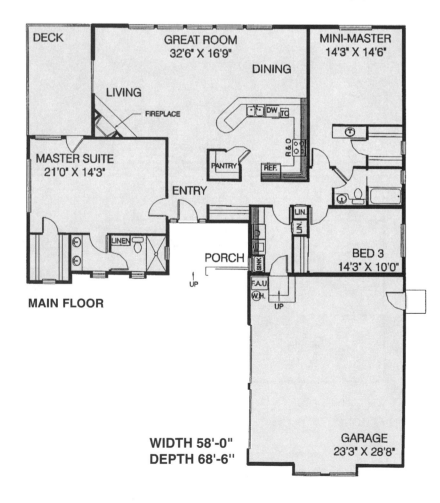

DECK

GREAT ROOM
32'6" X 16'9"

MINI-MASTER
14'3" X 14'6"

DINING

LIVING

FIREPLACE

MASTER SUITE
21'0" X 14'3"

PANTRY

REF.

ENTRY

LINEN

LIN.

PORCH

BED 3
14'3" X 10'0"

SINK

UP

F.A.U.
W.H.

UP

MAIN FLOOR

WIDTH 58'-0"
DEPTH 68'-6"

GARAGE
23'3" X 28'8"

No. 98743

■ **This plan features:**

— Three bedrooms

— Two full baths

■ A vaulted ceiling in the richly illuminated Foyer, which presents three choices of direction

■ An eye-catching Great Room with a vaulted ceiling, a corner fireplace and a bank of windows on the rear wall

■ An efficient U-shaped Kitchen with an angled eating bar

■ A luxurious Master Suite that includes access to the rear deck and a private Bath

■ A Mini-Master Suite that includes a walk-in closet with a vanity right outside and private access to the hall Bath

■ No materials list is available for this plan

Main floor — 1,958 sq. ft.

Compact and Appealing

No. 20075

This plan features:

— Three bedrooms

— Two full baths

■ A fireplaced Living Room and formal Dining Room both have extra-wide doorways

■ The Kitchen is centrally-located for maximum convenience

■ The Master Bedroom has a vaulted ceiling and a private Master Bath plus a walk-in closet

■ Both secondary Bedrooms have ample closet space

Main floor — 1,682 sq. ft.
Basement — 1,682 sq. ft.
Garage — 484 sq. ft.

An
EXCLUSIVE DESIGN
By Karl Kreeger

■ *Total living area* 1,682 sq. ft. ■ *Price Code* B ■

MAIN FLOOR

Open Spaces

No. 98498

This plan features:

— Three bedrooms

— Two full baths

■ There is an open floor plan between the Family Room and the Dining Room

■ Vaulted ceilings add volume to the Family Room

■ Three Bedrooms including a Master Suite with a five-piece private Bath

■ A convenient Laundry Center is located outside the Bedrooms

■ No materials list is available for this plan

Main floor — 1,135 sq. ft.
Garage — 460 sq. ft.

■ *Total living area* 1,135 ■ *Price Code* A ■

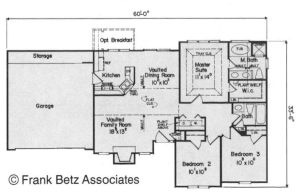

© Frank Betz Associates

FLOOR PLAN

Keystone Arches and Decorative Windows

■ *Total living area 1,666 sq. ft.* ■ *Price Code B* ■

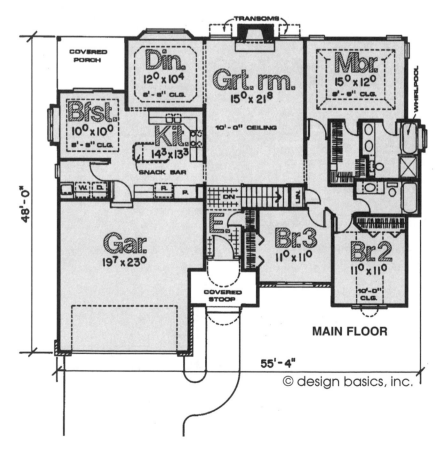

COVERED PORCH

Din.
12⁰ x 10⁴
9'-8" CLG.

Grt. rm.
15⁰ x 21⁸
10'-0" CEILING

Mbr.
15⁰ x 12⁰
9'-8" CLG.

TRANSOMS

WHIRLPOOL

Bfst.
10⁰ x 10⁰
9'-8" CLG.

Kit.
14³ x 13³

SNACK BAR

W. D.

Gar.
19⁷ x 23⁰

Br.3
11⁰ x 11⁰

Br.2
11⁰ x 11⁰
10'-0" CLG.

COVERED STOOP

48'-0"

55'-4"

MAIN FLOOR

© design basics, inc.

No. 94923

■ **This plan features:**

– Three bedrooms

– One full and one three-quarter baths

■ Brick and stucco enhance the dramatic front elevation and volume entrance

■ Inviting Entry leads into expansive Great Room with hearth fireplace framed by transom window

■ Dining Room topped by decorative ceiling is convenient to the Great Room and the Kitchen/ Breakfast Area

■ Corner Master Suite enjoys a tray ceiling, roomy walk-in closet and a plush Bath with a double vanity and whirlpool window tub

Main floor — 1,666 sq. ft.
Basement — 1,666 sq. ft.
Garage — 496 sq. ft.

Total living area 897 sq. ft. ■ *Price Code A* ■

No. 24309 ✕

■ This plan features:

— Two bedrooms

— One full bath

■ A wrap-around Deck equipped with a built-in grill for easy outdoor living

■ An entry, in a wall of glass, opens the Living Area to the outdoors

■ A large fireplace in the Living Area that opens into an efficient Kitchen, which has a built-in Pantry and serves the Nook area

■ Two Bedrooms share a centrally located full Bath with a window tub

■ A Loft Area ready for multiple uses

Main floor — 789 sq. ft.
Loft — 108 sq. ft.

An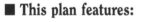
EXCLUSIVE DESIGN
By Marshall Associates

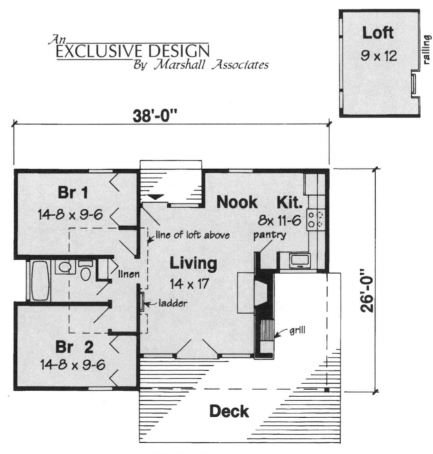

Loft
9 x 12
railing

38'-0"

Br 1
14-8 x 9-6

Nook   **Kit.**
8x 11-6

line of loft above
pantry

linen

Living
14 x 17

26'-0"

ladder

Br 2
14-8 x 9-6

grill

Deck

Main Floor

All On One Floor

■ *Total living area 1,768 sq. ft.* ■ *Price Code C* ■

No. 92805

■ This plan features:

— Three bedrooms

— Two full baths

■ The Living Room is topped by a cathedral ceiling and separated from the Family Room by a massive fieldstone fireplace

■ Sliding glass doors with windows above to optional Decks offering front to back natural lighting and views

■ An efficient, galley Kitchen adjacent to the Dining and Laundry areas

■ A private Master Bedroom with large windows, a walk-in closet and a full Bath

■ Two additional Bedrooms served by a full hall Bath

■ An optional basement, crawl or slab foundation — please specify when ordering

Main floor — 1,768 sq. ft.

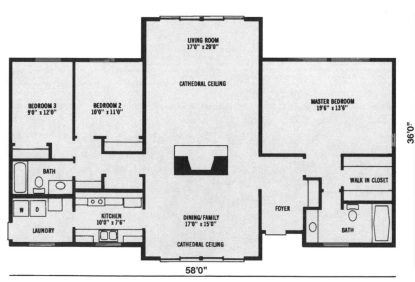

MAIN FLOOR

Small Yet Sophisticated

No. 92281

■ **This plan features:**

— Three bedrooms

— Two full baths

■ Spacious Great Room is highlighted by a fireplace and built-in shelving

■ The efficient, U-shaped Kitchen has ample work and storage space, a sliding glass door to Covered Patio and a Dining area with a window seat

■ The spacious Master Suite is enhanced by window seats, vaulted ceiling, a lavish Bath and large walk-in closet

■ Two additional Bedrooms share a full Bath

■ Convenient Utility area and Garage entry

■ No materials list is available for this plan

Main floor — 1,360 sq. ft.
Garage — 380 sq. ft.

■ Total living area 1,360 sq. ft. ■ Price Code A ■

MAIN FLOOR

For Today's Sophisticated Homeowner

No. 93027

■ **This plan features:**

— Three bedrooms

— Two full baths

■ A formal Dining Room opens off the Foyer and has a classic bay window

■ A Kitchen notable for its angled eating bar opens to the Living Room

■ A cozy fireplace in the Living Room, enjoyed also by the Kitchen

■ The Master Suite includes a whirlpool tub/shower combination and a walk-in closet

■ Ten-foot ceilings in the major living areas, including the Master Suite

■ No materials list is available for this plan

Main area — 1,500 sq. ft.
Garage — 437 sq. ft.

■ Total living area 1,500 sq. ft. ■ Price Code A ■

WIDTH 59-10

© Larry E. Belk

MAIN AREA

Comfort and Style

■ *Total living area 1,423 sq. ft.* ■ *Price Code A* ■

An EXCLUSIVE DESIGN
By Westhome Planners, Ltd.

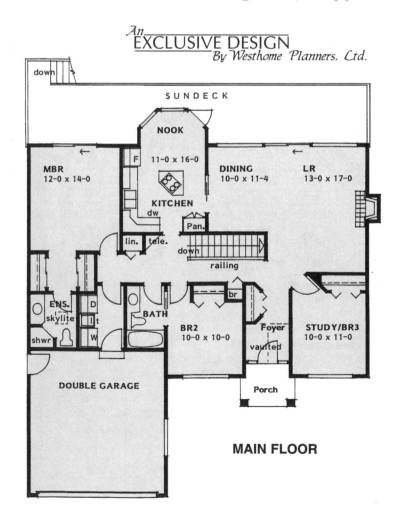

MAIN FLOOR

No. 90990

■ **This plan features:**

— Two bedrooms with possible third bedroom/den

— One full and one three-quarter baths

■ An unfinished daylight basement, provides possible space for family recreation

■ A Master Suite complete with private Bath and skylight

■ A large Kitchen includes an Eating Nook

■ The Sun Deck that is easily accessible from the Master Suite, Nook and the Living/Dining area

Main floor — 1,423 sq. ft.
Basement — 1,423 sq. ft.
Garage — 399 sq. ft.
Width — 46'-0"
Depth — 52'-0"

■ *Total living area 1,087 sq. ft.* ■ *Price Code A* ■

No. 93015

■ **This plan features:**

— Three bedrooms

— Two full baths

■ Sheltered Porch leads into the Entry with arches and a Great Room

■ Spacious Great Room with a 10-foot ceiling above a wall of windows and rear yard access

■ Efficient Kitchen with a built-in Pantry, a Laundry closet and a Breakfast Area accented by a decorative window

■ A bay of windows enhances the Master Bedroom which also contains a double vanity Bath and a walk-in closet

■ Two additional Bedrooms with ample closets share a full Bath

■ No materials list is available for this plan

Main floor — 1,087 sq. ft.

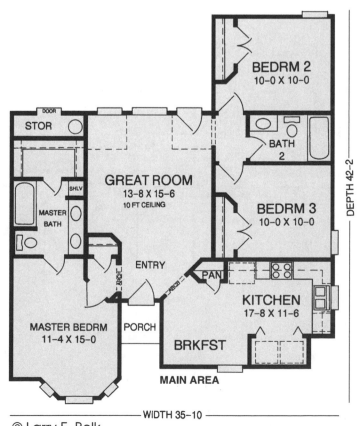

© Larry E. Belk

189

Arched Windows Make Wonderful Accents

©1997 Donald A. Gardner Architects, Inc.

■ *Total living area 1,542 sq. ft.* ■ *Price Code D* ■

No. 98005

■ This plan features

— Three bedrooms

— One full and one half baths

■ Privacy and openness are balanced in this efficient house designed with expansion in mind.

■ The combined Great Room and Dining Area feature a cathedral ceiling, a fireplace, and access to the Deck

■ An efficient, U-shaped Kitchen is convenient to dining and utility areas

■ Crowned with a tray ceiling, the Master Bedroom includes a walk-in closet and fully appointed Bath

Main floor—1,542 sq. ft.
Bonus —352 sq. ft.
Garage — 487 sq. ft.

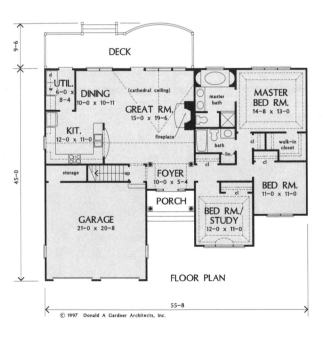

FLOOR PLAN

© 1997 Donald A Gardner Architects, Inc.

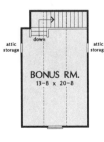

No. 24310 ⚒

■ This plan features:

— One bedroom

— One full bath

■ An abundance of glass enabling homeowners to view their scenic surroundings

■ Living Room with a circular fireplace and an entire wall of windows

■ Dining and Kitchen area flowing off the Living Room

■ Dining Area accesses the Deck for added living space

■ Studio area in Loft easily transformed into a second bedroom

Main floor — 598 sq. ft.
Upper floor — 290 sq. ft.

An
EXCLUSIVE DESIGN
By Marshall Associates

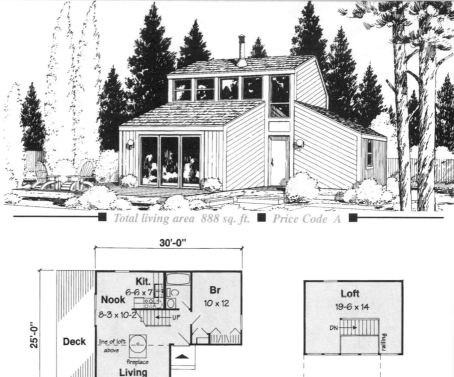

■ *Total living area 888 sq. ft.* ■ *Price Code A* ■

Impressive and Unique Design

No. 94312

■ This plan features:

— Two bedrooms

— One full and one three-quarter baths

■ Tiled entrance directing traffic into the Dining/Living Room, up the staircase or to the rear first floor Bedroom

■ Cozy wood stove warms the atmosphere of the Living Room which views the side yard

■ Sliding glass doors access the Deck from the Dining Room

■ Efficient U-shaped Kitchen flows easily into the Dining Room

■ First floor Bedroom is in close proximity to the full Bath and laundry center

■ Second floor Bedroom has full access to the three-quarter Bath and ample closet space

■ An optional basement or crawl space foundation — please specify when ordering

■ No materials list is available for this plan

Main level — 710 sq. ft.
Upper level — 314 sq. ft.
Basement — 700 sq. ft.

An
EXCLUSIVE DESIGN
By Marshall Associates

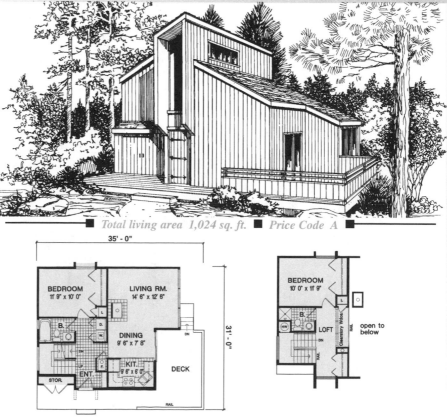

■ *Total living area 1,024 sq. ft.* ■ *Price Code A* ■

Your Classic Hideaway

■ *Total living area 1,773 sq. ft.* ■ *Price Code C* ■

No. 90423

■ **This plan features:**

— Three bedrooms

— Two full baths

■ A lovely fireplace in the Living Room which is both cozy and a source of heat

■ An efficient Country Kitchen, connects the large Dining and Living rooms

■ A lavish Master Suite enhanced by a step-up sunken tub, more than ample closet space, and separate shower

■ A screened Porch and Patio area for outdoor living

■ An optional basement, slab or crawl space foundation — please specify when ordering

Main area — 1,773 sq. ft.
Screened porch — 240 sq. ft.

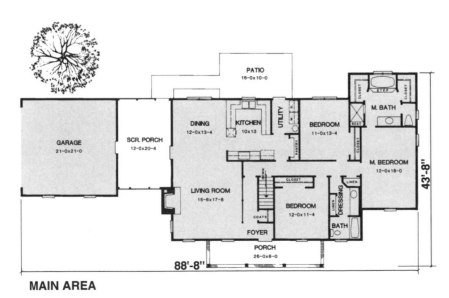

MAIN AREA

Snug Retreat With A View

■ *Total living area 880 sq. ft.* ■ *Price Code A* ■

No. 91031 ⚒

■ This plan features:

— One bedroom plus loft

— One full bath

■ A large front Deck provides views and an expansive entrance

■ A two-story Living/Dining Area with double glass doors leads out to the Deck

■ An efficient, U-shaped Kitchen has a pass-through counter to the Dining Area

■ The first floor Bedroom has ample closet space, located near a full shower Bath

■ A Loft/Bedroom on the second floor offering multiple uses

Main floor — 572 sq. ft.
Loft — 308 sq. ft.

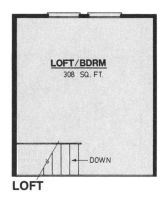

LOFT/BDRM
308 SQ. FT.

← DOWN

LOFT

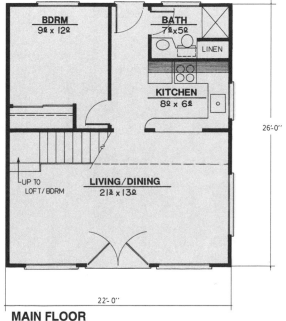

BDRM
9⁹ x 12⁹

BATH
7⁹ x 5⁹

LINEN

KITCHEN
8⁹ x 6⁹

UP TO
LOFT/BDRM

LIVING/DINING
21⁹ x 13⁹

26'-0''

22'-0''

MAIN FLOOR

Sunny Breakfast Bay

■ *Total living area 1,961 sq. ft.* ■ *Price Code C* ■

An
EXCLUSIVE DESIGN
By Marshall Associates

SECOND FLOOR

Alternate Foundation Plan

FIRST FLOOR

No. 24321

■ **This plan features:**

— Three bedrooms

— Three full baths

■ Three sides of windows fill breakfast bay with natural light

■ Formal Dining Room located to the other side of the Kitchen for ease in serving

■ Living Room open to the Dining Room highlighted by a cozy, corner fireplace

■ Den/Guest Room with easy access to full Bath

■ Master Suite with large whirlpool private Bath and walk-in closet

■ No materials list is available for this plan

First floor — 1,013 sq. ft.
Second floor — 948 sq. ft.
Garage — 393 sq. ft.

No. 91722 ⚒

■ This plan features:

— Three bedrooms

— One full bath

■ A Deck framing exterior to access views and provide entrance into the expansive Living Room with a cathedral ceiling

■ A double-sided fireplace with a tile hearth, separates the Living Room and Kitchen areas

■ An efficient U-shaped Kitchen has an open cooktop counter and adjoining Utility Area

■ Two bedrooms on the first floor with large closets share a full hall bath

■ A private bedroom and extensive storage space on the second floor

First floor — 972 sq. ft.
Second floor — 277 sq. ft.
Width — 24'-0"
Depth — 42'-0"

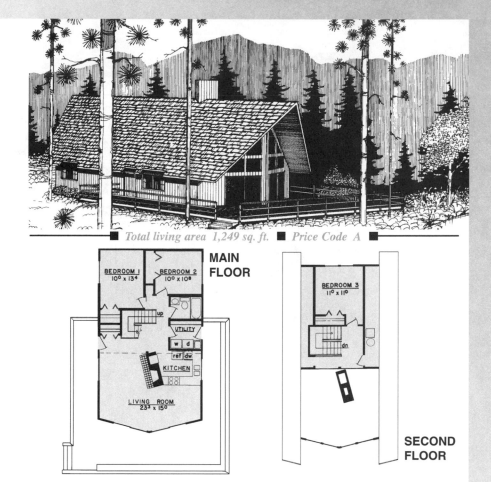

■ Total living area 1,249 sq. ft. ■ Price Code A ■

Captivating Sun-Catcher

No. 99303 ⚒

■ This plan features:

— Two bedrooms

— Two full baths

■ A glass-walled Breakfast Room adjoins the vaulted-ceiling Kitchen

■ A fireplaced, vaulted ceiling Living Room that flows from the Dining Room

■ A greenhouse window over the tub in the luxurious Master Bath

■ Two walk-in closets and glass sliders in the Master Bedroom

Main floor — 1,421 sq. ft.
Garage — 400 sq. ft.

■ Total living area 1,421 sq. ft. ■ Price Code A ■

Natural Light All Around

■ Total living area 1,841 sq. ft. ■ Price Code C ■

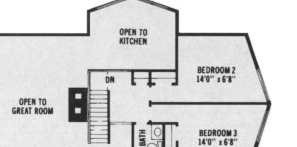

SECOND FLOOR

FIRST FLOOR

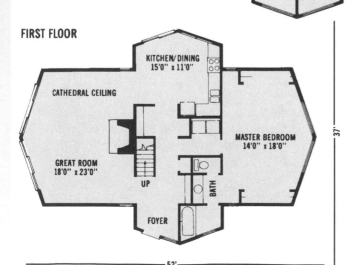

No. 92806

■ **This plan features:**

— Three bedrooms

— Two full baths

■ The Foyer leads into the Great Room with a fieldstone fireplace, a cathedral ceiling and an angled wall of windows

■ An L-shaped Kitchen/Dining area, adjacent to the laundry area,

■ The Master Suite has a private Bath, two closets and large angled windows

■ An optional basement, crawl space or slab foundation — please specify when ordering.

First floor — 1,323 sq. ft.
Second floor — 518 sq. ft.

■ *Total living area 1,911 sq. ft.* ■ *Price Code C* ■

No. 94966 ⚒

■ **This plan features:**

— Three bedrooms

— Two full baths

■ 10-foot ceilings top the Entry and the Great Room

■ A see-through fireplace is shared between the Great Room and the Hearth Room

■ A built-in entertainment center and bayed window in the Hearth Room

■ A Built-in Pantry and a corner sink enhance the efficiency of the Kitchen

■ Split bedroom plan assures privacy in the Master Suite, which includes a decorative ceiling, private Bath and a large walk-in closet

■ Two additional bedrooms at the opposite side of the home share a full, skylit Bath in the hall

Main floor — 1,911 sq. ft.
Garage — 481 sq. ft.

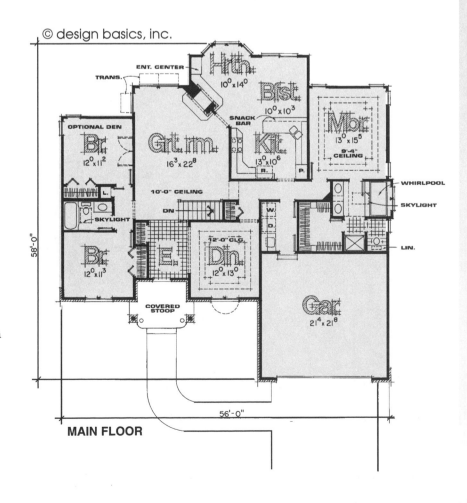

© design basics, inc.

MAIN FLOOR

Elegant Ceiling Treatments

■ *Total living area 1,692 sq. ft.* ■ *Price Code B* ■

No. 97254

■ This plan features:

— Three bedrooms

— Two full baths

■ A wrapping front Porch with six keystone arches

■ The Kitchen flows into the Breakfast Room

■ A vaulted ceiling highlights the Great Room

■ The Master Suite includes a tray ceiling

■ Two Bedrooms are located on the other side of the house

■ An optional basement or crawl space foundation — please specify when ordering

■ No materials list is available for this plan

Main floor — 1,692 sq. ft.
Bonus room — 358 sq. ft.
Basement — 1,705 sq. ft.
Garage — 472 sq. ft.

OPTIONAL BONUS ROOM PLAN

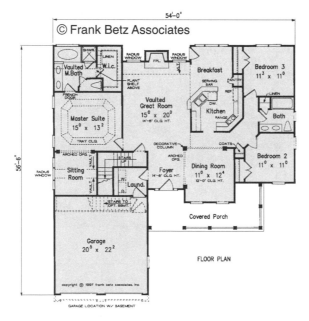

© Frank Betz Associates

FLOOR PLAN

GARAGE LOCATION W/ BASEMENT

Mountain Retreat

No. 34625

■ **This plan features:**

— Two bedrooms

— Two full baths

■ A Deck entrance through double sliding glass doors leads into a spacious Living Room with a cozy fireplace and a sloped ceiling

■ An efficient, U-shaped Kitchen has an open counter to the Living Room

■ The Master Bedroom has a double closet, a full Bath and a Laundry

■ The upper level has a Bedroom and a Loft that share a full Bath

Main level — 780 sq. ft

Upper level — 451 sq. ft.

Basement — 780 sq. ft.

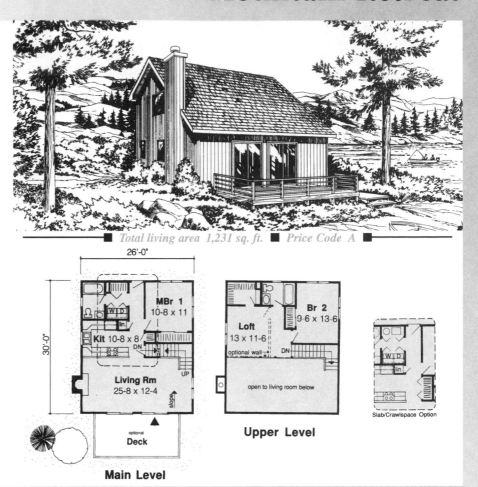

■ *Total living area 1,231 sq. ft.* ■ *Price Code A* ■

26'-0"

30'-0"

MBr 1 10-8 x 11

Kit 10-8 x 8

DN

Living Rm 25-8 x 12-4

UP

slope

optional **Deck**

Main Level

Br 2 9-6 x 13-6

Loft 13 x 11-6

optional wall

DN

open to living room below

Upper Level

W D

Slab/Crawlspace Option

Window Boxes Add Charm

No. 90684

■ **This plan features:**

— Three bedrooms

— Two full and one half baths

■ A spacious Living Room and formal Dining Room combination that is perfect for entertaining

■ The Family Room has a large fireplace and an expansive glass wall that overlooks the Patio

■ An informal Dining Bay is convenient to both the Kitchen and the Family Room

■ An efficient and well-equipped Kitchen has a peninsula counter that divides it from the Family Room

■ The Master Bedroom has his-n-her closets and a private Master Bath

Main area — 1590 sq. ft.

Basement — 900 sq. ft.

■ *Total living area 1,590 sq. ft.* ■ *Price Code B* ■

PATIO

LAV

KIT

FAMILY RM 19'0" x 15'4"

fireplace

BATH

MASTER BED RM 14'4" x 13'4"

MUD RM

TWO CAR GARAGE 19'0" x 20'6"

work shop or stor.

ref

DINING RM 10'6" x 13'4"

LIVING RM 13'4" x 17'4"

BATH

HALL

FOYER

BED RM 10'0" x 10'0"

BED RM 9'6" x 13'4"

27'-8"

FLOOR PLAN

PORCH

Classic Cottage

© 1998 Donald A. Gardner, Inc.

B. NATHAN

■ *Total living area 1,859 sq. ft.* ■ *Price Code D* ■

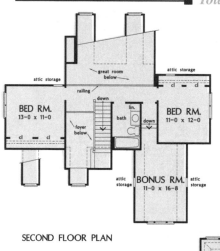

attic storage

great room below

attic storage

BED RM.
13-0 x 11-0

railing

down

lin.

foyer below

bath

down

BED RM.
11-0 x 12-0

cl   cl

BONUS RM.
11-0 x 16-8

attic storage

attic storage

SECOND FLOOR PLAN

PORCH

MASTER
BED RM.
13-0 x 15-0

GREAT RM.
19-0 x 17-0

fireplace

(cathedral ceiling)

DINING
11-0 x 10-0

KIT.
11-0 x 13-0

master bath

lin.

pd. rm.

lin.

pan.

d

UTIL.
9-1 x 5-8

w

storage

walk-in closet

FOYER
6-0 x 11-11

cl

up

53-0

GARAGE
21-0 x 21-0

PORCH

45-0

FIRST FLOOR PLAN

© 1998 Donald A. Gardner, Inc.

No. 98014

■ **This plan features:**

— Three bedrooms

— Two full and one half baths

■ An economic design for a narrow lot width

■ Twin dormers and a gabled Garage provide substantial curb appeal

■ Dramatic Great Room enhanced by two clerestory dormers and a balcony overhead on the second level

■ Crowned in an elegant tray ceiling, the first floor Master Suite has a private Bath and a walk-in closet

First floor — 1,336 sq. ft.
Second floor — 523 sq. ft.
Garage & storage — 492 sq. ft.
Bonus room — 225 sq. ft.

Fireplace-Equipped Family Room

■ *Total living area 1,505 sq. ft.* ■ *Price Code B* ■

No. 24326

■ This plan features:

— Four bedrooms

— One full, one three-quarter and one half baths

■ A lovely front Porch shading the entrance

■ A spacious Living Room that opens into the Dining Area which flows into the efficient Kitchen

■ A Family Room equipped with a cozy fireplace and sliding glass doors to a Patio

■ A Master Suite with a large walk-in closet and a private Bath with a step-in shower

■ Three additional Bedrooms share a full hall Bath

First floor — 692 sq. ft.
Second floor — 813 sq. ft.
Basement — 699 sq. ft.
Garage — 484 sq. ft.

An EXCLUSIVE DESIGN
By Marshall Associates

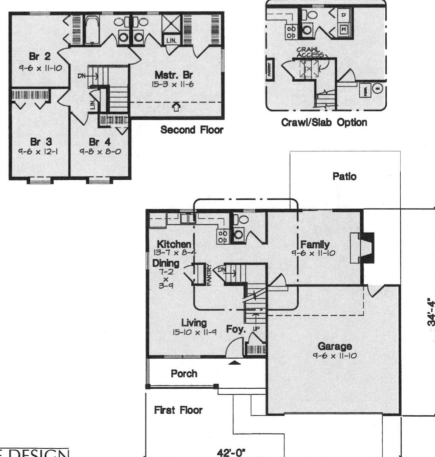

Br 2
9-6 x 11-10

Mstr. Br
15-3 x 11-6

Br 3
9-6 x 12-1

Br 4
9-8 x 8-0

Second Floor

CRAWL ACCESS

Crawl/Slab Option

Patio

Kitchen
13-7 x 8-4

Dining
7-2 x 3-9

Family
9-6 x 11-10

Living
15-10 x 11-9

Foy.

Garage
9-6 x 11-10

Porch

First Floor

34'-4"

42'-0"

Traditional Brick with Detailing

■ *Total living area 1,869 sq. ft.* ■ *Price Code D* ■

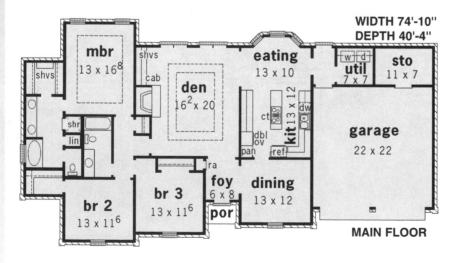

WIDTH 74'-10"
DEPTH 40'-4"

mbr
13 x 16⁸

shvs

den
16² x 20

eating
13 x 10

w d
util
7 x 7

sto
11 x 7

shvs
cab

ct

kit 13 x 12

dbl
ov

dw

shr
lin

pan

ref

garage
22 x 22

ra

br 2
13 x 11⁶

br 3
13 x 11⁶

foy
6 x 8

por

dining
13 x 12

MAIN FLOOR

No. 92536

■ **This plan features:**

— Three bedrooms

— Two full baths

■ Covered entry leads into the Foyer, the formal Dining Room and the Den

■ Expansive Den with a decorative ceiling over a hearth fireplace and sliding glass doors to the rear yard

■ Country Kitchen with a built-in Pantry, double ovens and a cooktop island easily serves the Breakfast Area and Dining Room

■ Private Master Suite with a decorative ceiling, a walk-in closet, a double vanity and a whirlpool tub

■ Two additional Bedrooms share a full Bath

■ An optional slab or crawl space foundation — please specify when ordering

Main floor — 1,869 sq. ft.
Garage — 561 sq. ft.

Compact And Open Cabin

No. 84020

■ **This plan features:**

— Three bedrooms

— One full bath

■ An open Living Room leads into an efficient Kitchen

■ Three Bedrooms, with ample closets, share a full hall Bath

■ A full basement option or a separate washer and dryer area

■ No materials list is available for this plan

Main floor — 768 sq. ft.

■ *Total living area 768 sq. ft.* ■ *Price Code A* ■

Slab/Crawlspace Option

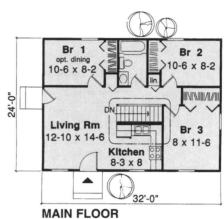

MAIN FLOOR

Let The Light Shine In

No. 99719

■ **This plan features:**

— Three bedrooms

— Two full baths

■ The main entry Deck provides expanded living space

■ A Solarium/Living area with windows and skylights surround a wood stove

■ An efficient Kitchen with a built-in Pantry, a garden window and a double sink island counter are convenient to the Dining Area

■ The first floor Bedroom has another skylight and ample closet space

■ The Master Suite has private access to a full Bath and an additional Bedroom on the second floor

First floor — 852 sq. ft.
Second floor — 414 sq. ft.
Width — 66'-0" (includes garage)
Depth — 26'-0"

■ *Total living area 1,266 sq. ft.* ■ *Price Code A* ■

FIRST FLOOR

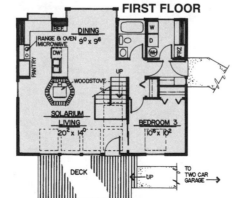

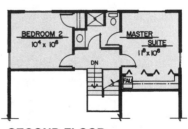

SECOND FLOOR

Unique Brick and Shake Siding

■ *Total living area 1,756 sq. ft.* ■ *Price Code C* ■

Main floor — 1,756 sq. ft.
Basement — 1,756 sq. ft.
Garage — 536 sq. ft.

MAIN FLOOR

WIDTH — 58'-0"
DEPTH — 55'-0"

No. 93104

■ **This plan features:**

— Three bedrooms

— Two full baths

■ Sheltered entrance surrounded by glass leads into the Foyer and the expansive Great Room

■ Windows surround a cozy fireplace in the Great Room topped by a vaulted ceiling

■ Well-appointed Kitchen with loads of counter and storage space, and a snackbar serving the bright Dining Area with access to the rear yard

■ French doors lead into the Master Suite with a huge walk-in closet and a double vanity Bath

■ Two additional Bedrooms with ample closets, share a full Bath

■ No materials list is available for this plan

Keystones, Arches and Gables

■ Total living area 1,642 sq. ft. ■ Price Code B ■

No. 93171

■ **This plan features:**

— Three bedrooms

— Two full and one half baths

■ Tiled Entry opens to Living Room with focal point fireplace

■ U-shaped Kitchen with a built-in Pantry, eating bar and nearby Laundry/Garage entry

■ Comfortable Dining Room with bay window and French doors to Screen Porch expanding living area outdoors

■ Corner Master Bedroom offers a great walk-in closet and private Bath

■ Two additional Bedrooms with ample closets and double windows share a full Bath

■ No materials list is available for this plan

Main floor — 1,642 sq. ft.
Basement — 1,642 sq. ft.

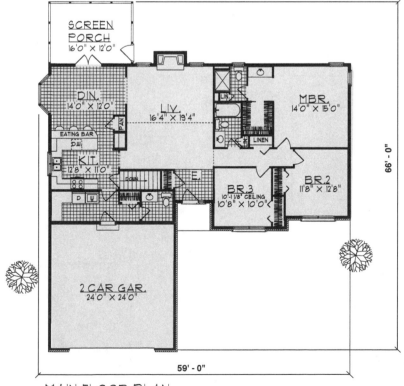

MAIN FLOOR PLAN

© 1995 Donald A Gardner Architects, Inc.

■ *Total living area 1,253 sq. ft.* ■ *Price Code C* ■

No. 99858

■ **This plan features:**

— Three bedrooms

— Two full baths

■ A continuous cathedral ceiling in the Great Room, Kitchen, and Dining Room giving a spacious feel to this efficient plan

■ A skylit Kitchen with a seven-foot high wall by the Great Room and a popular plant shelf

■ Master Suite opens up with a cathedral ceiling and contains walk-in and linen closets and a private Bath with garden tub and dual vanity

■ Cathedral ceiling as the crowning touch to the front Bedroom/Study

Main floor — 1,253 sq. ft.
Garage & Storage — 420 sq. ft.

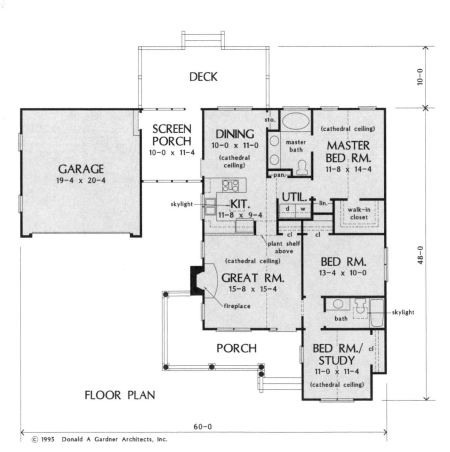

FLOOR PLAN

© 1995 Donald A Gardner Architects, Inc.

Spacious Simplicity

No. 24312

■ **This plan features:**

— Three bedrooms

— Two three-quarter baths

■ Spacious Living Room has wood burning stove or fireplace

■ Open layout between the Living Room and the Dining Room

■ Efficient Kitchen is larger than what is usually found in a vacation home

■ First floor Bedroom with direct access to a three-quarter Bath

■ Master Bedroom has a private Deck and direct access to a three-quarter Bath

First floor — 813 sq. ft.
Second floor — 485 sq. ft.

An **EXCLUSIVE DESIGN** *By Marshall Associates*

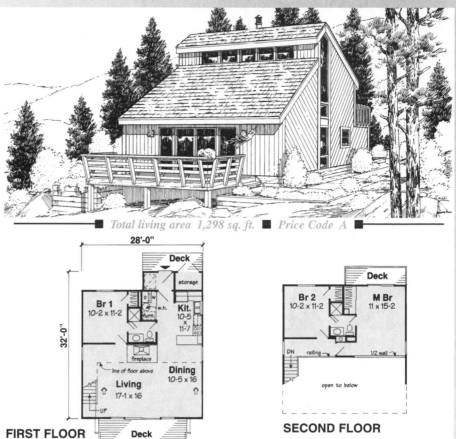

■ Total living area 1,298 sq. ft. ■ Price Code A ■

Compact Ranch

No. 99345

■ **This plan features:**

— Three bedrooms

— Two full baths

■ A Great Room and Dining Area with vaulted ceilings

■ The Great Room has a fabulous fireplace

■ The Kitchen and sunny Breakfast Area have access to a rear Deck

■ The Master Suite has a private full Bath and one wall of closet space

Main floor — 1,325 sq. ft.
Garage — 390 sq. ft.

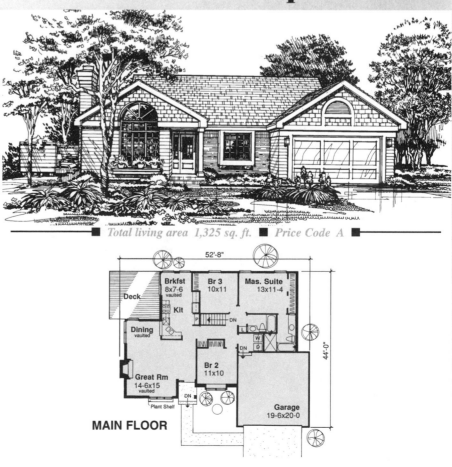

■ Total living area 1,325 sq. ft. ■ Price Code A ■

Angled Contemporary

■ *Total living area 1,798 sq. ft.* ■ *Price Code C* ■

No. 99633

■ This plan features:

— Three bedrooms

— Two full and one half baths

■ An angled shape that allows the house to be rotated on a site to give optimum orientation

■ A spacious Foyer that opens to the Living Room

■ A heat-circulating fireplace in the Living Room

■ Sliding glass doors in the Living Room and the Dining Room that lead to a partially covered Terrace

■ A cathedral ceiling in the Family Room which also has a heat-circulating fireplace

■ A Master Suite with a cathedral ceiling and private Bath with double vanity and whirlpool tub

Main area — 1,798 sq. ft.
Basement — 1,715 sq. ft.
Garage — 456 sq. ft.

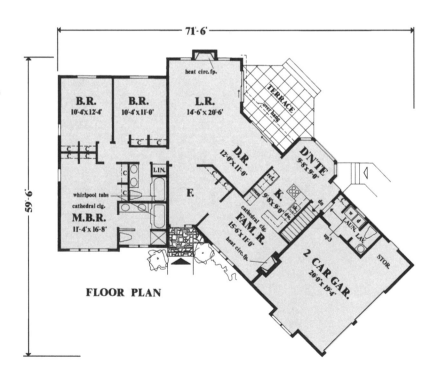

FLOOR PLAN

Quoin Accents Distinguish this Plan

© Larry E. Belk

■ *Total living area 1,142 sq. ft.* ■ *Price Code A* ■

No. 93017

■ This plan features:

— Three bedrooms

— Two full baths

■ A traditional brick elevation with quoin accents

■ A large Family Room with a corner fireplace and direct access to the outside

■ An arched opening leads to the Breakfast Area

■ A bay window illuminates the Breakfast Area with natural light

■ An efficiently designed, U-shaped Kitchen has ample cabinet and counter space

■ The Master Suite has a private Master Bath

■ Two additional Bedrooms share a full hall Bath

■ No materials list is available for this plan

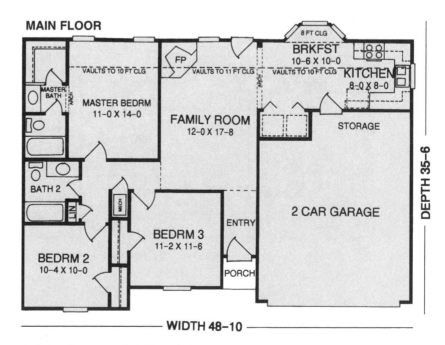

MAIN FLOOR

Main floor — 1,142 sq. ft.
Garage — 428 sq. ft.

Victorian Charm

S. NATHAN

© 1997 Donald A. Gardner Architects, Inc.

■ *Total living area 1,903 sq. ft.* ■ *Price Code E* ■

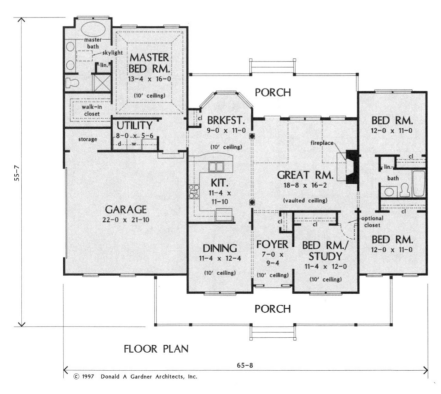

FLOOR PLAN

© 1997 Donald A Gardner Architects, Inc.

No. 96405

■ **This plan features:**

— Four bedrooms

— Two full baths

■ This home combines Victorian charm with today's lifestyle needs

■ Ceilings vaulted in Great Room and ten feet high in Foyer, Dining Room, Kitchen/Breakfast Bay and Bedroom/Study

■ Secluded Master Bedroom features a tray ceiling, a walk-in closet and a private, skylit Bath

■ Two additional Bedrooms, located in separate wing, share a full Bath

■ Front and rear Porches extend the living area outdoors

Main floor — 1,903 sq. ft.
Garage & storage — 531 sq. ft.

Rustic Charm In This Comfortable Cottage

No. 90855

This plan features:

— Two bedrooms

— One full and one half baths

■ An expansive two-level Sundeck across the front of the home, providing ample outdoor living

■ A vaulted ceiling with skylights and a fieldstone fireplace surrounded by glass accentuate the Living/Dining Room area

■ An open, L-shaped Kitchen with an Eating Nook, a built-in Pantry and a broom closet

■ The Master Bedroom has ample closet space, a half Bath and a sliding glass door to the Deck

■ A second Bedroom adjoins a full hall Bath with a laundry

Main floor — 1,186 sq. ft.
Width — 41'-0"
Depth — 40'-0"

An EXCLUSIVE DESIGN
By Westhome Planners, Ltd.

■ Total living area 1,186 sq. ft. ■ Price Code A ■

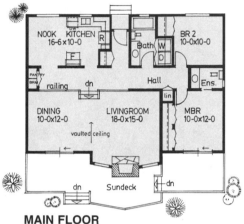

MAIN FLOOR

You've Got the Choice

No. 99241

This plan features:

— Three bedrooms

— Two full baths

■ A galley-style Kitchen with easy access to both the formal Dining Room, with built-in china closet, and the Eating Nook, with a sunny bay

■ A spacious Gathering Room with a raised hearth fireplace

■ A Master Bedroom with a walk-in closet, and a private Bath

■ Two additional Bedrooms served by a full hall Bath

Main floor — 1,366 sq. ft.
Basement — 1,281 sq. ft.
Garage — 484 sq. ft.

■ Total living area 1,366 sq. ft. ■ Price Code A ■

MAIN FLOOR

211

Caribbean Style Tower

■ *Total living area 1,876 sq. ft.* ■ *Price Code C* ■

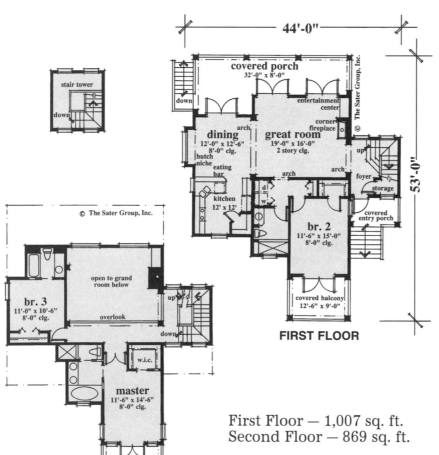

SECOND FLOOR

stair tower
down

FIRST FLOOR

44'-0"

covered porch
32'-0" x 8'-0"

down

entertainment center

dining
12'-0" x 12'-6"
8'-0" clg.

arch

corner fireplace

great room
19'-0" x 16'-0"
2 story clg.

up

hutch niche

eating bar

kitchen
12' x 12'

arch

arch

foyer

storage

covered entry porch

br. 2
11'-6" x 15'-0"
8'-0" clg.

53'-0"

covered balcony
12'-6" x 9'-0"

© The Sater Group, Inc.

open to grand room below

br. 3
11'-0" x 10'-6"
8'-0" clg.

overlook

up

down

w.i.c.

master
11'-6" x 14'-6"
8'-0" clg.

covered balcony

First Floor — 1,007 sq. ft.
Second Floor — 869 sq. ft.

No. 94249

■ **This plan features:**

— Three bedrooms

— Three full baths

■ A Porch with columns adds proportion and balance to the exterior

■ The Great Room has a two-story ceiling, an entertainment center and a fireplace

■ The Dining Room has a built-in hutch niche for your good china

■ The Kitchen is conveniently planned with its walk-in Pantry

■ The main floor Bedroom has a Bath and a private Covered Balcony

■ The upstairs Bedrooms each have a private Bath

■ Stairs lead from the second floor up to an Observation Tower Room

■ No material list is available for this plan

Brick Detail with Arches

■ *Total living area 1,987 sq. ft.* ■ *Price Code D* ■

No. 92544 ✕

■ This plan features:

— Four bedrooms

— Two full and one half baths

■ Front and back Porches expand the living space

■ Spacious Den with a fireplace flanked by built-in shelves and double access to the rear Porch

■ Formal Dining Room has an arched window

■ Efficient, U-shaped Kitchen with a snackbar counter, a bright Breakfast Area and an adjoining laundry and Garage

■ Secluded Master Suite

■ Three additional Bedrooms have walk-in closets, share one-and-a-half Baths

■ An optional slab or crawl space foundation available — please specify when ordering

Main floor — 1,987 sq. ft.
Garage/Storage — 515 sq. ft.

Home Builders on a Budget

© 1996 Donald A. Gardner Architects, Inc.

■ *Total living area 1,498 sq. ft.* ■ *Price Code C* ■

No. 99860

■ **This plan features:**

— Three bedrooms

— Two full baths

■ Down-sized Country style plan for a home builder on a budget

■ Columns punctuate open, one-level floor plan and connect Foyer with clerestory window dormers

■ Front Porch and large, rear Deck extend living space outdoors

■ Tray ceilings decorate Master Bedroom, Dining Room and Bedroom/Study

■ Private Master Bath features a garden tub, a dual vanity, a separate shower and skylights

Main floor — 1,498 sq. ft.
Garage & storage — 427 sq. ft.

FLOOR PLAN

© 1996 DONALD A. GARDNER ARCHITECTS, INC.

214

Practical Layout

No. 84330

This plan features:

— Three bedrooms

— One full bath

- The Living Room is enhanced by a fireplace and bright front window
- The U-shaped Kitchen has plenty of counter space for ease in meal preparation
- The Breakfast Nook is adjacent to the Kitchen and has a sliding door to the rear Deck
- All three Bedrooms have large closets
- No materials list is available for this plan

Main floor — 1,114 sq. ft.

Total living area 1,114 sq. ft. ■ Price Code A

ALTERNATE FLOOR PLAN for Crawl Space

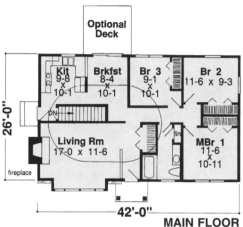

Optional Deck

Kit 9-8 x 10-1

Brkfst 8-4 x 10-1

Br 3 9-1 x 10-1

Br 2 11-6 x 9-3

DN

Living Rm 17-0 x 11-6

MBr 1 11-6 x 10-11

fireplace

26'-0"

42'-0"

MAIN FLOOR

Two Separate Dining Areas

No. 91349

This plan features:

— Two bedrooms

— One full and one three-quarter baths

- A vaulted ceiling entry
- The Living Room is accented with a vaulted ceiling and has a bay window and an optional fireplace
- A garden window, eating bar, and an abundance of storage space are in the efficient Kitchen
- The Master Bedroom has its own Bath, a double vanity and a walk-in closet
- The Library has a vaulted ceiling option and a window seat

Main floor — 1,694 sq. ft.

Total living area 1,694 sq. ft. ■ Price Code B

53'-0"

55'-0"

NOOK

VAULTED FAMILY RM

MSTR BDRM

KITCH

DINING RM

OPT VAULTED BDRM/LIBRARY

BDRM #2

VAULTED ENTRY

VAULTED LIVING RM

GARAGE

MAIN FLOOR

Two-Story Entry Adds Elegance

■ Total living area 2,667 sq. ft. ■ Price Code F ■

An
EXCLUSIVE DESIGN
By Marshall Associates

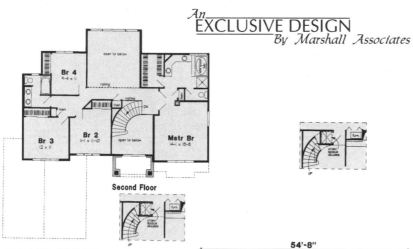

SECOND FLOOR

Second Floor

FIRST FLOOR

54'-8"

54'-6"

No. 24322

■ **This plan features:**

— Four bedrooms

— Three full baths

■ A two-story Entry with an elegant curved staircase

■ Formal Living and Dining Room with convenient built-ins

■ A spacious Family Room with direct access to rear yard

■ A well-appointed Kitchen with access to both Dining Room and Breakfast Area

■ A lavish Master Suite with a private Master Bath and walk-in closet

■ Three additional Bedrooms share a full Bath

■ No materials list is available for this plan

First floor — 1,499 sq. ft.
Second floor — 1,168 sq. ft.
Garage — 473 sq. ft.

All Seasons

■ Total living area 3,192 sq. ft. ■ Price Code H ■

No. 91319

■ This plan features:

— Three bedrooms

— One full, one three-quarter and one half baths

■ A wall of windows takes full advantage of the front view

■ A large, two-way staircase

■ The Master Bedroom has a private Master Bath and a walk-in wardrobe

■ An efficient Kitchen includes a breakfast bar that opens into the Dining Area

■ A formal Living Room with a vaulted ceiling and a stone fireplace

First floor — 1,306 sq. ft.
Second floor — 598 sq. ft.
Lower level — 1,288 sq. ft.

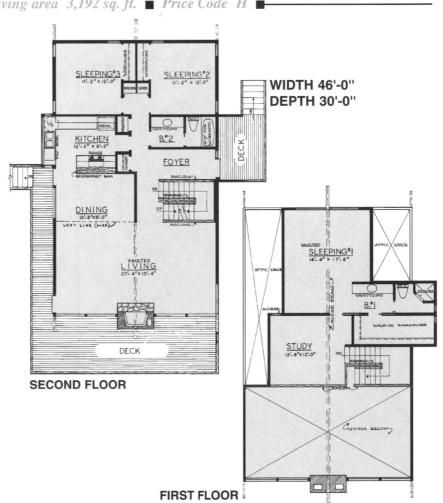

WIDTH 46'-0"
DEPTH 30'-0"

SECOND FLOOR

FIRST FLOOR

Ten Foot Entry

■ *Total living area 1,604 sq. ft.* ■ *Price Code B* ■

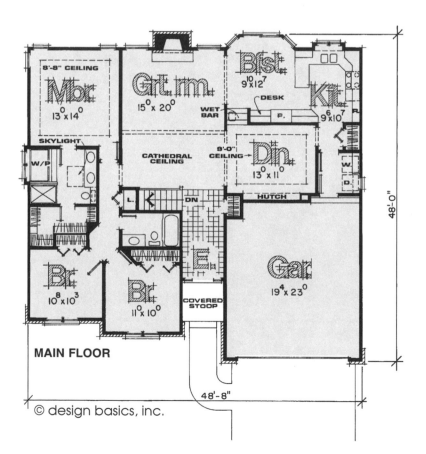

MAIN FLOOR

© design basics, inc.

No. 94986

■ This plan features:

— Three bedrooms

— Two full baths

■ Large volume Great Room highlighted by a fireplace flanked by windows

■ See-through wetbar enhances the Breakfast Area and the Dining Room

■ A decorative ceiling treatment adds elegance to the Dining Room

■ Fully equipped Kitchen has a planning desk and a Pantry

■ Roomy Master Suite has a skylighted dressing/bath area, a plant shelf, a double vanity and a whirlpool tub

■ Secondary Bedrooms share a convenient hall Bath

Main floor — 1,604 sq. ft.
Garage — 466 sq. ft.

Room for More

No. 24311

■ **This plan features:**

— Two bedrooms

— Two full baths

■ A Living Room with a fireplace and access to two Decks, expands the outdoor living space

■ An efficient Kitchen opens to the Dining Area

■ The Master Bedroom, includes a private Bath with a corner spa/tub

Main floor — 1,127 sq. ft.

■ Total living area 1,127 sq. ft. ■ Price Code A ■

Basement Option

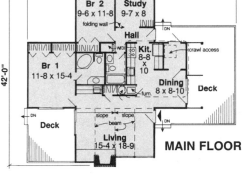

52'-0"

42'-0"

Br 2 9-6 x 11-8
folding wall

Study 9-7 x 8

Hall

Br 1 11-8 x 15-4

Kit. 8-8 x 10

crawl access

Dining 8 x 8-10

Deck

DN

Deck

slope   slope

beam

Living 15-4 x 18-9

furn.

MAIN FLOOR

Chalet Hide-Away

No. 99707

■ **This plan features:**

— One bedroom

— Two full baths

■ A wrap-around Deck provides expanded living space outdoors and access into the Kitchen/Dining area

■ The Living Area has windows on three sides, a fireplace with an over-sized hearth and a Dining area

■ An efficient, U-shaped Kitchen has ample counter space, and is convenient to the Dining Area and the Laundry

■ The first floor Bedroom has an over-sized closet, a private entrance, and is adjacent to a full Bath

■ The second floor Recreation Area has multiple uses and featurs a balcony at either end and a full Bath

First floor — 864 sq. ft.
Second floor — 612 sq. ft.

■ Total living area 1,476 sq. ft. ■ Price Code A ■

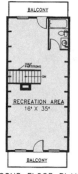

BALCONY

HALF PARTITIONS

RECREATION AREA 16' X 35'

BALCONY

SECOND FLOOR PLAN

WIDTH 24'-0"
DEPTH 36'-0"

BEDROOM 9' X 11'

DINING 9' X 9'

FIREPLACE

LIVING AREA 23' X 18'

DECK

FIRST FLOOR PLAN

Cabin in the Country

■ *Total living area 928 sq. ft.* ■ *Price Code A* ■

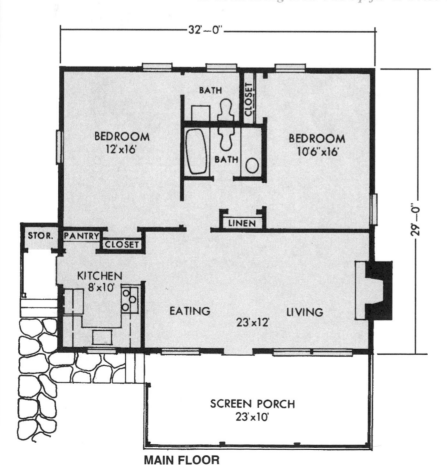

MAIN FLOOR

No. 90433

■ **This plan features:**

— Two bedrooms

— One full and one half baths

■ A screened Porch for enjoyment of your outdoor surroundings

■ A combination Living and Dining Area with cozy fireplace for added warmth

■ An efficiently laid out Kitchen with a built-in Pantry

■ Two large Bedrooms located at the rear of the home

■ An optional slab or crawl space foundation — please specify when ordering

Main floor — 928 sq. ft.
Screened porch — 230 sq. ft.
Storage — 14 sq. ft.

Cozy Three-Bedroom

■ *Total living area 1,515 sq. ft.* ■ *Price Code B* ■

No. 96522

■ This plan features:

— Three bedrooms

— Two full baths

■ The triple arched front Porch adds to the curb appeal of the home

■ The expansive Great Room is accented by a cozy gas fireplace

■ The efficient Kitchen includes an eating bar that separates it from the Great Room

■ The Master Bedroom is highlighted by a walk-in closet and a whirlpool Bath

■ Two secondary Bedrooms share use of the full hall Bath

■ The rear Porch extends dining to the outdoors

Main floor — 1,515 sq. ft.
Garage — 528 sq. ft.

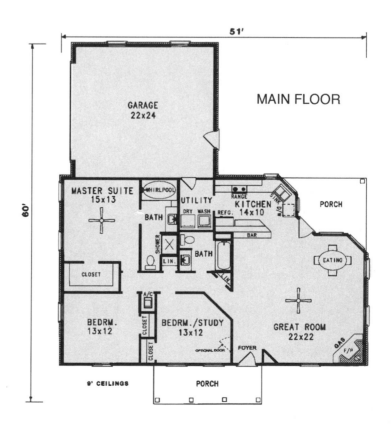

51'

MAIN FLOOR

GARAGE
22x24

60'

MASTER SUITE
15x13

WHIRLPOOL

UTILITY

RANGE
D/W

KITCHEN
14x10

REFG.

PORCH

BATH

DRY   WASH

BAR

SHOWER

BATH

EATING

CLOSET

LIN.

LIN.

GREAT ROOM
22x22

A/C

BEDRM.
13x12

CLOSET

BEDRM./STUDY
13x12

GAS
F/B

CLOSET

OPTIONAL DOOR

FOYER

9' CEILINGS

PORCH

Style and Practicality

© 1998 Donald A. Gardner, Inc.

B. NAT

■ *Total living area 1,795 sq. ft.* ■ *Price Code E* ■

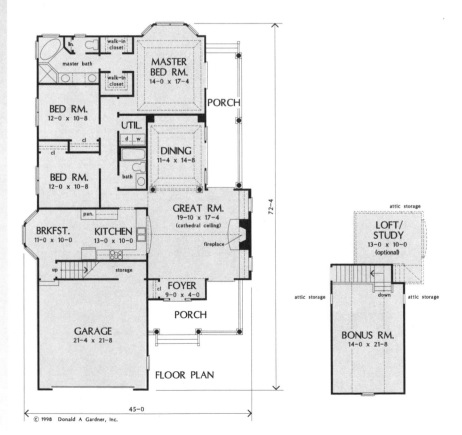

FLOOR PLAN

© 1998 Donald A. Gardner, Inc.

No. 98020

■ **This plan features:**

— Three bedrooms

— Two full baths

■ Slightly wrapping front and side Porches

■ Plan easily fits on a narrow lot

■ A cathedral ceiling enhancing the Great Room with fireplace and built-ins

■ An optional Loft/Study above the Kitchen overlooking the Great Room,

■ Columns framing entry to the formal Dining Room top by a tray ceiling

■ Complete Master Suite with tray ceiling, bay window, side Porch access, dual walk-in closets, and Bath with garden tub and separate shower

Main floor — 1,795 sq. ft.
Bonus room — 368 sq. ft.
Garage — 520 sq. ft.

Large Living in a Small Space

No. 24304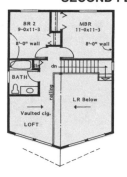

This plan features:

— Three bedrooms

— Two full baths

■ A sheltered entrance leads into an open Living Room with a corner fireplace and a wall of windows

■ A well-equipped Kitchen features a peninsula counter, a Laundry and clothes closet, and a built-in pantry

■ The Master Bedroom has a private Bath

■ Two additional Bedrooms share a full hall Bath

Main floor — 993 sq. ft.
Garage — 390 sq. ft.
Basement — 987 sq. ft.

An EXCLUSIVE DESIGN
By Marshall Associates

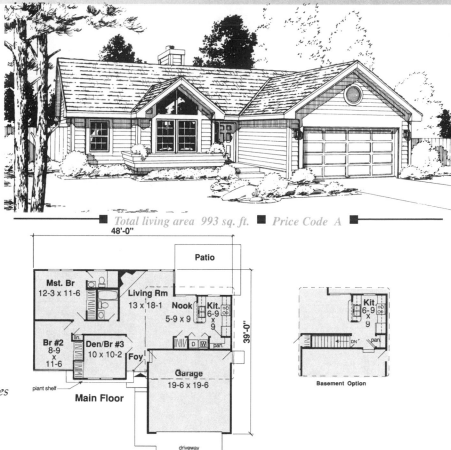

■ *Total living area 993 sq. ft.* ■ Price Code A ■

48'-0"

Mst. Br
12-3 x 11-6

Living Rm
13 x 18-1

Nook
5-9 x 9

Kit.
6-9 x 9

Patio

39'-0"

Br #2
8-9 x 11-6

Den/Br #3
10 x 10-2

Foy.

Garage
19-6 x 19-6

plant shelf

Main Floor

driveway

Kit
6-9 x 9

Basement Option

Enjoy The View

No. 90859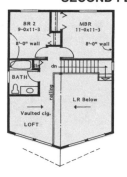

This plan features:

— Three bedrooms

— One full and one half baths

■ A wrap-around Sundeck

■ A spacious Living/Dining Room with a vaulted ceiling and a wood stove that is flanked by a wall of glass

■ The Mudroom/Utility has a Laundry Area and ample closets

■ An efficient, U-shaped Kitchen has a snack bar that separates the Dining Area

■ A first floor Bedroom is adjacent to a half Bath

■ The second floor Master Bedroom, Loft and secondary Bedroom share the full hall Bath

First floor — 843 sq. ft.
Second floor — 768 sq. ft.

An EXCLUSIVE DESIGN
By Westhome Planners, Ltd.

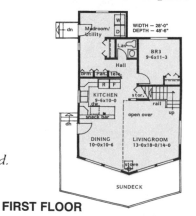

■ *Total living area 1,611 sq. ft.* ■ Price Code B ■

SECOND FLOOR

WIDTH — 28'-0"
DEPTH — 48'-6"

Mudroom/Utility

Hall

BR3
9-6x11-3

KITCHEN
9-6x10-0

snack bar

stor.

rail

open over

up

DINING
10-0x10-6

LIVINGROOM
13-0x18-0/14-0

stove

SUNDECK

FIRST FLOOR

BR 2
9-0x11-3

8'-0" wall

MBR
11-0x11-3

8'-0" wall

BATH

dn

LR Below

Vaulted clg.

LOFT

ceiling

Perfect Plan for Busy Family

■ *Total living area 1,756 sq. ft.* ■ *Price Code C* ■

No. 93191

■ **This plan features:**

— Three bedrooms

— Two full baths

■ Covered Entry opens to vaulted Foyer and Family Room

■ Family Room with a vaulted ceiling and central fireplace

■ Angular Kitchen with an eating bar, built-in desk and nearby Laundry and Garage entry

■ Secluded Master Bedroom with a large walk-in closet and double vanity Bath

■ Two additional Bedrooms with easy access to a full Bath

■ Plenty of room for growing family to expand on lower level

■ No materials list is available for this plan

Main floor — 1,756 sq. ft.
Basement — 1,756 sq. ft.

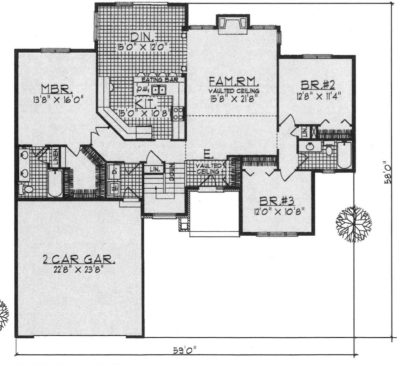

MAIN FLOOR PLAN

© 1995 Donald A. Gardner Architects, Inc.

■ *Total living area 1,561 sq. ft.* ■ *Price Code D* ■

No. 96417

■ This plan features:

— Three bedrooms

— Two full baths

■ Arched windows, dormers and charming front and back Porches with columns add country flavor

■ Central Great Room is topped by a cathedral ceiling

■ Breakfast Bay for casual dining is open to the Kitchen

■ Columns accent the entryway into the formal Dining Room

■ Cathedral ceiling crowns the Master Bedroom

■ Master Bath with skylights, whirlpool tub, shower, and a double vanity

Main floor — 1,561 sq. ft.
Garage & Storage — 346 sq. ft.

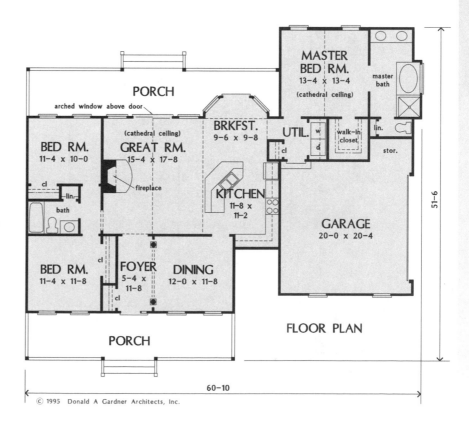

FLOOR PLAN

© 1995 Donald A Gardner Architects, Inc.

Covered Porch with Columns

■ *Total living area 1,856 sq. ft.* ■ *Price Code C* ■

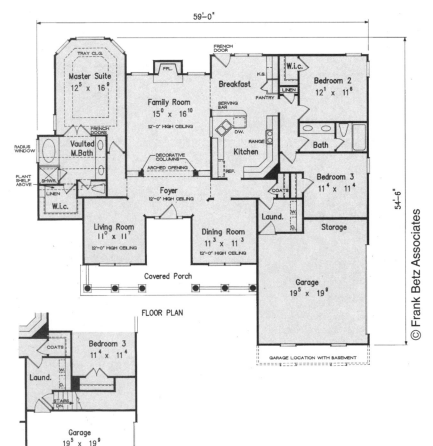

FLOOR PLAN

OPT. BASEMENT STAIR LOCATION

© Frank Betz Associates

No. 98408

This plan features:

— Three bedrooms

— Two full baths

■ The foyer with 12' ceiling leads past decorative columns into the Family Room with a center fireplace

■ The Living and Dining rooms are linked by Foyer and have windows overlooking the front Porch

■ The Kitchen has a serving bar and is adjacent to the Breakfast Nook which has a French door that opens to the backyard

■ The private Master Suite has a tray ceiling and a vaulted Bath with a double vanity

■ An optional basement, slab or a crawl space foundation — please specify when ordering

Main floor — 1,856 sq. ft.
Basement — 1,856 sq. ft.
Garage — 429 sq. ft.

House with a View

No. 90418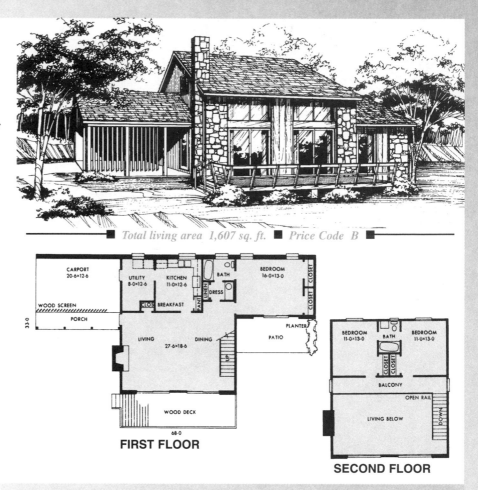

■ This plan features:

— Three bedrooms

— Two full baths

■ A large, open Living Room is accented by a fireplace and open stairs to the second floor

■ There is access to the Garage through the Utility Room which adjoins the Kitchen

■ A large Master Bedroom has a private Bath and dressing area, one wall of closets, and access to a private Patio

■ An optional basement, slab or crawl space foundation — please specify when ordering

First floor — 1,304 sq. ft.
Second floor — 303 sq. ft.

■ Total living area 1,607 sq. ft. ■ Price Code B ■

FIRST FLOOR

SECOND FLOOR

Didn't Waste An Inch of Space

No. 99834

■ This plan features:

— Three bedrooms

— Two full baths

■ Great Room with fireplace and built-in cabinets shares a cathedral ceiling with the angled Kitchen

■ Separate Dining Room allows for more formal entertaining

■ The Master Bedroom is topped by a cathedral ceiling and contains a walk-in closet and a well-appointed Bath

■ Front and rear covered Porches encourage relaxation

■ The skylit Bonus Room makes a great Recreation Room or Office in the future

First floor — 1,575 sq. ft.
Second floor — 276 sq. ft.
Garage — 536 sq. ft.

© 1994 Donald A. Gardner Architects, Inc.

■ Total living area 1,575 sq. ft. ■ Price Code D ■

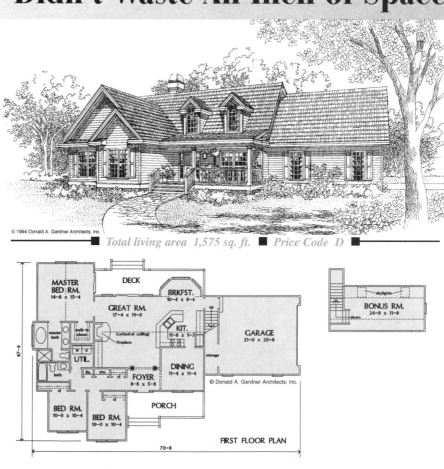

FIRST FLOOR PLAN

Spanish Style Affordable Home

■ *Total living area 1,111 sq. ft.* ■ *Price Code A* ■

No. 91340

■ This plan features:

— Two bedrooms

— Two full baths

■ The large Master Suite has vaulted ceilings and a handicap accessible private bath

■ Vaulted ceilings in the Great Room

■ An open Kitchen Area has an eating bar

Main area — 1,111 sq. ft.

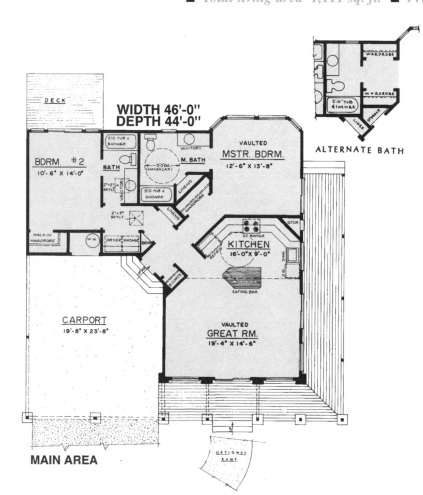

WIDTH 46'-0"
DEPTH 44'-0"

DECK

BDRM. #2
10'-6" X 14'-0"

BATH

M. BATH

VAULTED
MSTR. BDRM.
12'-6" X 13'-8"

WALK-IN
WARDROBE

W.H.

DRYER WASHER

KITCHEN
16'-0" X 9'-0"

BE RANGE

EATING BAR

STOR.

CARPORT
19'-8" X 23'-8"

VAULTED
GREAT RM.
19'-4" X 14'-6"

OPTIONAL
RAMP

MAIN AREA

ALTERNATE BATH

WARDROBE

WARDROBE

5'-0" TUB
& SHOWER

LINEN

L-Shaped Front Porch

■ *Total living area 1,280 sq. ft.* ■ *Price Code A* ■

No. 98747

■ This plan features:

— Three bedrooms

— Two full baths

■ Attractive wood siding and a large L-shaped covered Porch

■ Front entry leads to generous Living Room with a vaulted ceiling

■ Large two-car Garage with access through the Utility Room

■ Roomy secondary Bedrooms share the full Bath in the hall

■ Kitchen highlighted by a built-in Pantry and a garden window

■ Vaulted ceiling adds volume to the Dining Room

■ Master Suite is in an isolated location enhanced by abundant closet space, separate vanity and linen storage

Main floor — 1,280 sq. ft.

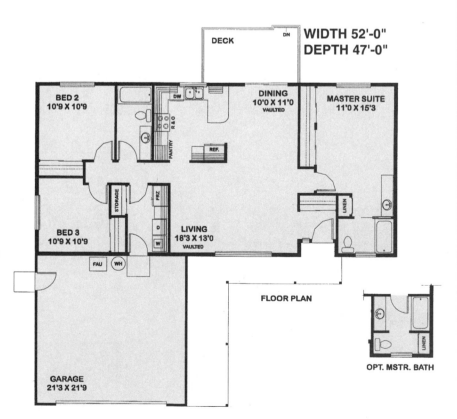

WIDTH 52'-0"
DEPTH 47'-0"

FLOOR PLAN

OPT. MSTR. BATH

Designed with Today's Active Family in Mind

■ Total living area 2,500 sq. ft. ■ Price Code E ■

An
EXCLUSIVE DESIGN
By Marshall Associates

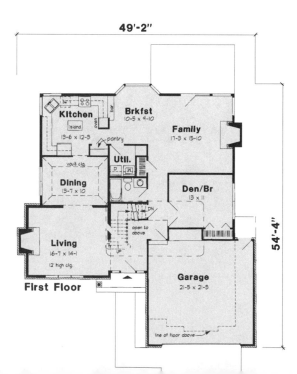

49'-2"

First Floor

Kitchen
island
13-6 x 12-3

Brkfst
10-5 x 9-10

Family
17-3 x 15-10

pantry

Dining
13-7 x 10
vault clg.

Util.

Den/Br
13 x 11

open to above

Living
16-7 x 14-1
12' high clg.

Garage
21-5 x 21-5

54'-4"

line of floor above

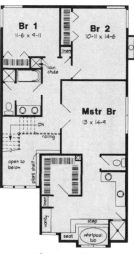

Second Floor

Br 1
11-6 x 9-11

Br 2
10-11 x 14-6

laun. chute

Mstr Br
13 x 14-9

open to below

plant shelf

railing

DN

step

seat

whirlpool tub

vanity

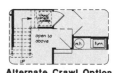

Alternate Crawl Option

open to above

w.h.   furn.

No. 24323

■ **This plan features:**

— Three or four bedrooms

— Three full baths

■ An open layout between the Kitchen, Breakfast Bay and Family Room gives a feeling of spaciousness

■ An island Kitchen with ample counter and storage space, a double sink, a built-in Pantry and an eating bar

■ A fireplace in the Family Room which has direct access to the rear yard

■ A vaulted ceiling adds a touch of elegance to the Dining Room

■ The luxurious Master Suite has a lavish, private Master Bath

■ No materials list is available for this plan

First floor — 1,420 sq. ft.
Second floor — 1,080 sq. ft.
Garage — 477 sq. ft.

Country Ranch

No. 91797

This plan features:

- Three bedrooms
- Two full baths

- A railed and covered wrap-around porch, adding charm to this country-styled home
- A high vaulted ceiling in the Living Room
- A smaller Kitchen with ample cupboard and counter space, that is augmented by a large pantry
- An informal Family Room with access to the wood Deck
- A private Master Suite with a spa tub and a walk-in closet
- Two family Bedrooms share a full hall Bath
- There is a shop and storage area in the two-car Garage

Main area — 1,485 sq. ft.
Garage — 701 sq. ft.

■ *Total living area 1,485 sq. ft.* ■ *Price Code A* ■

Clever Use of Interior Space

No. 99844

This plan features:

- Three bedrooms
- Two full baths

- Efficient interior with cathedral and tray ceilings create feeling of space
- Great Room boosts cathedral ceiling above cozy fireplace, built-in shelves and columns
- Octagon Dining Room and Breakfast alcove bathed in light and have easy access to the Porch
- Open Kitchen features an island counter sink and Pantry
- The Master Bedroom is enhanced by tray ceiling and plush Bath

Main floor — 1,737 sq. ft.
Garage & storage — 517 sq. ft.
Width — 65'-10"
Depth — 59'-8"

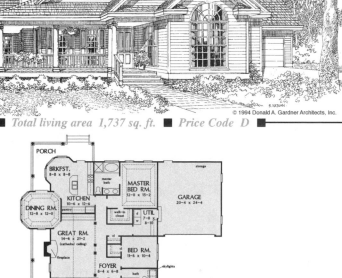

■ *Total living area 1,737 sq. ft.* ■ *Price Code D* ■

© 1994 Donald A. Gardner Architects, Inc.

Easy Living Cottage

■ *Total living area 1,706 sq. ft.* ■ *Price Code B* ■

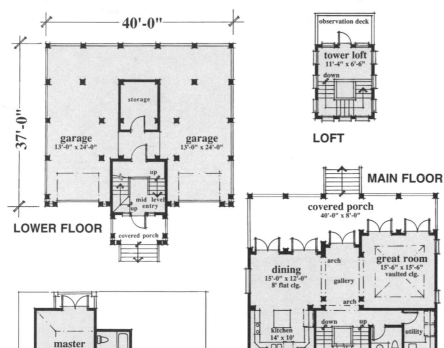

40'-0"

37'-0"

garage
13'-0" x 24'-0"

storage

garage
13'-0" x 24'-0"

up

mid
level
entry

up

covered porch

LOWER FLOOR

observation deck

tower loft
11'-4" x 6'-6"

down

up

LOFT

MAIN FLOOR

covered porch
40'-0" x 8'-0"

dining
15'-0" x 12'-0"
8' flat clg.

arch

gallery

arch

great room
15'-6" x 15'-6"
vaulted clg.

kitchen
14' x 10'

down

up

utility

master
12'-6" x 14'-0"
vaulted clg.

am
kitchen

built
ins

down

up

br. 2
10'-4" x 10'-0"
vaulted clg.

w d w
seat

UPPER FLOOR

No. 94250

■ **This plan features:**

— Two bedrooms

— Two full and one half baths

■ Lattice fretwork and a covered Porch accent this cottage

■ The Great Room has a vaulted ceiling and doors that open to the Porch

■ The Dining Room is open to the Kitchen

■ The Kitchen is U-shaped and features a center island

■ The Master Suite has a private balcony, a mini Kitchen and a full Bath

■ The vaulted secondary Bedroom has a window seat

■ A tower Loft with an Observation Deck affords panoramic views

■ No materials list is available for this plan

Main floor — 906 sq. ft.
Upper floor — 714 sq. ft.
Finished staircase — 86 sq. ft.
Lower floor — 155 sq. ft.
Garage — 950 sq. ft.

Moderate Ranch Has Features of a Larger Plan

■ *Total living area 1,811 sq. ft.* ■ *Price Code C* ■

No. 90441 ✖

■ This plan features:

— Three bedrooms

— Two full baths

■ The Great Room has a vaulted ceiling and a stone fireplace with bookshelves on either side

■ A spacious Kitchen with ample cabinet space conveniently located next to the large Dining Room

■ The Master Suite has a large Bath with a garden tub, a double vanity and a walk-in closet

■ Two other large Bedrooms, each with a walk-in closet and access to the full Bath

■ An optional basement, slab or crawl space foundation — please specify when ordering

Main floor — 1,811 sq. ft.
Basement — 1,811 sq. ft.
Garage — 484 sq. ft.

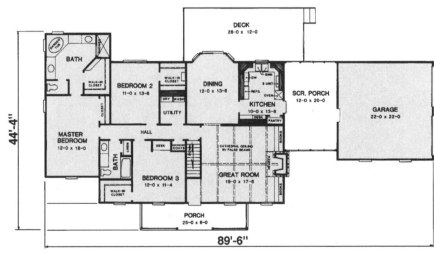

MAIN FLOOR

Charm and Personality

© 1996 Donald A. Gardner Architects, Inc.

■ *Total living area 1,655 sq. ft.* ■ *Price Code D* ■

No. 99871

■ **This plan features:**

— Three bedrooms

— Two full baths

■ Interior columns dramatically open the Foyer and Kitchen to the spacious Great Room

■ Drama is heightened by the Great Room cathedral ceiling and fireplace

■ Master Suite with a tray ceiling combines privacy with access to the rear Deck with spa

■ Tray ceilings with arched picture windows bring a special elegance to the Dining Room and the front Swing Room

■ An optional basement or crawl space foundation — please specify when ordering

Main floor — 1,655 sq. ft.
Garage — 434 sq. ft.

FLOOR PLAN

© 1996 Donald A Gardner Architects, Inc.

Small Scale, Lots of Space

No. 90390 ✖

■ This plan features:

— Two bedrooms with optional third bedroom/den

— Two full baths

■ Vaulted ceilings and corner windows

■ A Living Room enhanced by a cozy corner fireplace

■ A Master Suite featuring interesting angles and corner window treatments

Main area — 1,231 sq. ft.

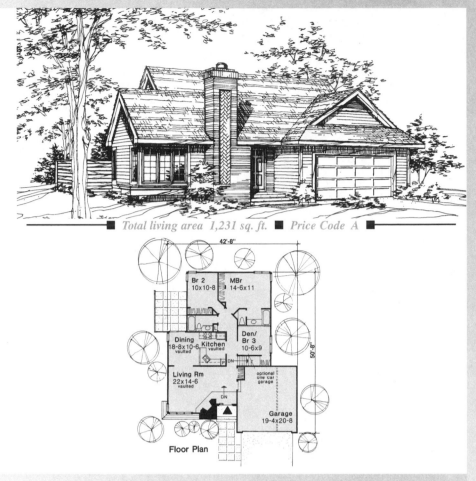

■ Total living area 1,231 sq. ft. ■ Price Code A ■

Floor Plan

An Earth Sheltered Home

No. 99745 ✖

■ This plan features:

— Two bedrooms

— Two full baths

■ The living spaces are placed all on the open side

■ A combined Kitchen/Living/Dining area, with a semicircle of tall windows, catches light from three sides

■ The Kitchen counters, sitting at the hinge of two wall angles, makes a lazy bend to create space for a media nook and Pantry

■ A luxurious Master Suite has an oversized tub, a walk-in closet and a vanity

■ An additional Bedroom with skylights has easy access to a full hall Bath

Main area — 1,482 sq. ft.
Garage — 564 sq. ft.
Width — 79'-0"
Depth — 50'-0"

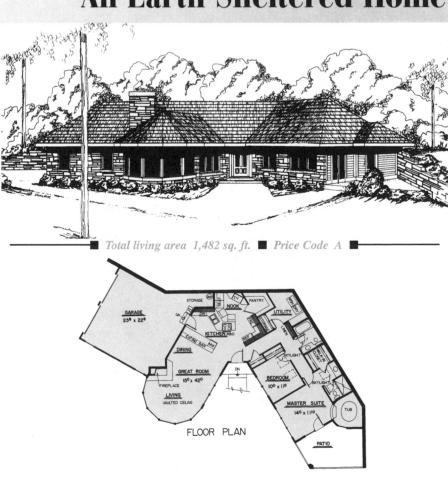

■ Total living area 1,482 sq. ft. ■ Price Code A ■

FLOOR PLAN

For the Empty-Nester

■ *Total living area 1,859 sq. ft.* ■ *Price Code C* ■

No. 98316

■ **This plan features:**

— Two bedrooms

— Two full baths

■ A Great Room with a thirteen-foot ceiling and access to the Lanai

■ An island Kitchen with a built-in Pantry, a desk, and an open layout to the Breakfast Area

■ A Master Suite with his-n-her walk-in closets and a private Master Bath

■ A Den that can function as a third Bedroom

Main floor — 1,859 sq. ft.
Garage — 393 sq. ft.

MAIN FLOOR

European Styling with a Georgian Flair

■ *Total living area 1,873 sq. ft.* ■ *Price Code D* ■

No. 92552 ✕

■ This plan features:

— Four bedrooms

— Two full baths

■ Elegant European styling spiced with Georgian styling

■ Arched windows, quoins and shutters on the exterior, a columned covered front and a rear Porch

■ Formal Foyer gives access to the Dining Room to the left and spacious Den straight ahead

■ Kitchen flows into the informal Eating Area and is separated from the Den by an angled extended counter eating bar

■ An optional crawl space or slab foundation — please specify when ordering

Main floor — 1,873 sq. ft.
Bonus area — 145 sq. ft.
Garage — 613 sq. ft.

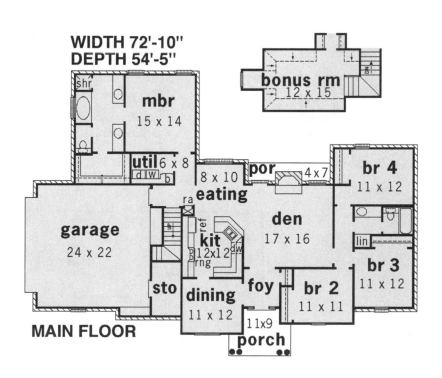

WIDTH 72'-10"
DEPTH 54'-5"

bonus rm
12 x 15

mbr
15 x 14

shr

util 6 x 8
d w b

garage
24 x 22

eating
8 x 10

por
4 x 7

br 4
11 x 12

ref
kit
12 x 12
rng
dw

den
17 x 16

lin

br 3
11 x 12

sto

dining
11 x 12

foy

br 2
11 x 11

porch
11x9

MAIN FLOOR

Focus on the Family

An EXCLUSIVE DESIGN
By Marshall Associates

■ *Total living area 1,800 sq. ft.* ■ *Price Code C* ■

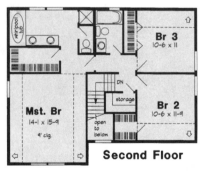

Second Floor

- whirlpool tub
- **Br 3** 10-6 x 11
- **Mst. Br** 14-1 x 15-9 9' clg.
- storage
- DN
- **Br 2** 10-6 x 11-9
- open to below

Alternate Crawl Option

- UP
- DN
- DN
- open to above
- crawl access
- furn. w/h

No. 24324

■ **This plan features:**

— Three bedrooms

— Two full and one half baths

■ Cozy front Porch

■ A fireplaced Family Room

■ The U-shaped Kitchen has a Pantry and ample cabinet space

■ A pan-vaulted ceiling in the formal Dining Room adds a decorative accent

■ The Living Room flows easily into the Dining Room

■ The Master Suite is enhanced with a walk-in closet, a double vanity and a whirlpool tub

■ No materials list is available for this plan

First floor — 916 sq. ft.
Second floor — 884 sq. ft.
Garage — 480 sq. ft.

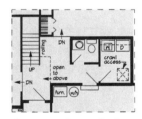

First Floor

40'-0"

48'-0"

- **Dining** 9-6 x 11
- pan vault clg.
- **Kit.** 10-4 x 11
- bar
- pantry
- **Family** 14 x 14-10
- **Living** 14-1 x 15-9
- railing
- open to above
- UP
- DN
- DN
- **Util.**
- **Garage** 14-5 x 23-8

Affordable Style

No. 91753

This plan features:

— Three bedrooms

— Two full baths

■ A country Porch welcomes you to an entry hall with a convenient closet

■ A well-appointed Kitchen boasts a double sink, ample counter and storage space, a peninsula eating bar and a built-in hutch

■ A terrific Master Suite including a private Bath and a walk-in closet

■ A Dining Room that flows from the Great Room and into the Kitchen that includes sliding glass doors to the Deck

■ The Great Room with a cozy fireplace can also be enjoyed from the Dining Area

■ Two additional Bedrooms share a full hall Bath

■ No materials list is available for this plan

Main floor — 1,490 sq. ft.
Covered porch — 120 sq. ft.
Basement — 1,490 sq. ft.
Garage — 579 sq. ft.
Width — 58'-0"
Depth — 61"-0"

■ *Total living area 1,490 sq. ft.* ■ *Price Code A* ■

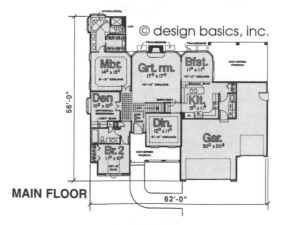

MAIN FLOOR

Impressive Brick and Wood Facade

No. 94921

This plan features:

— Two or three bedrooms

— Two full baths

■ Covered front and rear Porches expand the living space outside

■ A handy Serving Area is located between the Dining Room and the Great Room

■ Transom windows frame the hearth fireplace in the Great Room

■ A hub Kitchen has a built-in Pantry, snack bar and adjoining Laundry/Garage entry

■ French doors lead into the Den with a wetbar

■ An exclusive Master Suite includes a decorative ceiling, a walk-in closet, twin vanities and a corner whirlpool tub

Main floor — 1,651 sq. ft.
Basement — 1,651 sq. ft.
Garage — 480 sq. ft.

■ *Total living area 1,651 sq. ft.* ■ *Price Code B* ■

© design basics, inc.

MAIN FLOOR

Flexible Floor Plan

■ *Total living area 2,091 sq. ft.* ■ *Price Code C* ■

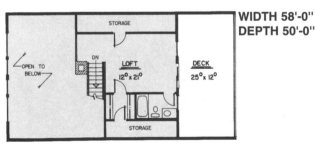

SECOND FLOOR

WIDTH 58'-0"
DEPTH 50'-0"

No. 99705 ☒

■ **This plan features:**

— Two bedrooms plus loft

— Three full and one half baths

■ An entrance through the Sun Porch into the Kitchen and Utility Area

■ An efficient Kitchen with an island sink/eating bar and a built-in Pantry

■ A expansive, two-story Living Room with a hearth fireplace and a wall of windows, providing access to a triangular Deck

■ Two first floor Bedrooms with over-sized closets, sliding glass doors to a Deck, and private Baths

■ A Loft area with a full Bath and a sliding glass door to a private Deck

First floor — 1,625 sq. ft.
Second floor — 466 sq. ft.
Garage — 742 sq. ft.

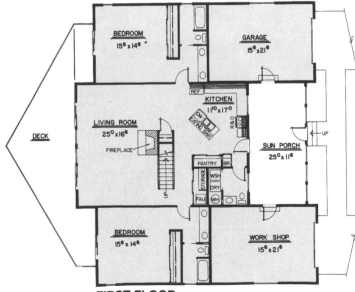

FIRST FLOOR

An Open Concept Home

■ *Total living area 1,282 sq. ft.* ■ *Price Code A* ■

No. 93021

■ This plan features:

— Three bedrooms

— Two full baths

■ An angled Entry creates the illusion of space

■ Two square columns flank the bar and separate the Kitchen from the Living Room

■ The Dining Room may service both formal and informal occasions

■ The Master Bedroom has a large walk-in closet

■ The large Master Bath has a double vanity, linen closet and whirlpool tub/shower combination

■ Two additional Bedrooms share a full Bath

■ No materials list is available for this plan

Main floor — 1,282 sq. ft.
Garage — 501 sq. ft.

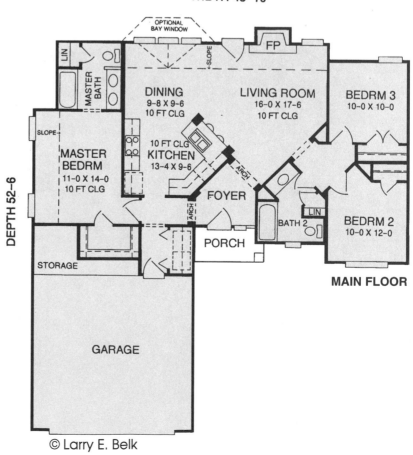

WIDTH 48–10

OPTIONAL BAY WINDOW

FP

LIN

MASTER BATH

DINING
9-8 X 9-6
10 FT CLG

LIVING ROOM
16-0 X 17-6
10 FT CLG

BEDRM 3
10-0 X 10-0

SLOPE

MASTER BEDRM
11-0 X 14-0
10 FT CLG

10 FT CLG
KITCHEN
13-4 X 9-6

ARCH

FOYER

BATH 2

LIN

BEDRM 2
10-0 X 12-0

DEPTH 52-6

ARCH

PORCH

MAIN FLOOR

STORAGE

GARAGE

© Larry E. Belk

Perfect Balance of Old and New

■ *Total living area 1,838 sq. ft.* ■ *Price Code C* ■

SECOND FLOOR

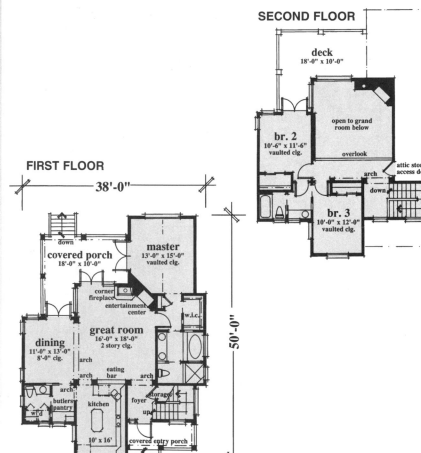

deck
18'-0" x 10'-0"

open to grand
room below

overlook

br. 2
10'-6" x 11'-6"
vaulted clg.

attic storage
access door

arch

down

br. 3
10'-0" x 12'-0"
vaulted clg.

FIRST FLOOR

38'-0"

50'-0"

down

covered porch
18'-0" x 10'-0"

master
13'-0" x 15'-0"
vaulted clg.

corner
fireplace

entertainment
center

w.l.c.

dining
11'-0" x 13'-0"
8'-0" clg.

great room
16'-0" x 18'-0"
2 story clg.

arch

arch

eating
bar

arch

arch

storage

foyer

up

arch

butlers
pantry

w/d

kitchen

10' x 16'

covered entry porch

No. 94251

■ **This plan features:**

— Three bedrooms

— Two full and one half baths

■ Horizontal siding compliments an insulated metal roof

■ The Great Room includes a corner fireplace, an entertainment center and an eating bar

■ Enter the Dining Room through an arched opening or from the French doors on the Porch

■ Access the Kitchen through two arched openings, one of which is from the Butler's Pantry

■ The first floor Master Suite has a walk-in closet and a private Bath

■ On the second floor find two Bedrooms a full Bath and an Observation Deck

■ No materials list is available for this plan

First Floor — 1,290 sq. ft.
Second Floor — 548 sq. ft.

Flexible Plan Creates Many Options

No. 90324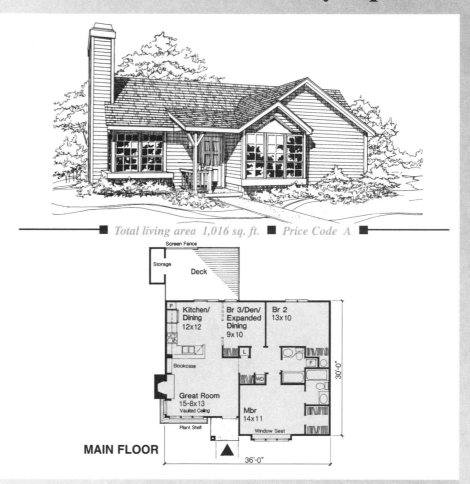

■ This plan features:

— Two bedrooms with optional third
bedroom/den

— Two full baths

■ The Great Room features a vaulted ceiling,
fireplace and built-in bookcase

■ The eat-in Kitchen opens onto a partially
enclosed Deck through sliding doors

■ The L-shaped design of the Kitchen
provides for easy meal preparation

■ The Master Bedroom has a private Bath, a
large walk-in closet and a window seat

Main floor — 1,016 sq. ft.

■ *Total living area 1,016 sq. ft.* ■ *Price Code A* ■

MAIN FLOOR

Large Feeling — Modest Square Footage

No. 96419

■ This plan features:

— Three bedrooms

— Two full baths

■ Arched windows, dormers, front and side
Porches, rear Deck, and an open interior
give this home a larger feeling

■ Elegant columns define the Dining Room,
while the Great Room gains an open and
airy feeling from the cathedral ceiling and
arched window above the sliding door

■ The Master Suite pampers the owner with
a private Bath which includes a whirlpool
tub, separate shower, double vanity, linen
closet and walk-in closet

■ An optional basement, slab or crawl space
foundation—please specify when ordering

Main floor — 1,541 sq. ft.
Garage & Storage — 446 sq. ft.

■ *Total living area 1,541 sq. ft.* ■ *Price Code D* ■

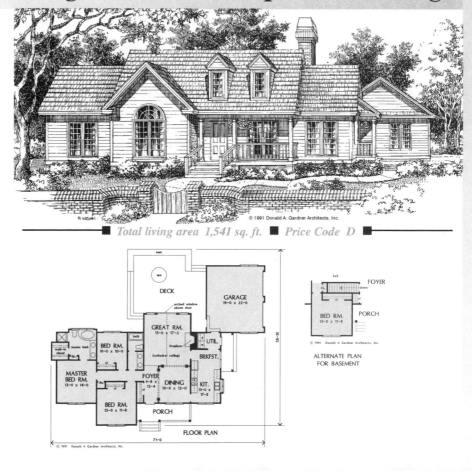

243

Style and Convenience

■ *Total living area 1,373 sq. ft.* ■ *Price Code A* ■

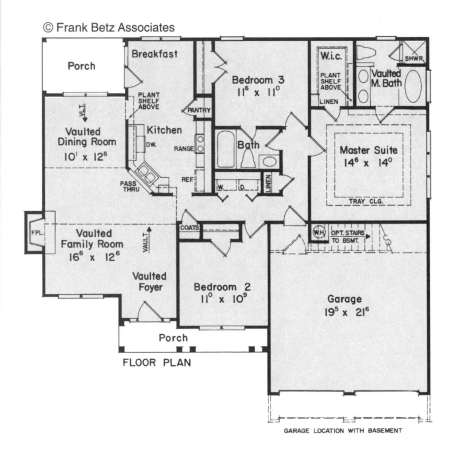

© Frank Betz Associates

FLOOR PLAN

GARAGE LOCATION WITH BASEMENT

No. 98411

This plan features:

— Three bedrooms

— Two full baths

■ Large front windows, dormers and an old-fashioned Porch

■ A vaulted ceiling in the Foyer

■ A formal Dining Room crowned in an elegant vaulted ceiling

■ An efficient Kitchen enhanced by a Pantry, and a pass-through to the Family Room

■ A decorative tray ceiling, a five-piece private Bath and a walk-in closet in the Master Suite

■ An optional basement or crawl space foundation available — please specify when ordering

Main floor — 1,373 sq. ft.
Basement — 1,386 sq. ft.
Width — 50'-4"
Depth — 45'-0"

244

■ *Total living area 1,325 sq. ft.* ■ *Price Code A* ■

No. 98912

■ This plan features:

— Three bedrooms

— Two full baths

■ Quaint front Porch shelters entry into the Living Area showcased by a massive fireplace and built-ins

■ Formal Dining Room is accented by a bay window

■ Efficient, galley Kitchen with Breakfast Area, laundry facilities and outdoor access

■ Secluded Master Bedroom offers a roomy walk-in closet and plush Bath with a dual vanity and a garden window tub

■ Two additional Bedrooms with ample closets share a full skylit Bath

Main floor — 1,325 sq. ft.
Basement — 556 sq. ft.
Garage — 724 sq. ft.

An
EXCLUSIVE DESIGN
By Jannis Vann & Associates, Inc.

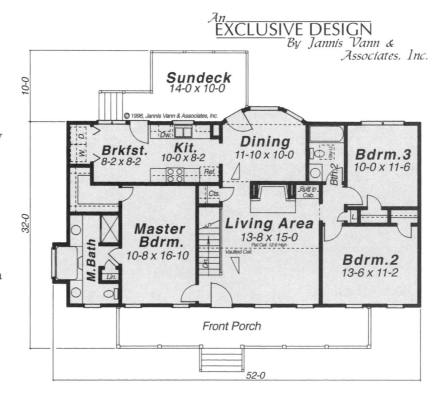

Elegant Brick Exterior

■ Total living area 1,390 sq. ft. ■ Price Code B ■

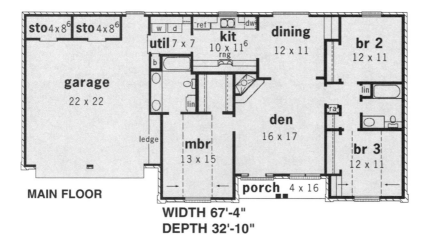

MAIN FLOOR

WIDTH 67'-4"
DEPTH 32'-10"

No. 92557

■ **This plan features:**

— Three bedrooms

— Two full baths

■ Detailing and accenting columns enhance the covered front Porch

■ Den has a corner fireplace and adjoins with the Dining Room

■ Efficient Kitchen is well-appointed and has easy access to the Utility/Laundry Room

■ Master Bedroom topped by a vaulted ceiling and pampered by a private Bath and a walk-in closet

■ Two secondary Bedrooms are located at the opposite end of home sharing a full Bath

■ An optional slab or crawl space foundation — please specify when ordering

Main floor — 1,390 sq. ft.
Garage — 590 sq. ft.

Interior and Exterior Unity Distinguishes Plan

No. 90398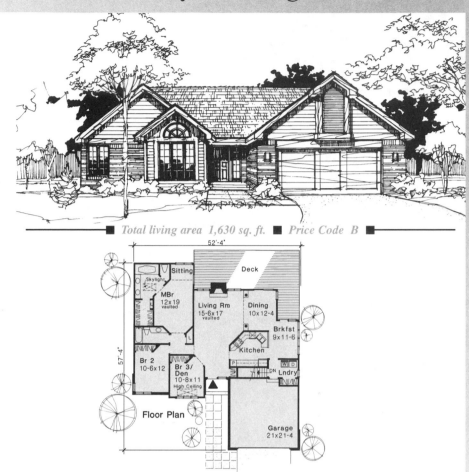

■ This plan features:

— Three bedrooms

— Two full baths

■ A vaulted ceiling Living Room with a cozy fireplace

■ Columns divide the Living and Dining Rooms; and half-walls separate the Kitchen and Breakfast Room

■ A luxurious Master Suite with a private sky-lit Bath, a double vanity and a generous walk-in closet

Main area —1,630 sq. ft.

■ Total living area 1,630 sq. ft. ■ Price Code B ■

Floor Plan

Barn With A Balcony

No. 91785

■ This plan features:

— Three bedrooms

— Two full baths

■ A gambrel roof and wrap-around Deck to expand the living space inside and out

■ An L-shaped Living/Dining Area with a fireplace and windows on three sides

■ An efficient galley Kitchen has ample counter and storage space

■ The first floor Bedroom has private access to a full hall Bath

■ Two large Bedrooms on the second floor, one with a private balcony, share a full hall Bath

First floor — 960 sq. ft.
Second floor — 720 sq. ft.
Width — 40'-0"
Depth — 24'-0"

■ Total living area 1,680 sq. ft. ■ Price Code B ■

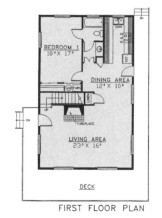

FIRST FLOOR PLAN

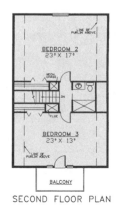

SECOND FLOOR PLAN

Homey Country Porch

■ *Total living area 1,816 sq. ft.* ■ *Price Code C* ■

An
EXCLUSIVE DESIGN
By Marshall Associates

Alternate Crawl Option

First Floor

45'-0"

50'-0"

Patio

Family 16-6 x 11-8

Dining 11-3 x 10

step

Kit. 11-3 x 11-8

Living 13-3 x 15-1

Porch

Garage 20-5 x 21-8

Second Floor

Br 3 11-3 x 4-3

linen

audio/video

Mst. Br 13-3 x 15-1

Br 2 11-3 x 15-2

First floor — 908 sq. ft.
Second floor — 908 sq. ft.
Garage — 462 sq. ft.

No. 24325

■ This plan features:

— Three bedrooms

— Two full and one half baths

■ A covered front Porch wraps around to connect with Patio that extends around back of home

■ A spacious Living Room with a cozy fireplace, triple front window and atrium door to Patio

■ The Family Room flows into the Dining Room and Kitchen

■ The efficient Kitchen includes a peninsula counter/snackbar, a double sink, a walk-in Pantry and a broom closet

■ The Master Suite has a walk-in closet, a private Bath and a built-in audio/video center

■ A laundry room ideally located near the Bedrooms

■ No materials list is available for this plan

■ *Total living area 1,345 sq. ft.* ■ *Price Code A* ■

No. 91342

■ This plan features:

— Three bedrooms

— Two full baths

■ A handicaped Master Bath plan is available

■ Vaulted Great Room, Dining Room and Kitchen areas

■ A Kitchen accented with angles and an abundance of cabinets for storage

■ A Master Bedroom with an ample sized wardrobe, large covered private Deck, and private Bath

Main area — 1,345 sq. ft.

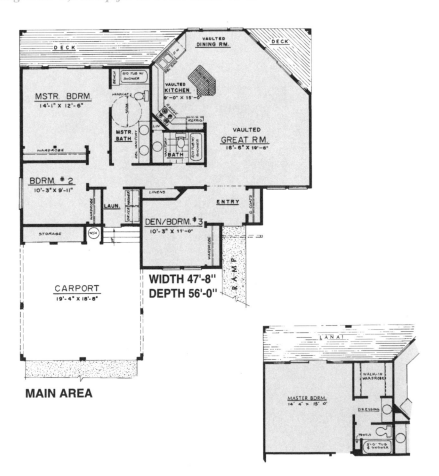

MAIN AREA

WIDTH 47'-8"
DEPTH 56'-0"

ALTERNATE BATH

Cathedral Ceiling

■ *Total living area 1,346 sq. ft.* ■ *Price Code A* ■

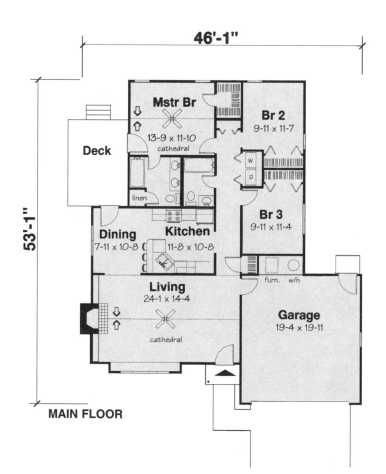

46'-1"

53'-1"

Mstr Br
13-9 x 11-10
cathedral

Deck

linen

Br 2
9-11 x 11-7

W
D

Br 3
9-11 x 11-4

Dining
7-11 x 10-8

Kitchen
11-8 x 10-8

Living
24-1 x 14-4
cathedral

furn.   w/h

Garage
19-4 x 19-11

MAIN FLOOR

No. 24402

■ **This plan features:**

— Three bedrooms

— Two full baths

■ A spacious Living Room with a cathedral ceiling and elegant fireplace

■ A Dining Room that adjoins both the Living Room and the Kitchen

■ An efficient Kitchen, with double sinks, ample cabinet space and peninsula counter that doubles as an eating bar

■ A convenient hallway laundry center

■ A Master Suite with a cathedral ceiling and a private Master Bath

Main floor — 1,346 sq. ft.
Garage — 449 sq. ft.

An
EXCLUSIVE DESIGN
By Upright Design

Cozy Rustic Exterior

No. 24313

■ This plan features:

— Two bedrooms

— Two full baths

■ The front Deck has a double glass door entrance and large windows to either side

■ An open layout creates space and efficiency between the Kitchen and the Living Room

■ The first floor Bedroom has a double closet and a full Bath

■ The second floor Bedroom has double closets

First floor — 781 sq. ft.

Second floor — 429 sq. ft.

An EXCLUSIVE DESIGN *By Marshall Associates*

Total living area 1,210 sq. ft. ■ Price Code A ■

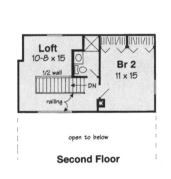

Second Floor

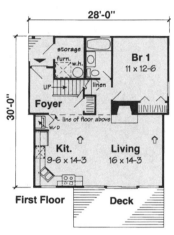

First Floor   **Deck**

Year Round Retreat

No. 90613

■ This plan features:

— Three bedrooms

— Two full baths

■ The Living Room has a dramatic sloping ceiling and a wood burning stove

■ The Kitchen and Living Room open onto the rear Deck

■ The Master Suite has a full Bath, linen closet and ample closet space

First floor — 967 sq. ft.

Second floor — 465 sq. ft.

Basement — 811 sq. ft.

Garage — 234 sq. ft.

Total living area 1,432 sq. ft. ■ Price Code A ■

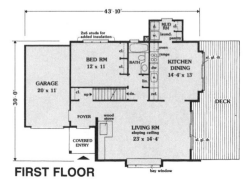

FIRST FLOOR

SECOND FLOOR

Turret Study Adds Drama

■ *Total living area 3,714 sq. ft.* ■ *Price Code J* ■

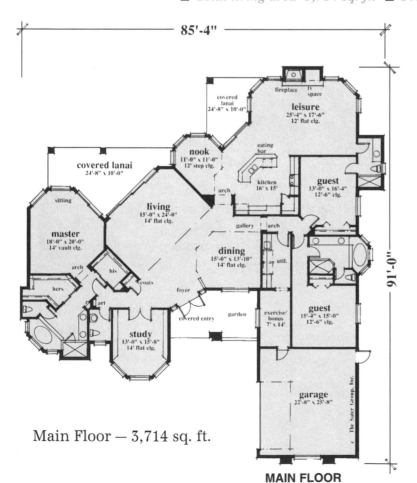

Main Floor — 3,714 sq. ft.

MAIN FLOOR

No. 94252

■ **This plan features:**

— Three bedrooms

— Three full and one half baths

■ The Covered Entry has an area for a garden

■ The Living and Dining rooms are open to each other and the Foyer

■ The rear Covered Lanai can be accessed from three different rooms

■ There is a Leisure Room with a fireplace and a built-in space for a television

■ One wing of the home is devoted to Guest Rooms; each with a Bath

■ The Master Suite is huge and luxurious

■ Enter the Study through French doors where the front wall is lavished with windows

■ No materials list is available for this plan

■ *Total living area 1,292 sq. ft.* ■ *Price Code A* ■

No. 93222

■ This plan features:

— Three bedrooms

— Two full baths

■ An expansive Living Room enhanced by natural light streaming in from the large front window

■ A bayed formal Dining Room with direct access to the Sun Deck and the Living Room for entertainment ease

■ An efficient, galley Kitchen, convenient to both formal and informal eating areas

■ An informal Breakfast Room with direct access to the Sun Deck

■ A large Master Suite equipped with a walk-in closet and a full private Bath

Main area — 1,276 sq. ft.
Finished staircase — 16 sq. ft.
Basement — 392 sq. ft.
Garage — 728 sq. ft.

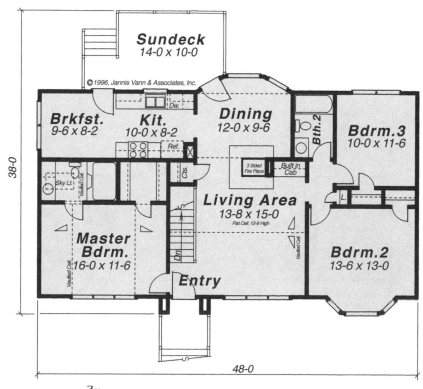

Sundeck
14-0 x 10-0

© 1996, Jannis Vann & Associates, Inc.

Brkfst.
9-6 x 8-2

Kit.
10-0 x 8-2

Dining
12-0 x 9-6

Bth.2

Bdrm.3
10-0 x 11-6

38-0

Sky Lt.

Ref.

3 Sided Fire Place

Built in Cab

Living Area
13-8 x 15-0
Flat Ceil. 12-9 High

Master Bdrm.
16-0 x 11-6

Dn

Bdrm.2
13-6 x 13-0

Entry

48-0

An
EXCLUSIVE DESIGN
By Jannis Vann &
Associates, Inc.

Split Bedroom Ranch

■ *Total living area 1,804 sq. ft.* ■ *Price Code C* ■

Main floor — 1,804 sq. ft.
Basement — 1,804 sq. ft.
Garage — 506 sq. ft.

No. 90476

■ **This plan features:**

— Three bedrooms

— Two full baths

■ The Foyer opens into the Great Room which features a vaulted ceiling and a hearth fireplace

■ The U-shaped Kitchen is located between the Dining Room and the Breakfast Nook

■ The secluded Master Bedroom is spacious and includes amenities such as walk-in closets and a full Bath

■ Two secondary Bedrooms have ample closet space and share a full Bath

■ The covered front Porch and rear Deck provide additional space for entertaining

■ An optional basement, slab or a crawl space foundation — please specify when ordering

MAIN FLOOR

Towering Windows

No. 91071

This plan features:

— Three bedrooms

— Two full baths

■ A wrap-around Deck above a three-car Garage that has plenty of work/storage space

■ Both the Dining and Living areas claim vaulted ceilings above French doors to the Deck

■ An octagon-shaped Kitchen has a cooktop peninsula and an open counter to the Dining Area

■ The Master Bedroom on the upper floor has an over-sized closet, a private Bath and an optional Loft

■ Two additional Bedrooms share a full hall Bath

■ An optional crawl space or slab foundation — please specify when ordering

■ No materials list is available for this plan

Main floor — 1,329 sq. ft.
Upper floor — 342 sq. ft.
Garage — 885 sq. ft.
Deck — 461 sq. ft.

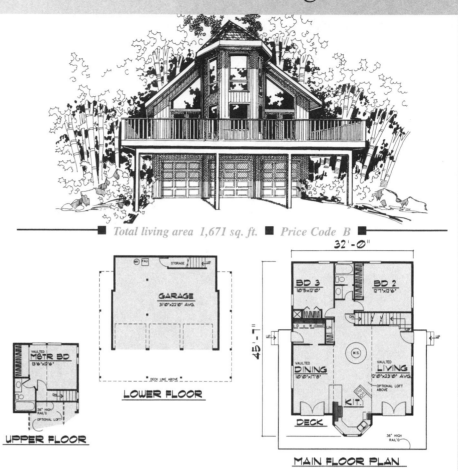

■ *Total living area 1,671 sq. ft.* ■ *Price Code B* ■

UPPER FLOOR

LOWER FLOOR

MAIN FLOOR PLAN

Leisure Time Getaway

No. 24308

This plan features:

— One bedroom

— One full bath

■ The simplicity of an A-frame with a spacious feeling achieved by the large, two-story Living Room

■ An entrance deck leads into the open Living Room accented by a spiral staircase to the Loft

■ A small, but efficient Kitchen serves the Living Area easily, and provides access to the full Bath with a shower and a storage area

■ A first floor Bedroom and a Loft Area provide the sleeping quarters

Main floor — 660 sq. ft.
Loft — 163 sq. ft.

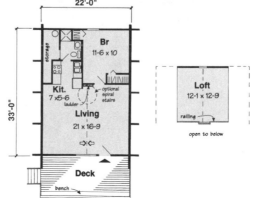

■ *Total living area 823 sq. ft.* ■ *Price Code A* ■

Main Floor

An EXCLUSIVE DESIGN *By Marshall Associates*

Exciting Ceiling Treatments And Open Spaces

© 1995 Donald A. Gardner Architects, Inc.

■ *Total living area 1,298 sq. ft.* ■ *Price Code C* ■

No. 99828

■ This plan features:

— Three bedrooms

— Two full baths

■ Double gables and a covered Porch add charm to the exterior

■ Common living areas are in an open format and are topped by a cathedral ceiling

■ Front Bedroom, doubling as a Study, topped by a cathedral ceiling and accented by an arched picture window

■ The Master Bedroom is crowned in a cathedral ceiling pampered by a lavish Bath

Main floor — 1,298 sq. ft.
Garage — 287 sq. ft.

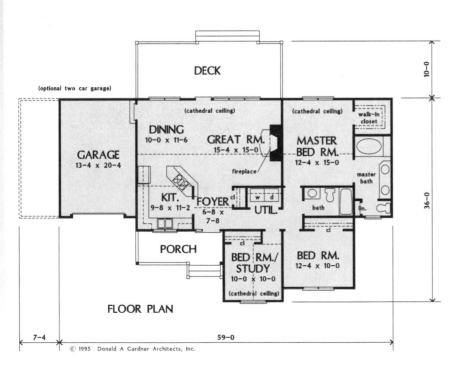

FLOOR PLAN

© 1995 Donald A Gardner Architects, Inc.

■ *Total living area 1,665 sq. ft.* ■ *Price Code B* ■

No. 91418

■ This plan features:

— Three bedrooms

— Two full baths

■ A dramatic vaulted Foyer

■ A range-top island Kitchen with a sunny Eating Nook surrounded by a built-in planter

■ A vaulted ceiling in the Great Room with a built-in bar and corner fireplace

■ A bayed Dining Room that combines with the Great Room for a spacious feeling

■ A Master Bedroom with a private Reading Nook, vaulted ceiling, walk-in closet and a well-appointed private Bath

■ Two additional Bedrooms sharing a full hall Bath

■ An optional basement, crawl space or slab foundation — please specify when ordering

Main area — 1,665 sq. ft.

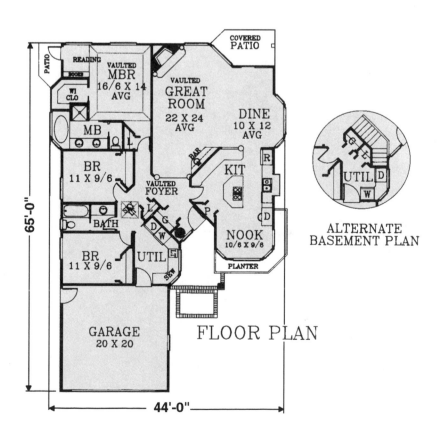

FLOOR PLAN

ALTERNATE BASEMENT PLAN

Three Bedroom Ranch

■ *Total living area 1,575 sq. ft.* ■ *Price Code B* ■

No. 98414

■ This plan features:

— Three bedrooms

— Two full baths

■ Formal Dining Room enhanced by a plant shelf and a side window

■ Wetbar located between the Kitchen and the Dining Room

■ Built-in Pantry, a double sink and a snack bar highlight the Kitchen

■ Breakfast Room containing a radius window and a French door to the rear yard

■ Large cozy fireplace framed by windows in the Great Room

■ Master Suite with a vaulted ceiling over the Sitting Room, a Master Bath and a walk-in closet

■ An optional basement or crawl space foundation available — please specify when ordering

Main floor — 1,575 sq. ft.
Garage — 459 sq. ft.
Basement — 1,658 sq. ft.

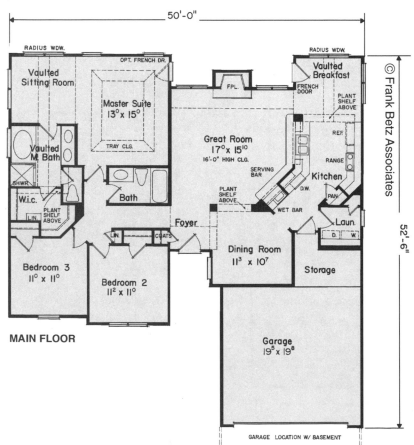

MAIN FLOOR

Country Charm

No. 99635

■ This plan features:

— Three bedrooms

— Two full and one half baths

■ A large heat-circulating fireplace

■ The Master Bedroom has a private Bath including a separate stall shower and whirlpool tub

■ A comfortable lifestyle by separating the formal and informal areas

■ Access to the Garage through the Mud Room, which contains laundry facilities and extra closet space

Main area — 1,650 sq. ft.
Garage — 491 sq. ft.

■ Total living area 1,650 sq. ft. ■ Price Code B ■

FLOOR PLAN

Soaring Ceilings Add Space and Drama

No. 90288

■ This plan features:

— Two bedrooms (with optional third bedroom)

— Two full baths

■ A sunny Master Suite with a sloping ceiling, private terrace entry, and luxurious garden bath with an adjoining Dressing Room

■ The Gathering Room has a fireplace, study and formal Dining Room, flowing together for a more spacious feeling

■ A convenient pass-through adds to the efficiency of the galley Kitchen and adjoining Breakfast Room

Main area — 1,387 sq. ft.
Garage — 440 sq. ft.

■ Total living area 1,387 sq. ft. ■ Price Code A ■

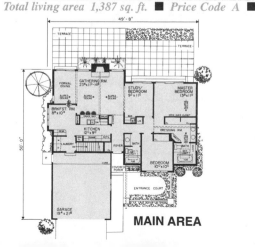

MAIN AREA

Theatrical Tiled Roof

■ Total living area 3,285 sq. ft. ■ Price Code F ■

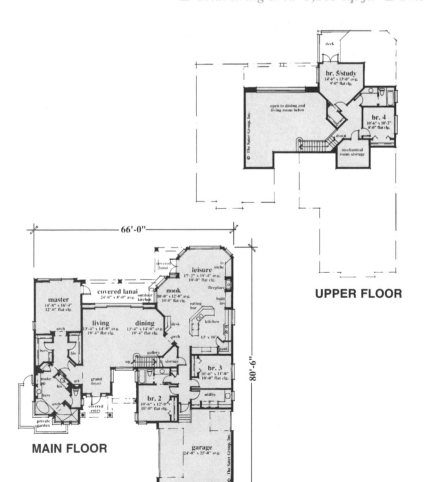

UPPER FLOOR

MAIN FLOOR

No. 94253

■ **This plan features:**

— Five bedrooms

— Three full baths

■ The tiled roof adds theatrical drama to this stucco home

■ The Living and Dining Rooms are combined and they access the Lanai

■ The informal area includes the Kitchen, Nook and Leisure Room

■ The incomparable Master Suite has left nothing to chance

■ Upstairs find two more Bedrooms; one with a private Deck

■ The Garage has space to store not only two cars, but a golf cart as well

■ No materials list is available for this plan

Main Floor — 2,747 sq. ft.
Upper Floor — 538 sq. ft.
Garage — 616 sq. ft.

Covered Front and Rear Porches

■ *Total living area 1,660 sq. ft.* ■ *Price Code C* ■

No. 92560 ☒

■ This plan features:

— Three bedrooms

— Two full baths

■ Traditional Country styling with front and rear covered Porches

■ Peninsula counter/eating bar in Kitchen for meals on the go

■ Formal Dining Room with built-in cabinet

■ Vaulted ceiling and cozy fireplace highlight the Den

■ Private Master Suite pampered by five-piece Bath

■ Two Bedrooms at the opposite end of home sharing a full Bath

■ An optional slab or crawl space foundation — please specify when ordering

Main floor — 1,660 sq. ft.
Garage — 544 sq. ft.

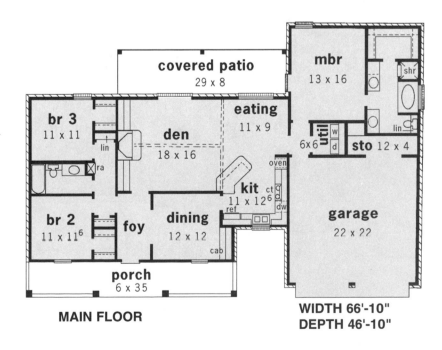

MAIN FLOOR

WIDTH 66'-10"
DEPTH 46'-10"

Cozy Homestead

■ *Total living area 1,821 sq. ft.* ■ *Price Code C* ■

An
EXCLUSIVE DESIGN
By Plan One Homes, Inc.

No. 24651

■ **This plan features:**

— Three bedrooms

— Two full baths

■ Multi-paned windows and a country Porch set the theme for this comfortable home

■ A spacious Living Room is enhanced by the natural light from the front window and a fireplace

■ An efficient U-shaped Kitchen is located next to the Dining Room and contains a walk-in Pantry, a double sink and a Breakfast Nook

■ The private Master Suite has a whirlpool tub, a separate shower, a walk-in closet and a tray ceiling

■ No materials list is available for this plan

Main area — 1,821 sq. ft.
Garage — 1,075 sq. ft.
Basement — 742 sq. ft.

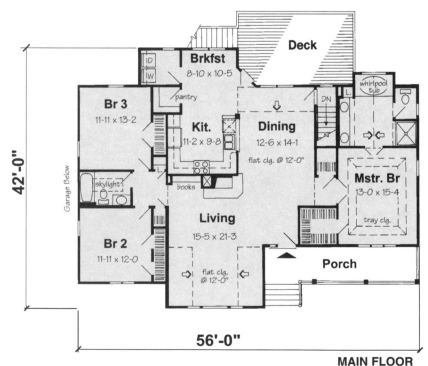

MAIN FLOOR

High Ceilings and Arched Windows

No. 98441

■ This plan features:

— Three bedrooms

— Two full baths

■ Natural illumination streams into the Dining Room and Sitting Area of the Master Suite through large, arched windows

■ The Kitchen has a convenient pass through to the Great Room and a serving bar for the Breakfast Room

■ The Great Room is topped by a vaulted ceiling and is further accented by a fireplace and a French door

■ Decorative columns accent the entrance of the Dining Room

■ A tray ceiling over the Master Suite and a vaulted ceiling is over the Sitting Room and the Master Bath

■ An optional basement or crawl space foundation — please specify when ordering

■ No materials list is available for this plan

Main floor — 1,502 sq. ft.
Garage — 448 sq. ft.
Basement — 1,555 sq. ft.

■ *Total living area 1,502 sq. ft.* ■ *Price Code B* ■

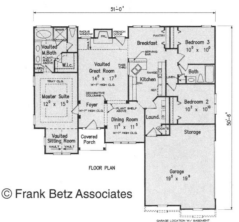

© Frank Betz Associates

Passive Solar and Contemporary Features

No. 26110

■ This plan features:

— Two bedrooms (with possible third bedroom/den)

— One full and one half baths

■ Numerous glass doors, windows, and a greenhouse

■ 2 x 6 studs, R-19 insulation in the exterior walls, and R-33 insulation in all sloping ceilings

■ A Living Room with a concrete slab floor for solar gain

■ A sky-lit Living Room ceiling which slants two stories

First floor — 902 sq. ft.
Second floor — 567 sq. ft.

■ *Total living area 1,469 sq. ft.* ■ *Price Code A* ■

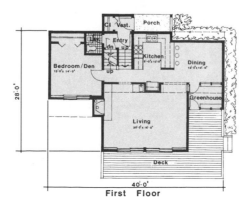

First Floor

Second Floor

Cozy Country Ranch

■ *Total living area 1,576 sq. ft.* ■ *Price Code B* ■

No. 24708

■ This plan features:

— Three bedrooms

— Two full baths

■ Front Porch shelters outdoor entrance into Living Room

■ Expansive Living Room highlighted by a boxed window and hearth fireplace between built-ins

■ Columns frame entrance to Dining Room which has access to backyard

■ Efficient, U-shaped Kitchen with direct access to the Screened Porch and the Dining Room

■ Master Bedroom wing enhanced by a large walk-in closet and a double vanity Bath with a whirlpool tub

■ Two additional Bedrooms with large closets share a double vanity Bath with Laundry center

■ No materials list is available for this plan

Main Floor

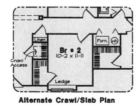

Alternate Crawl/Slab Plan

Main floor — 1,576 sq. ft.
Garage — 576 sq. ft.
Basement — 1,454 sq. ft.

Drive Under Garage

■ *Total living area 1,208 sq. ft.* ■ *Price Code A* ■

No. 98915 ⚒

■ **This plan features:**

— Three bedrooms

— Two full baths

■ Porch shelters Entry into Living Area with an inviting fireplace

■ Convenient Dining Area opens to Living Room, Kitchen and Sun Deck

■ Efficient, U-shaped Kitchen serves Dining Area and Sun Deck beyond

■ Pampering Master Bedroom with a vaulted ceiling, two closets and a double vanity Bath

■ Two additional Bedrooms share a full Bath and convenient laundry center

Main floor — 1,208 sq. ft.
Basement — 728 sq. ft.
Garage — 480 sq. ft.

An EXCLUSIVE DESIGN
By Jannis Vann & Associates, Inc.

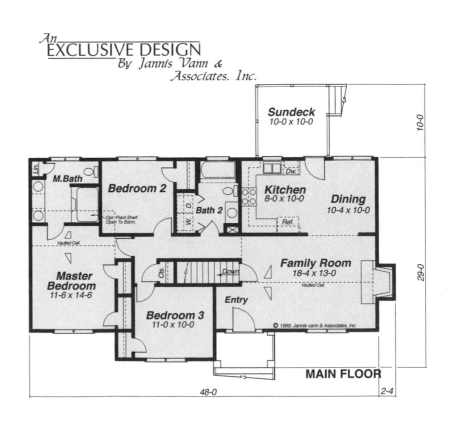

Exciting Ceilings Add Appeal

©1994 Donald A. Gardner Architects, Inc.

■ *Total living area 1,475 sq. ft.* ■ *Price Code C* ■

No. 96452

■ **This plan features:**

— Three bedrooms

— Two full baths

■ Open design enhanced by cathedral and tray ceilings and arched windows

■ Foyer with columns defines Great Room with a central fireplace and Deck access

■ Cooktop island in Kitchen provides great cooks with convenience and company

■ The ultimate Master Suite offers a walk-in closet, a tray ceiling and a whirlpool bath

■ Front Bedroom/Study offers multiple uses with tray ceiling and arched window

Main floor — 1,475 sq. ft.
Garage & storage — 478 sq. ft.

© Donald A. Gardner Architects, Inc.

High Windows Add Light

No. 26114

Total living area 1,112 sq. ft. ■ *Price Code A*

■ **This plan features:**

— Three bedrooms

— One full and one half baths

■ A covered Entry steps down into the spacious Living/Dining Room featuring a vaulted ceiling, a fireplace and sliding glass doors to expansive Deck area

■ An efficient, U-shaped Kitchen with a peninsula counter adjoining the Dining Room

■ A first floor Bedroom/Den with a triple window and a walk-in closet

■ Two additional Bedrooms on the second floor share a balcony and a full Bath

First floor — 696 sq. ft.
Second floor — 416 sq. ft.
Basement — 696 sq. ft.

FIRST FLOOR

SECOND FLOOR

Window Design Highlights Plan

No. 90348

Total living area 1,149 sq. ft. ■ *Price Code A*

■ **This plan features:**

— Two bedrooms plus loft

— Two full baths

■ An airy Living Room with glass on three sides and a fireplace tucked into the corner

■ An efficient Kitchen serving the Living and Dining rooms easily

■ First floor Bedrooms featuring a private Bath and a walk-in closet connected to Storage area

■ A landing staircase leading to a second Bedroom with a walk-in closet, a Laundry and a full Bath

■ A ladder to top-of-the-tower Loft with loads of light and multiple uses

First floor — 729 sq. ft.
Second floor — 420 sq. ft.
Width — 42'-0"
Depth — 32'-8"

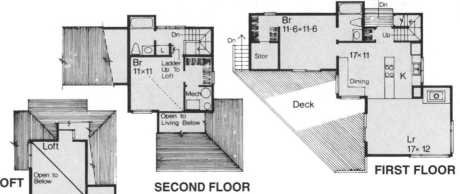

LOFT

SECOND FLOOR

FIRST FLOOR

Beautiful From Front to Back

B. NATHAN

■ *Total living area 1,632 sq. ft.* ■ *Price Code D* ■

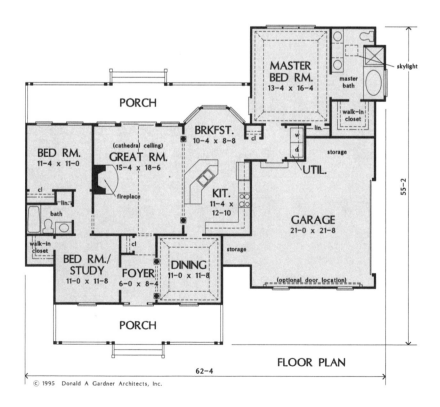

PORCH

BED RM.
11-4 x 11-0

cl

(cathedral ceiling)
GREAT RM.
15-4 x 18-6

fireplace

BRKFST.
10-4 x 8-8

cl

**MASTER
BED RM.**
13-4 x 16-4

skylight

master
bath

walk-in
closet

lin.

w
d

storage

lin.

UTIL.

KIT.
11-4 x
12-10

GARAGE
21-0 x 21-8

lin.

bath

walk-in
closet

BED RM./
STUDY
11-0 x 11-8

cl

FOYER
6-0 x 8-4

DINING
11-0 x 11-8

storage

(optional door location)

PORCH

55-2

62-4

FLOOR PLAN

No. 99840

■ **This plan features:**

— Three bedrooms

— Two full baths

■ Porches, gables and dormers provide special charm

■ The central Great Room has a cathedral ceiling, a fireplace, and a clerestory window

■ Columns divide the open Great Room from the Kitchen and the Breakfast Bay

■ A tray ceiling and columns dress up the formal Dining Room

■ Skylit Master Bath with a shower, a whirlpool tub, a dual vanity and a spacious walk-in closet

Main floor — 1,632 sq. ft.
Garage & Storage — 561 sq. ft.

© Larry E. Belk

■ *Total living area 1,955 sq. ft.* ■ *Price Code C* ■

No. 93030

■ **This plan features:**

— Three bedrooms

— Two full baths

■ A columned Dining Room and an expansive Great Room with a large hearth fireplace

■ The Kitchen has a built-in Pantry, a peninsula sink and an octagon-shaped Breakfast Area

■ The Master Bedroom wing has French doors, a vaulted ceiling, a plush Master Bath with a huge walk-in closet, a double vanity and a window tub

■ Two Bedrooms with walk-in closets share a full hall Bath

■ No materials list is available for this plan

Main floor — 1,955 sq. ft.
Garage — 561 sq. ft.

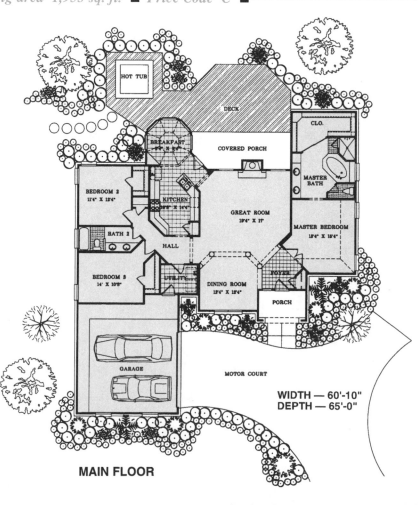

WIDTH — 60'-10"
DEPTH — 65'-0"

MAIN FLOOR

Especially for You

■ *Total living area 3,296 sq. ft.* ■ *Price Code F* ■

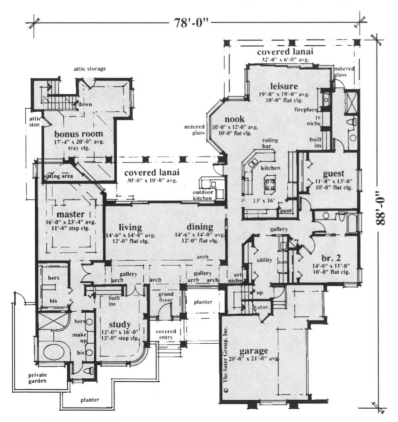

MAIN FLOOR

Main floor — 3,296 sq. ft.
Bonus room — 407 sq. ft.
Garage — 549 sq. ft.

No. 94255

■ **This plan features:**

— Three bedrooms

— Three full baths

■ From the grand Foyer enter the gallery with numerous decorative arches

■ On one of the rear Covered Lanais you will find an outdoor Kitchen

■ Built-ins and a curved window wall dominate the Study

■ The Master Suite has a tray ceiling amongst its luxurious features

■ The Kitchen is a delight with its center island and a walk-in Pantry

■ The Leisure Room lives up to its name with a fireplace and television niche

■ There is a Bonus Room above the oversized two-car Garage

■ No materials list is available for this plan

One Floor Convenience

No. 98443

■ This plan features:

— Three bedrooms

— Two full baths

■ The vaulted Foyer blends with the vaulted Great Room giving a larger feeling to the home

■ The Formal Dining Room opens into the Great Room allowing for a terrific living area in which to entertain

■ The Kitchen includes a serving bar and easy flow into the Breakfast Room

■ The Master Suite is topped by a decorative tray ceiling and a vaulted ceiling in the Master Bath

■ Two additional Bedrooms share the full Bath in the hall

■ An optional slab or crawl space foundation — please specify when ordering

■ No materials list is available for this plan

Main floor — 1,359 sq. ft.
Garage — 439 sq. ft.

■ *Total living area 1,359 sq. ft.* ■ *Price Code A* ■

FLOOR PLAN

© Frank Betz Associates

Contemporary Ranch Design

No. 26740

■ This plan features:

— Three bedrooms

— Two full baths

■ Sloping cathedral ceilings

■ An efficient, centrally-located Kitchen

■ A Daylight Room for dining pleasure

■ A secluded Master Bedroom with Master Bath and access to private Deck

■ The Great Hall has a fireplace

Main floor — 1,512 sq. ft.
Garage — 478 sq. ft.

■ *Total living area 1,512 sq. ft.* ■ *Price Code B* ■

MAIN FLOOR

Quaint and Cozy

© 1993 Donald A. Gardner Architects, Inc.

B. NATHAN

■ *Total living area 1,864 sq. ft.* ■ *Price Code E* ■

No. 99878

■ **This plan features:**

— Three bedrooms

— Two full and one half baths

■ Spacious floor plan with large Great Room crowned by cathedral ceiling

■ Central Kitchen with angled counter opens to the Breakfast Area and Great Room

■ Privately located Master Bedroom has a cathedral ceiling

■ Operable skylights over the tub accent the luxurious Master Bath

■ Bonus Room over the Garage makes expanding easy

■ An optional crawl space or basement foundation — please specify when ordering

Main floor — 1,864 sq. ft.
Garage — 614 sq. ft.
Bonus — 420 sq. ft.

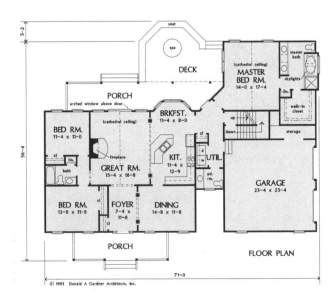

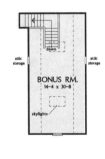

FLOOR PLAN

© 1993 Donald A Gardner Architects, Inc.

Varied Roof Heights Create Interesting Lines

■ *Total living area 1,613 sq. ft.* ■ *Price Code B* ■

No. 90601 ✕

■ This plan features:

— Three bedrooms

— Two full and one half baths

■ The spacious Family Room has a heat-circulating fireplace, which is visible from the Foyer

■ A large Kitchen with a cooktop island, opening into the Dinette bay

■ The Master Suite has his-n-her closets and a private Master Bath

■ Two additional Bedrooms share a full hall Bath

■ Formal Dining and Living Rooms, flow into each other for easy entertaining

Main floor — 1,613 sq. ft.
Basement — 1,060 sq. ft.
Garage — 461 sq. ft.

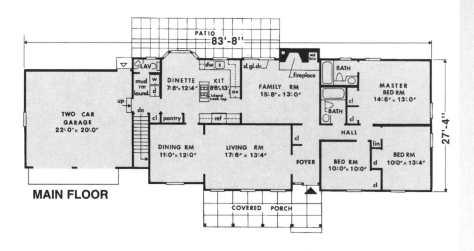

Country Style Charm

■ *Total living area 1,857 sq. ft.* ■ *Price Code C* ■

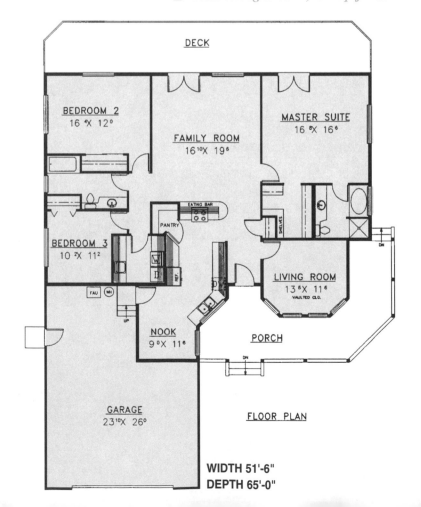

DECK

BEDROOM 2
16⁴X 12⁰

FAMILY ROOM
16¹⁰X 19⁶

MASTER SUITE
16⁸X 16⁶

EATING BAR

PANTRY

BEDROOM 3
10²X 11²

SHELVES

LIVING ROOM
13⁸X 11⁶
VAULTED CLG.

FAU   WH

UP

DN

NOOK
9⁰X 11⁶

PORCH

DN

GARAGE
23¹⁰X 26⁰

FLOOR PLAN

WIDTH 51'-6"
DEPTH 65'-0"

No. 91731 ⚒

■ **This plan features:**

— Three bedrooms

— Two full baths

■ Brick accents, front facing gable, and railed wrap-around covered Porch

■ A built-in range and oven in a dog-leg shaped Kitchen

■ A Nook with garage access for convenient unloading of groceries and other supplies

■ A bay window wrapping around the front of the formal Living Room

■ A Master Suite with French doors opening to the Deck

Main area — 1,857 sq. ft.
Garage — 681 sq. ft.

Roof Lines Attract the Eye

No. 26113 ⚒

■ This plan features:

— Three bedrooms

— One full and one three-quarter baths

■ Unusual roof lines which are both pleasing and balanced

■ An open floor plan shared by the Kitchen, Dining Room, Living Room and split Entry spaces

■ An optional Den/Bedroom on the first floor

■ A wrap-around Deck and two-car Garage add the finishing touches to this design

First floor — 846 sq. ft.
Second floor — 492 sq. ft.
Basement — 846 sq. ft.
Garage — 540 sq. ft.
Deck — 423 sq. ft.

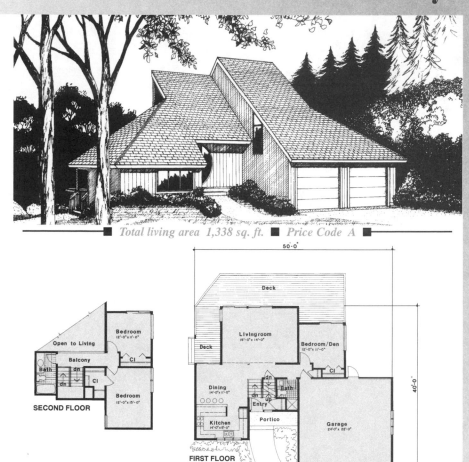

■ *Total living area 1,338 sq. ft.* ■ *Price Code A* ■

Rustic Vacation House

No. 90004 ⚒

■ This plan features:

— Three bedrooms

— One full and one half baths

■ Two Porches and an outdoor balcony for entertaining, relaxing or just enjoying a sunset

■ A spiral stairway leading to the balcony and upstairs Bedroom

■ A Living Room with a massive stone fireplace, floor-to-ceiling windows at the gable end, and sliding glass doors to a rear Porch

■ A Pantry adjoining the Kitchen, which has a small bay window over the sink

First floor — 1,020 sq. ft.
Second floor — 265 sq. ft.

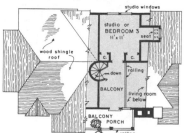

■ *Total living area 1,285 sq. ft.* ■ *Price Code A* ■

Ceiling Treatments Add Interest

■ *Total living area 1,553 sq. ft.* ■ *Price Code B* ■

No. 98412

■ This plan features:

— Three bedrooms

— Two full baths

■ A vaulted ceiling over the Family Room and a tray ceiling over the Master Suite

■ Decorative columns accent the entrance into the Dining Room

■ Great Room has a pass-through from the Kitchen and a fireplace framed by a window to one side and a French door

■ A built-in Pantry and desk add convenience to the Kitchen

■ An optional basement, slab or crawl space foundation — please specify when ordering

Main floor — 1,553 sq. ft.
Basement — 1,605 sq. ft.
Garage — 434 sq. ft.

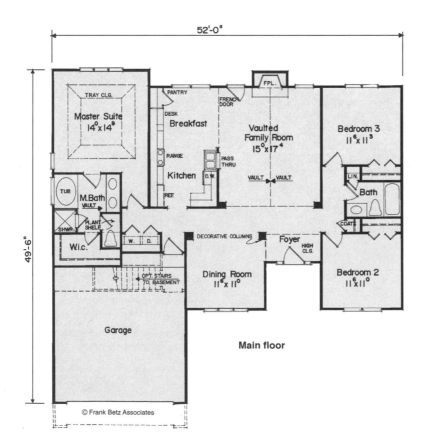

Main floor

© Frank Betz Associates

Bay Windows and a Terrific Front Porch

■ *Total living area 1,778 sq. ft.* ■ *Price Code C* ■

No. 93261

An
EXCLUSIVE DESIGN
*By Jannis Vann &
Associates, Inc.*

■ **This plan features:**

— Three bedrooms

— Two full baths

■ A Country style front Porch

■ An expansive Living Area that includes a fireplace

■ The Master Suite has a private Master Bath and a walk-in closet, as well as a bay window view of the front yard

■ An efficient Kitchen serves the sunny Breakfast Area and the Dining Room with equal ease

■ A built-in Pantry and a desk add to the conveniences in the Breakfast Area

■ Two additional Bedrooms share the full hall Bath

Main area — 1,778 sq. ft.
Basement — 1,008 sq. ft.
Garage — 728 sq. ft.

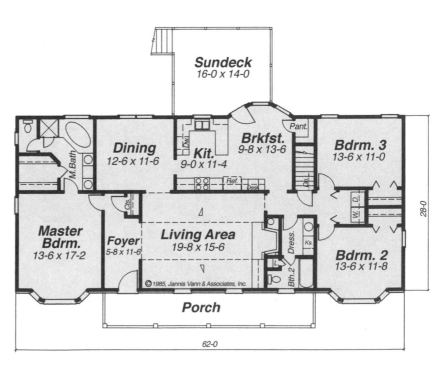

Sundeck
16-0 x 14-0

Pant.

Dining
12-6 x 11-6

Kit.
9-0 x 11-4

Brkfst.
9-8 x 13-6

Bdrm. 3
13-6 x 11-0

M. Bath

Ref.

Desk

W. D.

28-0

Master
Bdrm.
13-6 x 17-2

Foyer
5-8 x 11-6

Living Area
19-8 x 15-6

Dress.

Cls.

Bth.2

© 1985, Jannis Vann & Associates, Inc.

Bdrm. 2
13-6 x 11-8

Porch

62-0

MAIN AREA

Split Bedroom Plan

■ *Total living area 1,429 sq. ft.* ■ *Price Code A* ■

MAIN FLOOR
WIDTH 49'-0"
DEPTH 53'-0"

© Frank Betz Associates

No. 98415

■ **This plan features:**

— Three bedrooms

— Two full baths

■ A tray ceiling adds a decorative touch to the Master Bedroom

■ A full Bath is located between the secondary Bedrooms

■ A corner fireplace and a vaulted ceiling highlight the Family Room

■ A wetbar/serving bar in the Family Room and a built-in Pantry add to the convenience of the Kitchen

■ The Dining Room is crowned by an elegant high ceiling

■ An optional basement, crawl space or slab foundation — please specify when ordering

Main floor — 1,429 sq. ft.
Basement — 1,472 sq. ft.
Garage — 438 sq. ft.

Compact Country Cottage

No. 99856

This plan features:

— Three bedrooms

— Two full baths

■ The foyer opens to a large Great Room with a fireplace and a cathedral ceiling

■ An efficient U-shaped Kitchen with a peninsula counter extends work space and separates it from the Dining Room

■ Two front bedrooms, one with a bay window, the other with a walk-in closet, share a full Bath in the hall

■ The Master Suite is located in the rear and has a walk-in closet and a private Bath with a double vanity

■ A partially covered Deck with skylights is accessible from the Dining Room, Great Room and the Master Bedroom

Main floor — 1,310 sq. ft.
Garage & storage — 455 sq. ft.

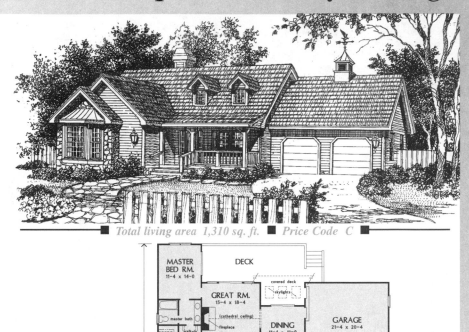

■ *Total living area 1,310 sq. ft.* ■ *Price Code C* ■

FLOOR PLAN

© 1991 Donald A Gardner Architects, Inc.

Master Suite Offers Privacy

No. 24318

This plan features:

— Four bedrooms

— Two full baths

■ A large covered Porch and dormer windows, creating a friendly invitation to enter

■ The Living Room has a beamed ceiling and access to the Patio through an atrium door

■ The Dining Room adjoins the Living Room and Kitchen making entertaining easy

■ An efficient, U-shaped Kitchen has a curved counter that serves as a pass-through and a snack bar

■ An exclusive Master Suite with a double vanity Bath is on the second floor offering a quiet place

■ Three Bedrooms on the first floor share a full hall Bath

First floor — 1,044 sq. ft.
Second floor — 354 sq. ft.

■ *Total living area 1,398 sq. ft.* ■ *Price Code A* ■

Second Floor

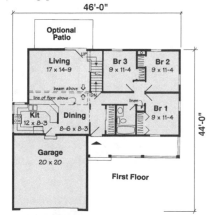

First Floor

An EXCLUSIVE DESIGN *By Marshall Associates*

279

Spectacular Scenes

Total living area 1,855 sq. ft. ■ Price Code C

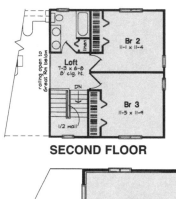

SECOND FLOOR

Br 2
11-1 x 11-4

Loft
7-3 x 6-6
8' clg. ht.

Br 3
11-5 x 11-4

railing open to
Great Rm below

linen

DN

1/2 wall

First floor — 913 sq. ft.
Second floor — 516 sq. ft.
Lower level — 426 sq. ft.
Basement — 487 sq. ft.

LOWER LEVEL

Mech.
13-6 x 6-6

Recreation
17-10 x 22-6

Unfinished
Basement

patio below deck

railing

UP

line of floor
above

FIRST FLOOR

Deck

Deck

Dining Rm
13-0 x 8-6

Kitchen
12-4 x 6-6

Great Rm
18-3 x 14-11

Master Br
13-6 x 12-0

ent.
cntr.

books

ref.

linen

8' clg. ht.

UP

DN

railing

private
terrace

line of floor
above

cut-outs

27'-0"

40'-0"

No. 24704

■ **This plan features:**

— Three bedrooms

— Two full and one half baths

■ Exceptional Great Room and Dining Room with central fireplace, glass from the floor to the vaulted ceiling and Deck access

■ Efficient Kitchen has a peninsula counter serving the Dining Room

■ First floor Master Bedroom has a private Deck, a walk-in closet and a double vanity Bath

■ Two second floor Bedrooms have large closets and share a double vanity Bath

■ Lower level Recreation Room with utilities, Unfinished Basement and Patio access

■ No materials list is available for this plan

An Affordable Floor Plan

■ *Total living area 1,410 sq. ft.* ■ *Price Code A* ■

No. 91807 ✂

■ This plan features:

— Three bedrooms

— One full and one three-quarter baths

■ A covered Porch entry

■ An old-fashioned hearth fireplace in the Living Room

■ An efficient Kitchen with U-shaped counter that is accessible from the Dining Room

■ The Master Bedroom has a large walk-in closet and private Bath

■ An optional crawl space and slab foundation available — please specify when ordering

Main floor — 1,410 sq. ft.
Garage — 484 sq. ft.

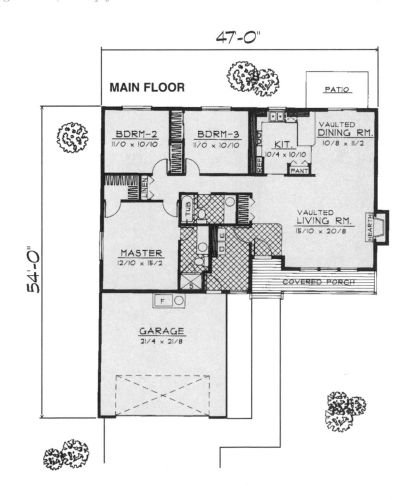

MAIN FLOOR

47'-0"

54'-0"

BDRM-2
11/0 x 10/10

BDRM-3
11/0 x 10/10

KIT.
10/4 x 10/10

PATIO

VAULTED
DINING RM.
10/8 x 11/2

PANT

REF

LINEN

TUB

MASTER
12/10 x 15/2

VAULTED
LIVING RM.
15/10 x 20/8

HEARTH

COVERED PORCH

F

GARAGE
21/4 x 21/8

Cozy Traditional with Style

■ Total living area 1,830 sq. ft. ■ Price Code C ■

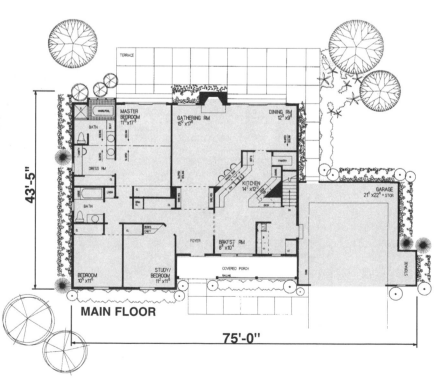

MAIN FLOOR

43'-5"

75'-0"

No. 99208

■ **This plan features:**

— Three bedrooms

— Two full baths

■ A convenient one-level design

■ A galley-style Kitchen that shares a snack bar with the spacious Gathering Room

■ Inviting focal point fireplace in Gathering Room

■ An ample Master Suite with a luxurious Bath which includes a whirlpool tub and separate Dressing Room

■ Two additional Bedrooms, one that could double as a Study, located at the front of the house

Main floor — 1,830 sq. ft.
Basement — 1,830 sq. ft.

Year Round Leisure

No. 90630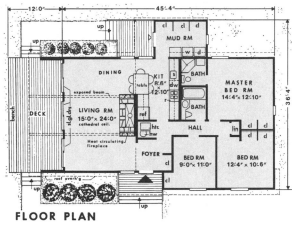

This plan features:

— Three bedrooms

— One full bath and one three-quarter baths

■ A cathedral ceiling with exposed beams and a stone wall with heat-circulating fireplace in the Living Room

■ Three sliding glass doors lead from the Living Room to a large Deck

■ A built-in Dining area that separates the Kitchen from the far end of the Living Room

■ The Master Suite has his-n-her closets and a private Bath

■ Two additional Bedrooms, one double sized, sharing a full hall Bath

Main floor — 1,207 sq. ft.

■ Total living area 1,207 sq. ft. ■ Price Code A ■

FLOOR PLAN

Truly Western Approach to the Ranch House

No. 90007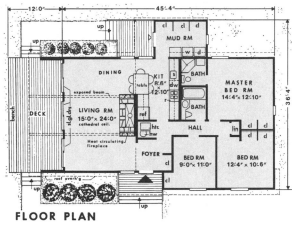

This plan features:

— Four bedrooms

— Three full baths

■ Authentic ranch styling with long Loggia, posts and braces, hand-split shake roof and cross-buck doors

■ A Texas-sized, hexagonal, sunken Living Room with two solid walls, one with a fireplace, and two 10' walls of sliding glass doors

■ A porch surrounding the Living Room on three sides

■ A Master Suite with a private Master Bath

■ An efficient well-equipped Kitchen flowing into the Family Room

Main floor — 1,830 sq. ft.
Basement — 1,830 sq. ft.
Garage — 540 sq. ft.

■ Total living area 1,830 sq. ft. ■ Price Code C ■

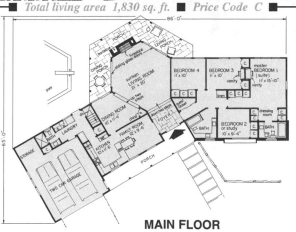

MAIN FLOOR

283

Rustic Simplicity

© 1987 Donald A. Gardner Architects, Inc.

■ *Total living area 1,426 sq. ft.* ■ *Price Code C* ■

No. 99864

■ This plan features:

— Three bedrooms

— Two full and one half baths

■ The central living area is large and boasts a cathedral ceiling, exposed wood beams and a clerestory

■ A long screened Porch has a bank of skylights

■ The open Kitchen contains a convenient serving and eating counter

■ The generous Master Suite opens to the screened Porch, and is enhanced by a walk-in closet and a whirlpool tub

■ Two more Bedrooms share a second full Bath

Main floor — 1,426 sq. ft.

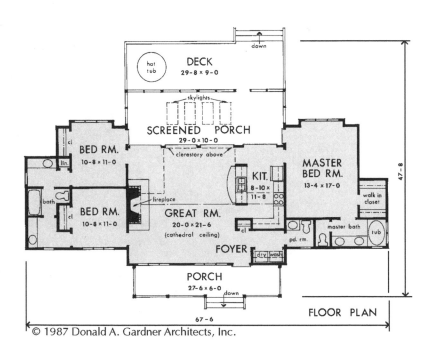

© 1987 Donald A. Gardner Architects, Inc.

One-Level with a Twist

■ *Total living area 1,575 sq. ft.* ■ *Price Code B* ■

No. 20083

■ This plan features:

— Three bedrooms

— Two full baths

■ Wide-open active areas that are centrally-located

■ A spacious Dining, Living, and Kitchen Area

■ The Master Suite at the rear of the home has a full Bath

■ Two additional Bedrooms share a full hall Bath

Main floor — 1,575 sq. ft.
Basement — 1,575 sq. ft.
Garage — 475 sq. ft.

An
EXCLUSIVE DESIGN
By Karl Kreeger

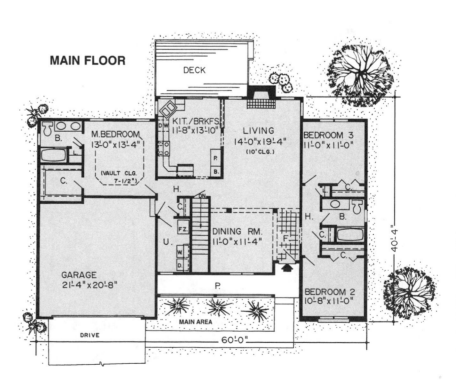

MAIN FLOOR

DECK

KIT./BRKFS
11'-8"x13'-10"

LIVING
14'-0"x19'-4"
(10'CLG.)

B.

M.BEDROOM
13'-0"x13'-4"

(VAULT CLG.
7-1/2')

BEDROOM 3
11'-0"x11'-0"

C.

H.

DN

C.

FZ.

DINING RM.
11'-0"x11'-4"

H.

B.

C.

U.

W.
D.

GARAGE
21'-4"x20'-8"

P.

MAIN AREA

BEDROOM 2
10'-8"x11'-0"

40'-4"

DRIVE

60'-0"

Facade Highlights Classic Home

■ *Total living area 2,594 sq. ft.* ■ *Price Code D* ■

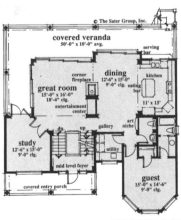

MAIN FLOOR

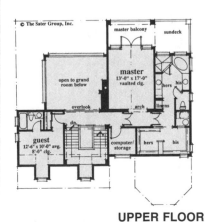

UPPER FLOOR

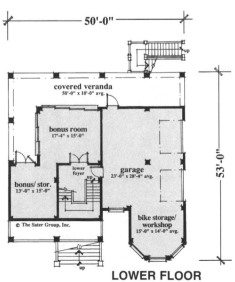

LOWER FLOOR

Main Floor — 1,655 sq. ft.
Upper Floor — 939 sq. ft.
Bonus — 532 sq. ft.
Garage — 667 sq. ft.

No. 94257

■ This plan features:

— Three bedrooms

— Three full and one half baths

■ Exterior highlights include a metal roof, and covered Verandahs

■ The main level Study is accessed in two locations by French doors

■ Two walls of glass brighten the Great Room

■ A corner fireplace warms the Dining Room and the Kitchen beyond

■ An island with an eating bar highlights the Kitchen

■ The upstairs Master Suite has a lavish Bath and a his-n-her walk-in closet

■ Two Guest Rooms with private Baths complete this home

■ No materials list is available for this plan

Pleasing to the Eye

No. 93073

This plan features:

- Three bedrooms
- Two full baths
- A large covered front Porch opens to the foyer with a nine-foot ceiling
- The Kitchen has a dining bay, a built-in desk and a sunny window over the sink
- The Living Room includes a corner fireplace and ten-foot ceilings
- Bedrooms are grouped for homeowner convenience
- The Master Suite is topped by a sloped ceiling and is pampered by a private Bath and walk-in closet
- The two-car Garage has an optional door location at the rear of the home
- An optional slab or crawl space foundation — please specify when ordering
- No materials list is available for this plan

Main floor — 1,202 sq. ft.
Garage — 482 sq. ft.

■ Total living area 1,202 sq. ft. ■ Price Code A ■

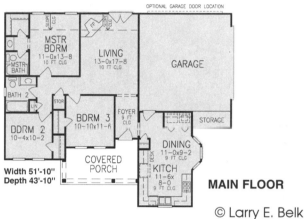

MAIN FLOOR

© Larry E. Belk

Suited for a Hill

No. 90822

This plan features:

- Three bedrooms
- One full and one half baths
- Vaulted ceilings and a fieldstone fireplace in the Living/Dining Room
- Two first floor Bedrooms that have ample closet space and share a full hall Bath
- The Master Bedroom on the loft level includes a private Bath
- A wrap-around Sun Deck offers an abundance of outdoor living space

Main floor — 925 sq. ft.
Loft — 338 sq. ft.
Basement — 864 sq. ft.
Width — 33'-0"
Depth — 47'-0"

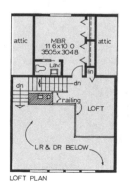

■ Total living area 1,263 sq. ft. ■ Price Code A ■

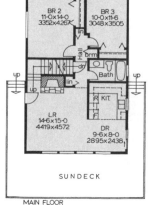

MAIN FLOOR

LOFT PLAN

An EXCLUSIVE DESIGN
By Westhome Planners, Ltd.

287

Keystones and Arched Windows

■ Total living area 1,670 sq. ft. ■ Price Code B ■

No. 98432

■ This plan features:

— Three bedrooms

— Two full baths

■ A decorative column helps to define the Dining Room from the Great Room

■ A fireplace and French door can be found in the Great Room

■ An efficient Kitchen includes a serving bar, Pantry and pass-through to the Great Room

■ A vaulted ceiling over the Breakfast Room

■ A plush Master Suite includes a private Bath and a walk-in closet

■ Two additional Bedrooms share a full Bath in the hall

■ An optional basement, slab or crawl space foundation — please specify when ordering

Main floor — 1,670 sq. ft.
Garage — 240 sq. ft.

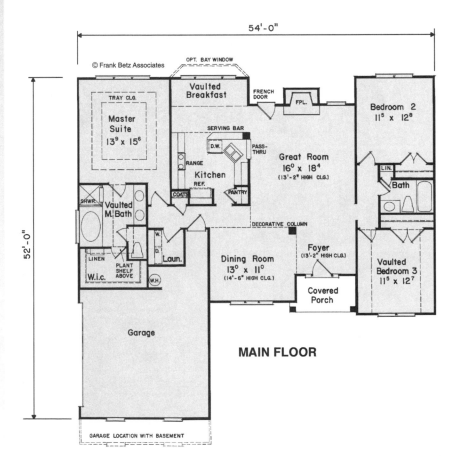

MAIN FLOOR

Step Saving Convenience

■ *Total living area 1,955 sq. ft.* ■ *Price Code C* ■

No. 92617

■ This plan features:

— Three bedrooms

— Two full baths

■ A covered Porch leads into the Foyer

■ A corner fireplace and a wall of windows with an atrium door to the Patio in the Great Room

■ An efficient Kitchen with a built-in pantry, a peninsula counter/snack bar separating it from the Breakfast alcove

■ Topped by a tray ceiling, a private Master Bedroom offers an ultra Bath with a walk-in closet, a double vanity and a window tub

■ Two additional Bedrooms, one with a sloped ceiling, share a full hall Bath

■ No materials list is available for this plan

Main floor — 1,955 sq. ft.

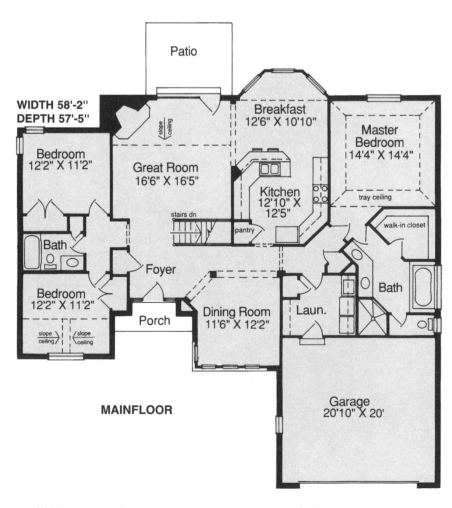

WIDTH 58'-2"
DEPTH 57'-5"

Patio

Breakfast 12'6" X 10'10"

Master Bedroom 14'4" X 14'4"

tray ceiling

Bedroom 12'2" X 11'2"

Great Room 16'6" X 16'5"

Kitchen 12'10" X 12'5"

slope ceiling

walk-in closet

stairs dn

pantry

Bath

Foyer

Bath

Bedroom 12'2" X 11'2"

Dining Room 11'6" X 12'2"

Laun.

Porch

slope ceiling

slope ceiling

Garage 20'10" X 20'

MAINFLOOR

Arches are Appealing

■ *Total living area 1,642 sq. ft.* ■ *Price Code B* ■

Main floor — 1,642 sq. ft.
Garage — 420 sq. ft.
Basement — 1,642 sq. ft.

Optional Basement Stairs

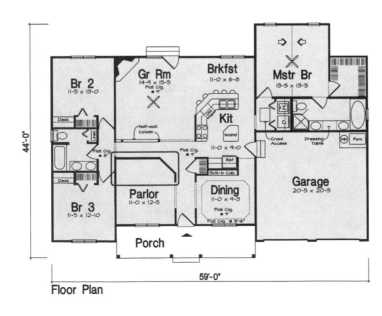

Floor Plan

No. 24717

■ **This plan features:**

— Three bedrooms

— Two full baths

■ Welcoming front Porch enhanced by graceful columns and curved windows

■ Parlor and Dining Room frame entry hall

■ Expansive Great Room accented by a corner fireplace and outdoor access

■ Open and convenient Kitchen with a work island, angled, peninsula counter/eating bar, and nearby Laundry and Garage entry

■ Secluded Master Bedroom with a large walk-in closet and luxurious Bath with a dressing table

■ Two additional Bedrooms with ample closets, share a double vanity Bath

■ No materials list is available for this plan

No. 94300

■ **This plan features:**

— Two bedrooms

— Two full baths

■ A welcoming Porch into an air-lock Entry

■ Open Living/Dining Room with a circular fireplace and a wall of windows with Deck access

■ Private Deck with covered and open areas, offers comfortable outdoor living space

■ Compact Kitchen with a wonderful view, easily serves Dining and Deck areas

■ Two Bedrooms, one with a walk-in closet and private Bath, have double windows

■ An optional Carport offers sheltered space and Storage access

■ No materials list is available for this plan

Main floor — 950 sq. ft.

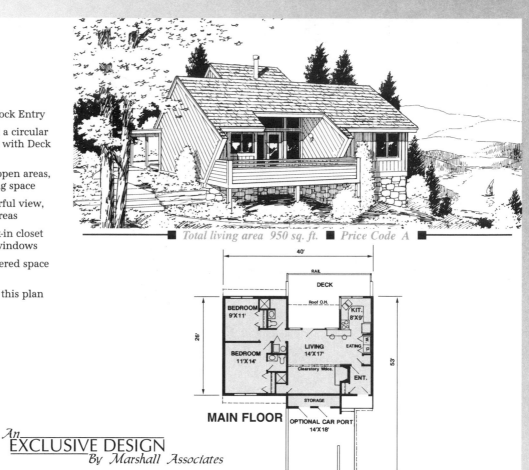

■ *Total living area 950 sq. ft.* ■ *Price Code A* ■

An EXCLUSIVE DESIGN *By Marshall Associates*

Step Saving, One-Floor Convenience

No. 94982

■ **This plan features:**

— Three bedrooms

— One full and one three-quarter baths

■ The covered Porch leads to a short entry way with a convenient coat closet

■ The fireplace with transoms to either side highlights the Great Room

■ The Kitchen/Breakfast area features a pantry, an extended counter/snack bar and a double sink

■ The Laundry Room doubles as a Mud Room from the Garage

■ The Master Suite includes a private Bath and a large walk-in closet

■ Two secondary Bedroom are located in close proximity to a full Bath

Main floor — 1,360 sq. ft.
Garage — 544 sq. ft.

■ *Total living area 1,360 sq. ft.* ■ *Price Code A* ■

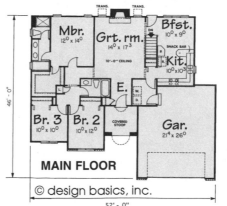

© design basics, inc.

Southern Hospitality

■ Total living area 1,830 sq. ft. ■ Price Code C ■

No. 92220

■ This plan features:

— Three bedrooms

— Two full baths

■ Covered Veranda catches breezes

■ Tiled Entry leads into Great Room with fieldstone fireplace, a cathedral ceiling and atrium door to another Covered Veranda

■ A bright Kitchen/Dining Room includes a stovetop island/snackbar, built-in Pantry and desk

■ Vaulted ceiling crowns Master Bedroom that offers a plush Bath and huge walk-in closet

■ Two additional Bedrooms with ample closets share a double vanity Bath

■ No materials list is available for this plan

Main floor — 1,830 sq. ft.
Garage — 759 sq. ft.

Open Spaces

■ *Total living area 1,388 sq. ft.* ■ *Price Code A* ■

No. 93279

■ This plan features:

— Three bedrooms

— Two full baths

■ A central, double-sided fireplace adds atmosphere to the Family Room, Kitchen and the Breakfast Area

■ An efficient Kitchen is highlighted by a peninsula counter that doubles as a snack bar

■ The Master Suite includes a walk-in closet, a double vanity, separate shower and tub in the Bath

■ Two additional Bedrooms share a full hall Bath

■ A wooden Deck can be accessed from the Breakfast Area

■ An optional crawl space or slab foundation — please specify when ordering

Main floor — 1,388 sq. ft.
Garage — 400 sq. ft.

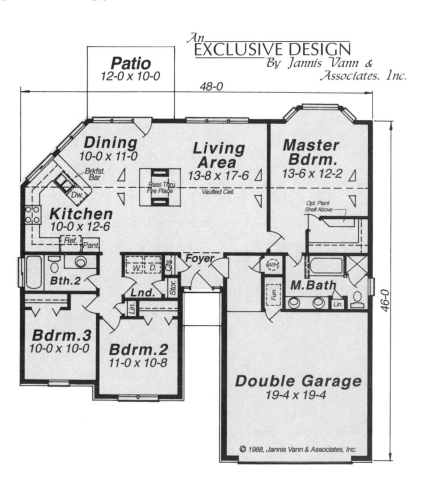

An EXCLUSIVE DESIGN
By Jannis Vann & Associates, Inc.

Patio
12-0 x 10-0

48-0

Dining
10-0 x 11-0

Living Area
13-8 x 17-6

Master Bdrm.
13-6 x 12-2

Brkfst. Bar

Pass Thru Fire Place

Vaulted Ceil.

Dw.

Opt. Plant Shelf Above

Kitchen
10-0 x 12-6

Ref. Pant.

Foyer

W.H.

Bth.2

W. D.   Cls.

Fum.

M.Bath

Lin.

Lnd.

Lin.   Stor.

Bdrm.3
10-0 x 10-0

Bdrm.2
11-0 x 10-8

Double Garage
19-4 x 19-4

46-0

© 1988, Jannis Vann & Associates, Inc.

293

Easy One Floor Living

■ *Total living area 1,671 sq. ft.* ■ *Price Code B* ■

WIDTH 50'-0"
DEPTH 51'-0"

© Frank Betz Associates

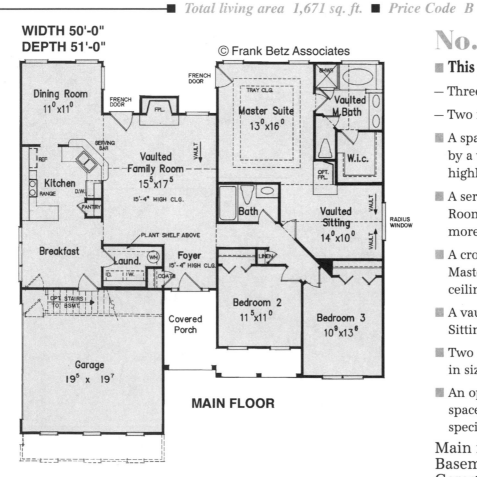

MAIN FLOOR

No. 98423

■ **This plan features:**

— Three bedrooms

— Two full baths

■ A spacious Family Room is topped by a vaulted ceiling and highlighted by a large fireplace

■ A serving bar open to the Family Room and the Dining Room adds more efficiency to the Kitchen

■ A crowning tray ceiling over the Master Bedroom and a vaulted ceiling over the Master Bath

■ A vaulted ceiling over the cozy Sitting Room in the Master Suite

■ Two additional Bedrooms, roomy in size, share the full hall Bath

■ An optional basement, crawl space or slab foundation — please specify when ordering

Main floor — 1,671 sq. ft.
Basement — 1,685 sq. ft.
Garage — 400 sq. ft.

Great Room With Cathedral Ceiling

No. 94970 ✂

■ This plan features:

— Three bedrooms

— One full and one three-quarter baths

■ A convenient split ranch design with three steps up from the Entry to the Great Room

■ A Bay window, fireplace and an outstanding volume ceiling highlight the Great Room

■ The Dinette's angled shape is accented by windows on the corner angles and a vaulted ceiling

■ An efficient family Kitchen has a snackbar/island counter plus a corner sink and built-in Pantry

■ The Master Bedroom is enhanced by a tiered ceiling, three-quarter Bath and a boxed window

■ Two additional Bedrooms share a full Bath in the hall

Main floor — 1,385 sq. ft.
Garage — 658 sq. ft.

■ Total living area 1,385 sq. ft. ■ Price Code A ■

© design basics, inc.

MAIN FLOOR

Ideal for Coastal View

No. 92802 ✂

■ This plan features:

— Three bedrooms

— Two full baths

■ A wrap-around Deck and windows to the summit of the cathedral ceiling in the Dining/Living areas

■ An efficient, U-shaped Kitchen has a pass-through counter to the Dining Area

■ A private Bath, and ample closet space in the Master Bedroom

■ Two additional Bedrooms share a full hall Bath

■ A Loft Area expands the living space or storage

■ An optional slab, crawl or pole foundation — please specify when ordering

First floor — 1,320 sq. ft.
Second floor — 185 sq. ft.

■ Total living area 1,505 sq. ft. ■ Price Code B ■

SECOND FLOOR

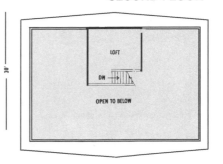

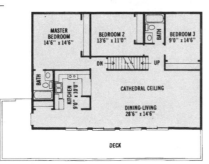

FIRST FLOOR

Natural Light and Views

■ *Total living area 2,023 sq. ft.* ■ *Price Code C* ■

No. 26760

■ **This plan features:**

— Three bedrooms

— Two full and one half baths

■ A sheltered entrance enhanced by skylight

■ An adjoining Living and Dining Room for easy entertaining

■ A prow-shaped Family Room highlighted by beamed ceiling, cozy fireplace and sliding glass door to multi-level Deck

■ An open Kitchen with a cook island and Breakfast Area with access to the Deck

■ A Master Bedroom with a private Deck and a Bath with a walk-in closet

■ Two additional Bedrooms near a full Bath

Main floor — 2,023 sq. ft.
Decks — 589 sq. ft.

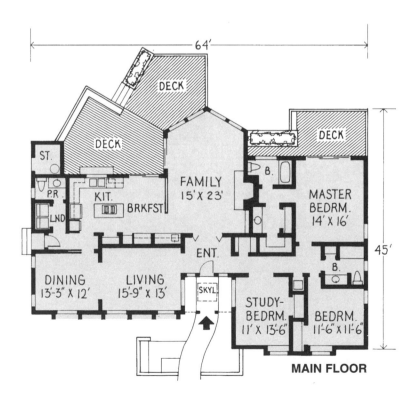

MAIN FLOOR

© 1995 Donald A Gardner Architects, Inc.

■ *Total living area 1,246 sq. ft.* ■ *Price Code C* ■

No. 99806

■ This plan features:

— Three bedrooms

— Two full baths

■ Great Room topped by a cathedral ceiling and enhanced by a fireplace

■ Great Room, Dining Room and Kitchen open to each other for a feeling of spaciousness

■ Pantry, skylight and peninsula counter add to the comfort and efficiency of the Kitchen

■ Cathedral ceiling crowns the Master Suite which has many amenities; walk-in and linen closets, a luxurious private Bath

■ The Swing Room, Bedroom or Study is topped by a cathedral ceiling

■ A skylight over the full hall Bath naturally illuminates the room

Main floor — 1,246 sq. ft.
Garage — 420 sq. ft.

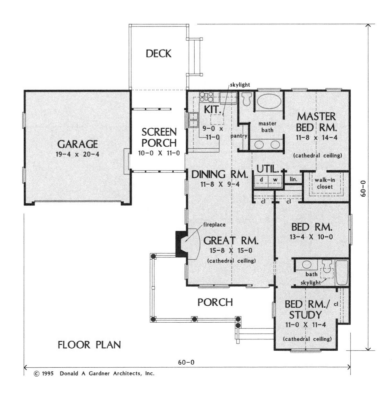

FLOOR PLAN

© 1995 Donald A Gardner Architects, Inc.

Energy Efficient Air-Lock Entry

■ *Total living area 1,771 sq. ft.* ■ *Price Code C* ■

No. 24714

■ **This plan features:**

— Two bedrooms

— Two full baths

■ The attractive covered Porch highlights the curb appeal of this charming home

■ A cozy window seat and a vaulted ceiling enhance the private Den

■ The sunken Great Room is accented by a fireplace that is nestled between windows

■ A screened Porch, accessed from the Dining Room, extends the living space to the outdoors

■ The Master Bath features a garden tub, separate shower, his-n-her walk-in closets and a skylight

■ No materials list is available for this plan

Main floor — 1,771 sq. ft.
Basement — 1,194 sq. ft.
Garage — 517 sq. ft.

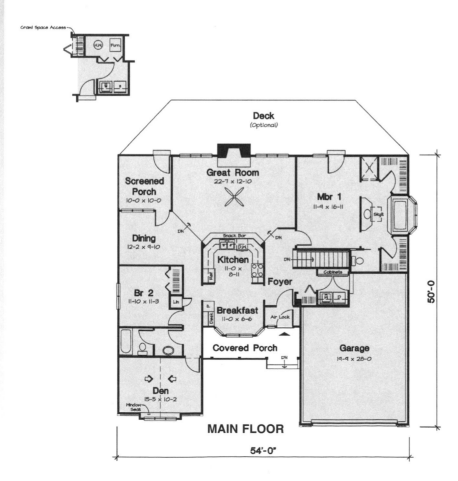

MAIN FLOOR

Home-Sweet-Home

No. 24723

This plan features:

– Three bedrooms

– Two full baths

■ Single level format allows for step-saving convenience

■ Large Living Room, highlighted by a fireplace and built-in entertainment center, adjoins the Dining Room

■ Skylights, a ceiling fan and room defining columns accent the Dining Room

■ A serving bar to the Dining Room, and ample counter and cabinet space in the Kitchen

■ Decorative ceiling treatment over the Master Bedroom and a private Master Bath

■ Two secondary Bedrooms with easy access to the full Bath in the hall

■ No materials list is available for this plan

Main floor — 1,112 sq. ft.
Garage — 563 sq. ft.

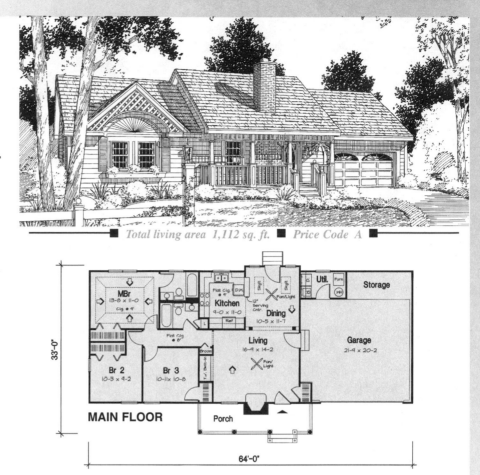

Total living area 1,112 sq. ft. ■ Price Code A

MAIN FLOOR

Key West Inspired

No. 94256

This plan features:

– Three bedrooms

– Two full and one three-quarter baths

■ A covered Porch and an Observation Deck above it add to the allure of this home

■ The Dining Room is separated from the Kitchen by an arched opening

■ The Kitchen is conveniently arranged and has a center island

■ The Great Room has French doors to the Porch, a fireplace and built-ins

■ The identical secondary Bedrooms each have a window seat and a built-in desk

■ The Master Suite offers a walk-in closet, a private Bath and access to the Deck

■ No materials list is available for this plan

Main Floor — 1,046 sq. ft.
Upper Floor — 638 sq. ft.

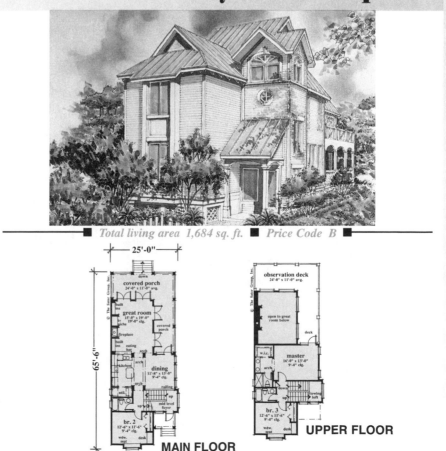

Total living area 1,684 sq. ft. ■ Price Code B

MAIN FLOOR

UPPER FLOOR

Seaside Splendor

■ *Total living area 1,824 sq. ft.* ■ *Price Code C* ■

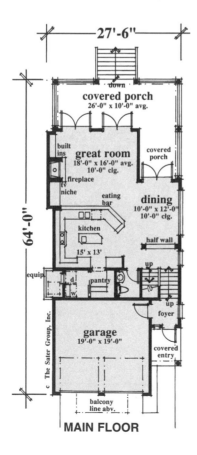

MAIN FLOOR

- 27'-6"
- 64'-0"
- covered porch
  26'-0" x 10'-0" avg.
- built ins
- great room
  18'-0" x 16'-0" avg.
  10'-0" clg.
- fireplace
- tv niche
- covered porch
- eating bar
- dining
  10'-0" x 12'-0"
  10'-0" clg.
- kitchen
  15' x 13'
- half wall
- equip.
- pantry
- up
- up
- foyer
- garage
  19'-0" x 19'-0"
- covered entry
- balcony line abv.

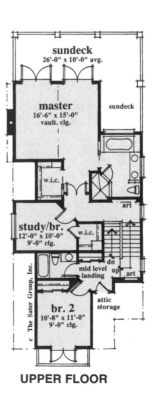

UPPER FLOOR

- sundeck
  26'-0" x 10'-0" avg.
- master
  16'-6" x 15'-0"
  vault. clg.
- sundeck
- w.i.c.
- art
- study/br.
  12'-0" x 10'-0"
  9'-0" clg.
- w.i.c.
- dn
- up
- mid level landing
- art
- br. 2
  10'-8" x 11'-0"
  9'-0" clg.
- attic storage

c The Sater Group, Inc.

No. 94258

■ **This plan features:**

— Three bedrooms

— Two full and one half baths

■ The Great Room and the Dining Room both access the covered Porch

■ The Kitchen is open to the living area and they share an eating bar

■ The Master Suite has a vaulted ceiling and a private Sun Deck

■ Both secondary Bedrooms have nine-foot ceilings

■ There is a Utility Room that has room set aside for a Pantry

■ No materials list is available for this plan

Main Floor — 876 sq. ft.
Upper Floor — 948 sq. ft.
Garage — 361 sq. ft.

Affordable Energy-Saver

■ *Total living area 1,393 sq. ft.* ■ *Price Code A* ■

No. 90680 ✖

■ This plan features:

— Three bedrooms

— Two full baths

■ The covered Porch leads into an open Foyer and Living/Dining Room with skylights and front to back exposure

■ An efficient Kitchen with a bay window Dinette Area, and a walk-in Pantry is adjacent to the Mud Room and Garage area

■ The private Master Bedroom with a luxurious Master Bath leading to a private Deck complete with a pampering Hot Tub

■ Two additional Bedrooms with access to a full hall Bath

Main floor — 1,393 sq. ft.
Basement — 1,393 sq. ft.
Garage — 542 sq. ft.

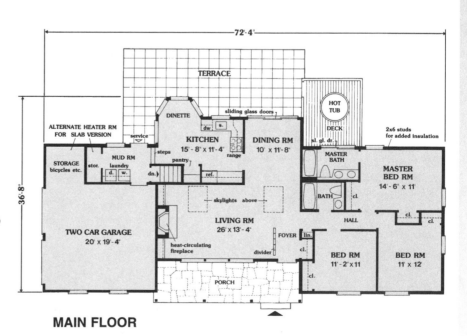

MAIN FLOOR

Columns Punctuate the Interior Space

© 1997 Donald A Gardner Architects, Inc.

S. NATHAN

■ *Total living area 2,188 sq. ft.* ■ *Price Code G* ■

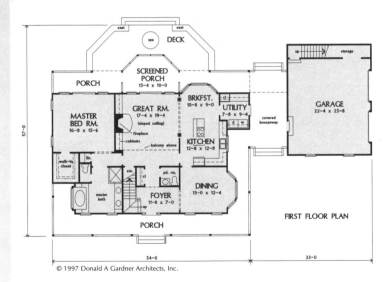

© 1997 Donald A Gardner Architects, Inc.

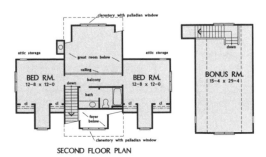

SECOND FLOOR PLAN

No. 99801

■ **This plan features:**

— Three bedrooms

— Two full and one half baths

■ A two-story Great Room and Foyer, both with dormer windows

■ Large Kitchen, featuring a center cooking island with counter and large Breakfast Area

■ Columns punctuate interior spaces

■ Master Bedroom, privately situated on the first floor, has a dual vanity, garden tub and separate shower

First floor — 1,618 sq. ft.
Second floor — 570 sq. ft.
Bonus room — 495 sq. ft.
Garage & storage — 649 sq. ft.

Modified A-Frame at Home Anywhere

No. 90309

■ This plan features:

— One or two bedrooms

— One full and one half baths

■ A combined Living Room/Dining Room with a ceiling that reaches to the second floor loft

■ A galley-styled Kitchen is conveniently arranged and open to the Dining Room

■ The Living Room area has sliding glass doors to the Deck and a fireplace

■ The loft has a half Bath and an optional Bedroom

Main floor — 735 sq. ft.
Second floor — 304 sq. ft.

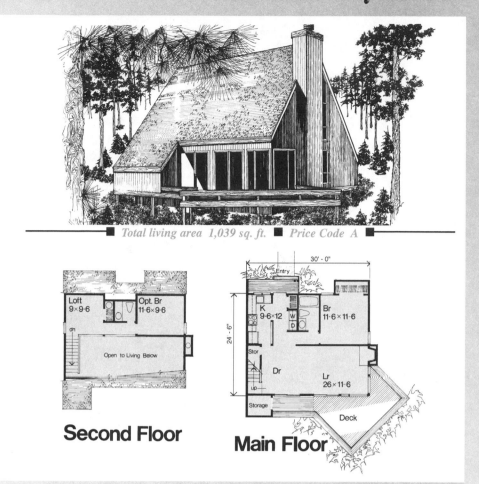

■ *Total living area 1,039 sq. ft.* ■ *Price Code A* ■

Second Floor

Main Floor

Cozy Vacation Hide-Away

No. 94309

■ This plan features:

— Two bedrooms

— One full and one three-quarter baths

■ Highly windowed Living Room offers an unrestricted view of the surroundings

■ Spacious Deck expands living space to the outdoors and has a built-in grill

■ Efficient Kitchen is highlighted by a corner double sink and an eating bar

■ The Master Bedroom is equipped with a walk-in closet and a private three-quarter Bath

■ Spiral staircase gains access to Loft area overlooking the Living Room

■ No materials list is available for this plan

Main floor — 1,028 sq. ft.
Loft — 187 sq. ft.

An
EXCLUSIVE DESIGN
By Marshall Associates

■ *Total living area 1,215 sq. ft.* ■ *Price Code A* ■

MAIN FLOOR

LOFT

Ranch with Handicapped Access

Total living area 1,734 sq. ft. ■ Price Code B

No. 20403

■ This plan features:

— Three bedrooms

— One full and one three-quarter baths

■ Ramps into the front Entry from the Porch; the Utility Area and the Kitchen from the Garage; and the Family Room from the Deck

■ An open area topped by a sloped ceiling for the Family Room, the Dining Room, the Kitchen and the Breakfast alcove

■ Kitchen with a built-in Pantry and an open counter

■ A Master Bedroom Suite accented by a sloping ceiling above a wall of windows, offering access to the Deck

■ Two front Bedrooms with sloped ceilings share a full hall

Main floor — 1,734 sq. ft.
Garage — 606 sq. ft.

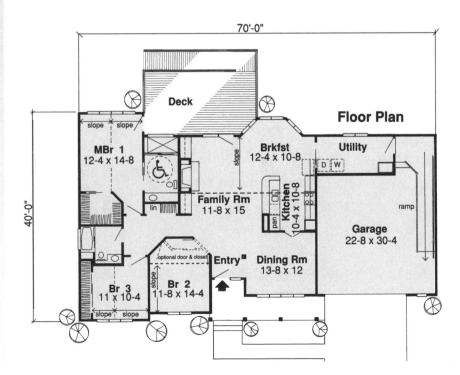

Floor Plan

70'-0"

40'-0"

Deck

MBr 1
12-4 x 14-8

Br 3
11 x 10-4

Br 2
11-8 x 14-4

optional door & closet

Entry

Family Rm
11-8 x 15

Dining Rm
13-8 x 12

Brkfst
12-4 x 10-8

Kitchen
10-4 x 10-8

pan

Utility

D W

Garage
22-8 x 30-4

ramp

slope

lin

©1996 Donald A. Gardner Architects, Inc.

B. NATHAN

■ *Total living area 1,864 sq. ft.* ■ *Price Code D* ■

No. 96468

■ This plan features:

— Three bedrooms

— Two full baths

■ Sunlit Foyer flows easily into the generous Great Room

■ Great Room crowned in a cathedral ceiling and accented by a fireplace

■ Accent columns define the open Kitchen and Breakfast Bay

■ Master Bedroom topped by a tray ceiling and highlighted by a well-appointed Master Bath

■ Two additional Bedrooms and a skylit Bath in the hall create the children's wing

Main floor — 1,864 sq. ft.
Bonus room — 319 sq. ft.
Garage — 503 sq. ft.

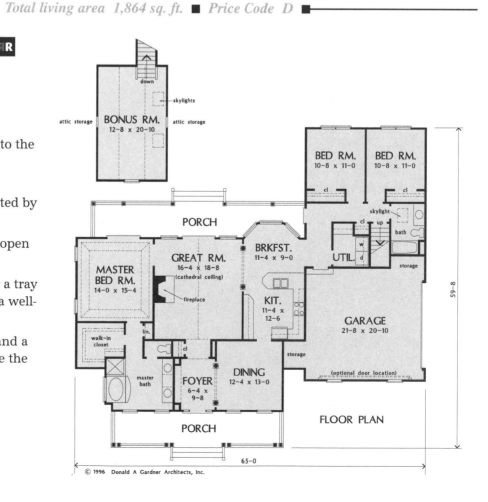

BONUS RM.
12-8 x 20-10

attic storage   skylights   attic storage

down

PORCH

MASTER BED RM.
14-0 x 15-4

GREAT RM.
16-4 x 18-8
(cathedral ceiling)

fireplace

BRKFST.
11-4 x 9-0

KIT.
11-4 x 12-6

UTIL.

skylight

cl   up

bath

w   d

storage

BED RM.
10-8 x 11-0

BED RM.
10-8 x 11-0

cl   cl

GARAGE
21-8 x 20-10

59-8

walk-in closet

lin.

master bath

cl

FOYER
6-4 x 9-8

DINING
12-4 x 13-0

storage

(optional door location)

PORCH

FLOOR PLAN

65-0

© 1996 Donald A Gardner Architects, Inc.

Master Suite on a Private Level

■ *Total living area 2,843 sq. ft.* ■ *Price Code G* ■

Recreation
22 x 26

Br 2
11-6 x 11-6

storage

furn.

Ldry

w.h.

Br 3
14 x 11

Lower Floor

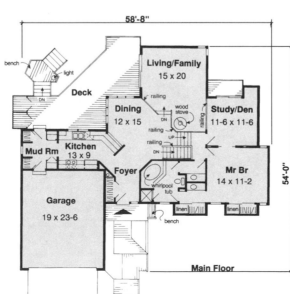

58'-8"

bench

light

Deck

DN

Living/Family
15 x 20

railing

Dining
12 x 15

wood stove

Study/Den
11-6 x 11-6

railing

railing

DN

Mud Rm

Kitchen
13 x 9

UP

DN

Foyer

whirlpool tub

Mr Br
14 x 11-2

linen

linen

54'-0"

Garage
19 x 23-6

bench

Main Floor

No. 26810

■ **This plan features:**

— Three bedrooms

— Two full baths

■ A Dining Room and sunken Living Room on a space-expanding diagonal

■ A corridor Kitchen extends into a traffic-free space open to the living areas

■ A Deck, making the outdoors a natural part of all social areas

■ A Master Bedroom connects to a Study and a Deck

■ A Recreation Area is located in the basement level

Main floor — 1,423 sq. ft.
Lower floor — 1,420 sq. ft.
Garage — 478 sq. ft.

A Compact Home

No. 93018

This plan features:

— Three bedrooms

— Two full baths

▪ Siding with brick wainscoting distinguishes the elevation

▪ A large Family Room with a corner fireplace and direct access to the outside

▪ An arched opening leads to the Breakfast Area

▪ A bay window illuminates the Breakfast Area with natural light

▪ An efficiently designed, U-shaped Kitchen has ample cabinet and counter space

▪ The Master Suite has a private Master Bath

▪ Two additional Bedrooms share a full hall Bath

▪ No materials list is available for this plan

Main floor — 1,142 sq. ft.
Garage — 428 sq. ft.

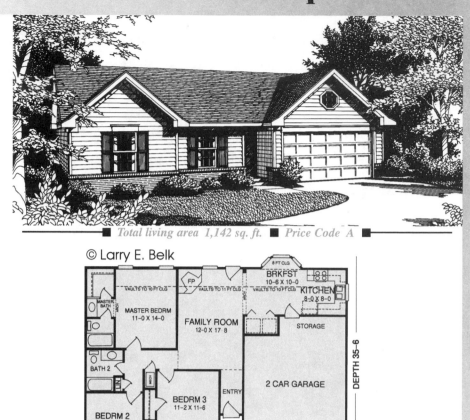

■ Total living area 1,142 sq. ft. ■ Price Code A ■

© Larry E. Belk

MAIN FLOOR

Four Bedroom Stucco

No. 94240

This plan features:

— Three bedrooms

— Two full baths

▪ Fits easily on narrow depth lots

▪ Grand Room layout has vaulted ceiling that includes the Foyer and Dining Room

▪ Grand Room is highlighted by a built-in entertainment center and access to Lanai

▪ Compact Kitchen opens to glass Nook and formal Dining Area

▪ Private Master Suite has glass doors to the Lanai Area and a plush Bath

▪ Two Bedrooms and a Study or third Bedroom located on the opposite side have ample closet space

▪ Guest Bath has outdoor access to the pool area

▪ No materials list is available for this plan

Main floor — 1,647 sq. ft.
Garage — 427 sq. ft.

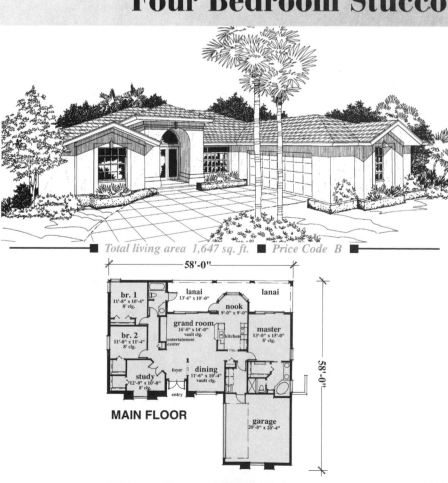

■ Total living area 1,647 sq. ft. ■ Price Code B ■

MAIN FLOOR

Recreation Room Houses Fireplace

■ *Total living area 1,956 sq. ft.* ■ *Price Code C* ■

No. 9964

■ This plan features:

— Four bedrooms

— Two full baths

■ A wood-burning fireplace warms the Living/Dining Room, which is accessible to the large wooden Sun Deck

■ Two first-floor Bedrooms have access to a full hall Bath

■ Two ample-sized second floor Bedrooms

■ The Recreation Room has a cozy fireplace and convenient half Bath

First floor — 906 sq. ft.
Second floor — 456 sq. ft.
Lower floor — 594 sq. ft.
Basement — 279 sq. ft.

■ *Total living area 1,367 sq. ft.* ■ *Price Code A* ■

No. 99639

■ This plan features:

— Three bedrooms

— Two full baths

■ The Living Room has a high ceiling that slopes and a decorative heat-circulating fireplace on the rear wall

■ An efficient Kitchen that adjoins the Dining Room

■ A Dinette Area for informal eating in the Kitchen can comfortably seat six people

■ The Master Suite is arranged with a large dressing area that has a walk-in closet plus two linear closets and space for a vanity

Main area — 1,367 sq. ft.
Basement — 1,267 sq. ft.
Garage — 431 sq. ft.

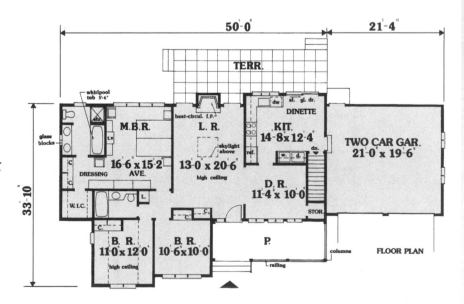

Easy Everyday Living and Entertaining

■ *Total living area 1,664 sq. ft.* ■ *Price Code B* ■

No. 92238

■ **This plan features:**

— Three bedrooms

— Two full baths

■ Front entrance accented by segmented arches, a sidelight and transom windows

■ Open Living Room with a focal point fireplace, a wetbar and access to the Patio

■ Dining Area open to both the Living Room and the Kitchen

■ Efficient Kitchen with a cooktop island, walk-in Pantry and Utility Area with a Garage entry

■ Large walk-in closet, double vanity Bath and access to Patio featured in the Master Bedroom

■ No materials list is available for this plan

Main floor — 1,664 sq. ft.
Basement — 1,600 sq. ft.
Garage — 440 sq. ft.

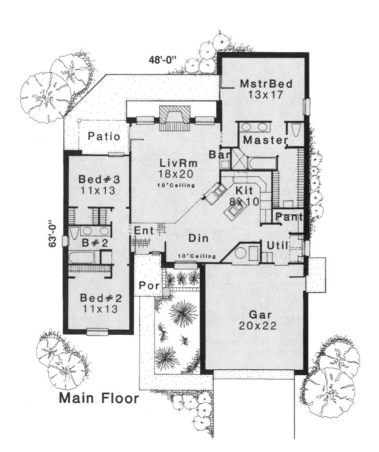

Main Floor

Gabled Roofline and Arched Windows

No. 91063

■ **This plan features:**

— Three bedrooms

— Two full baths

■ Vaulted ceilings and an open interior creates a spacious feeling

■ A private Master Bedroom with a generous closet and Master Bath

■ Two additional Bedrooms shares the second full Bath

■ A Kitchen with ample storage, countertops and a built-in Pantry

■ No materials list is available for this plan

Main floor — 1,207 sq. ft.
Garage — 440 sq. ft.

■ *Total living area 1,207 sq. ft.* ■ *Price Code A* ■

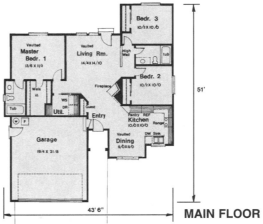

MAIN FLOOR

Popular Floor Plan For Young Families

No. 94316

■ **This plan features:**

— Four bedrooms

— Two full and one half baths

■ With all of the Bedrooms on one floor, this home is perfect for families with small children

■ A private Master Bath and a walk-in closet are found in Master Bedroom

■ An open layout between the Kitchen and Living Room affords a spacious and airy feeling

■ The convenient Laundry Center is located in the hall outside Kitchen

■ An expansive Family Room has a cozy fireplace and access to the rear Patio

■ No material list is available for this plan

First floor — 736 sq. ft.
Second floor — 788 sq. ft.
Basement — 746 sq. ft.
Garage — 400 sq. ft.

An
EXCLUSIVE DESIGN
By Marshall Associates

■ *Total living area 1,524 sq. ft.* ■ *Price Code B* ■

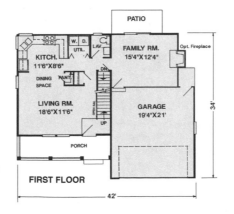

FIRST FLOOR

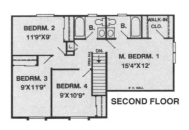

SECOND FLOOR

Elegant Row House

■ *Total living area 2,520 sq. ft.* ■ *Price Code F* ■

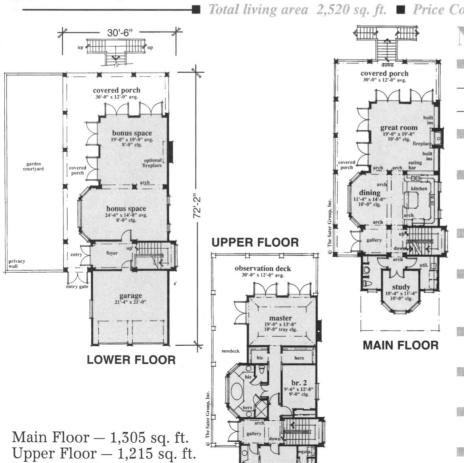

30'-6"

up   up

covered porch
30'-0" x 12'-0" avg.

bonus space
19'-0" x 19'-0" avg.
8'-0" clg.

optional 'fireplace

garden courtyard

covered porch

arch

bonus space
24'-6" x 14'-0" avg.
8'-0" clg.

72'-2"

entry   foyer   up

privacy wall

entry gate

garage
21'-4" x 21'-0"

LOWER FLOOR

© The Sater Group, Inc.

UPPER FLOOR

observation deck
30'-0" x 12'-0" avg.

master
19'-0" x 13'-8"
10'-0" tray clg.

sundeck

his   hers

his

br. 2
9'-6" x 12'-8"
9'-0" clg.

hers

arch

gallery   down

guest
10'-4" x 15'-8"
9'-0" clg.

equip.

covered porch
30'-0" x 12'-0" avg.

down

great room
19'-0" x 19'-0"
10'-0" clg.

built ins

fireplace

built ins

covered porch

arch   arch

eating bar

dining
11'-4" x 14'-0"
10'-0" clg.

arch

kitchen

arch

gallery

up
down

arch

util.

study
10'-4" x 11'-4"
10'-0" clg.

MAIN FLOOR

© The Sater Group, Inc.

No. 94259

■ **This plan features:**

— Three bedrooms

— Two full and one half baths

■ Arched columns define the formal and casual spaces

■ Wrap-around Porticos on two levels provide views to the living areas

■ Four sets of French doors let the outside in to the Great Room

■ The Master Suite features a private Bath designed for two people

■ Generous bonus space awaits your ideas for completion

■ The Guest Bedroom leads to a gallery hallway with Deck access

■ No materials list is available for this plan

■ An optional slab or post/pier foundation — please specify when ordering

Main Floor — 1,305 sq. ft.
Upper Floor — 1,215 sq. ft.
Bonus — 935 sq. ft.
Garage — 480 sq. ft.

Breakfast Bar Sets Off Dining Area

■ Total living area 1,174 sq. ft. ■ Price Code A ■

No. 10054

■ This plan features:

— Four bedrooms

— One full bath

■ Chalet styling and romantic balconies add to the attractive features of this elevation

■ A front Deck extends living space to the outdoors

■ A large Living/Dining Room area provides an expansive, open space for get-togethers

■ A well-appointed Kitchen with a breakfast bar for informal eating

■ Two first floor Bedrooms are conveniently located near a full hall Bath

■ Two second floor Bedrooms are highlighted by private balconies

First floor — 768 sq. ft.
Second floor — 406 sq. ft.

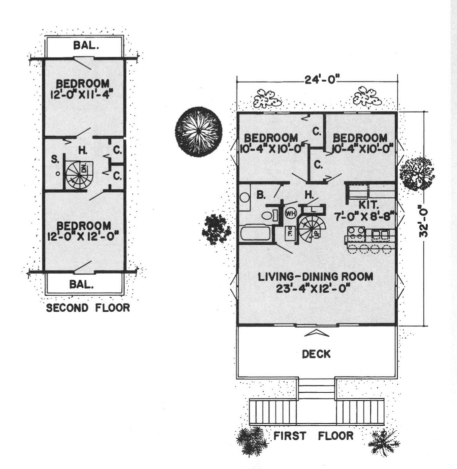

SECOND FLOOR

BAL.

BEDROOM
12'-0" X 11'-4"

S. H. C.
o C.

BEDROOM
12'-0" X 12'-0"

BAL.

FIRST FLOOR

24'-0"

BEDROOM
10'-4" X 10'-0"   C.   BEDROOM
10'-4" X 10'-0"

C.

B.   H.   KIT.
7'-0" X 8'-8"

WH

32'-0"

LIVING-DINING ROOM
23'-4" X 12'-0"

DECK

Charming Brick Ranch

■ *Total living area 1,782 sq. ft.* ■ *Price Code C* ■

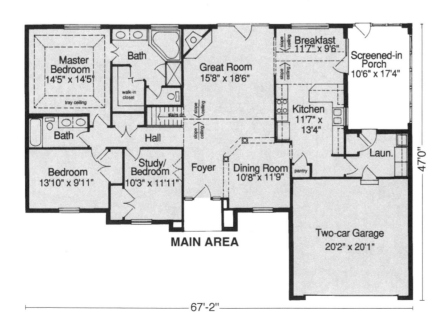

MAIN AREA

67'-2"

47'0"

Master Bedroom 14'5" x 14'5"
tray ceiling

Bath

walk-in closet

Great Room 15'8" x 18'6"

Breakfast 11'7" x 9'6"

Screened-in Porch 10'6" x 17'4"

Kitchen 11'7" x 13'4"

Bath

ship ld

Hall

Foyer

Study/ Bedroom 10'3" x 11'11"

Bedroom 13'10" x 9'11"

Dining Room 10'8" x 11'9"

pantry

Laun.

Two-car Garage 20'2" x 20'1"

Main area — 1,782 sq. ft.
Garage — 407 sq. ft.
Basement — 1,735 sq. ft.

No. 92630

■ **This plan features:**

— Three bedrooms

— Two full baths

■ Sheltered entrance leads into open Foyer and Dining Room defined by columns

■ Vaulted ceiling spans Foyer, Dining Room and Great Room with corner fireplace and atrium door to rear yard

■ Central Kitchen with separate Laundry and Pantry easily serves Dining Room, Breakfast Area and Screened Porch

■ Luxurious Master Bedroom offers a tray ceiling and French doors to the Bath with a double vanity, a walk-in closet and a whirlpool tub

■ Two additional Bedrooms, one which easily converts to a Study, share a full Bath

■ No materials list is available for this plan

One-Level Contemporary

No. 24327

This plan features:

— Three bedrooms

— Two full baths

- A vaulted ceiling and elegant fireplace in the Living Room

- An open layout between the Living Room, Dining Room and Kitchen gives a more spacious feeling to these areas

- A well-equipped Kitchen with a double sink and a peninsula counter that may be used as an eating bar

- A Master Suite that includes a walk-in closet and a private Bath with a double vanity

- Two additional Bedrooms that have ample closet space and share a full hall Bath

Main area — 1,266 sq. ft.
Garage — 443 sq. ft.
Basement — 1,266 sq. ft.

An EXCLUSIVE DESIGN
By Marshall Associates

■ *Total living area 1,266 sq. ft.* ■ *Price Code A* ■

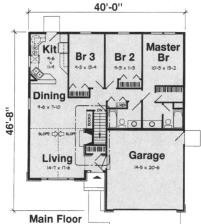

Main Floor

Open Floor Plan Enhances Home

No. 90307

This plan features:

— One bedroom

— Two full baths

- A Fireside Room with a vaulted ceiling and a unique built-in sofa enclosed in glass with a focal point fireplace

- A centrally-located island Kitchen efficiently laid out and flowing into the Dining Room

- A second floor Bedroom incorporates a bump-out window and a Sitting Room

Main floor — 768 sq. ft.
Loft — 419 sq. ft.

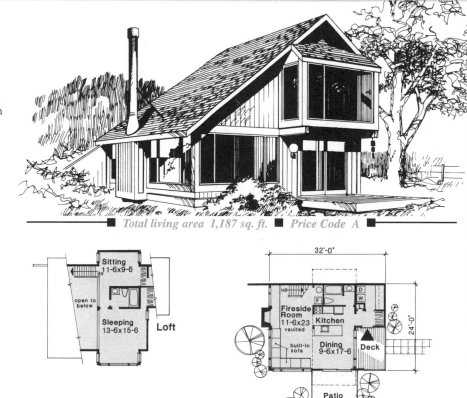

■ *Total living area 1,187 sq. ft.* ■ *Price Code A* ■

Small, Yet Lavishly Appointed

■ Total living area 1,845 sq. ft. ■ Price Code C ■

No. 98425

■ This plan features:

— Three bedrooms

— Two full and one half baths

■ The Dining Room, Living Room, Foyer and Master Bath all topped by high ceilings

■ Master Bedroom includes a decorative tray ceiling and a walk-in closet

■ Kitchen open to the Breakfast Room and is enhanced by a serving bar and a Pantry

■ Living Room with a large fireplace and a French door to the rear yard

■ An optional basement or crawl space foundation — please specify when ordering

Main floor — 1,845 sq. ft.
Bonus — 409 sq. ft.
Basement — 1,845 sq. ft.
Garage — 529 sq. ft.

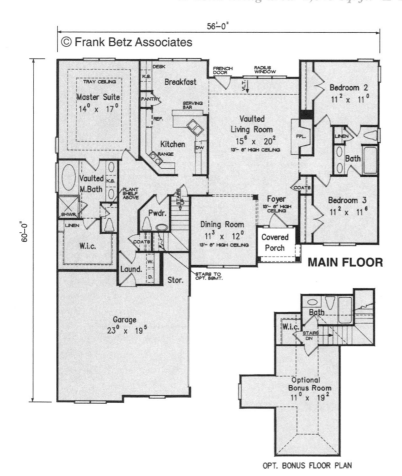

© Frank Betz Associates

56'-0"

60'-0"

TRAY CEILING
Master Suite
14⁰ x 17⁰

Breakfast

Vaulted Living Room
15⁶ x 20²
13'- 6" HIGH CEILING

Bedroom 2
11² x 11⁰

Kitchen

Bath

Vaulted M.Bath

Foyer
13'- 6" HIGH CEILING

Bedroom 3
11² x 11⁶

Pwdr.

Dining Room
11³ x 12⁰
13'- 6" HIGH CEILING

W.i.c.

Covered Porch

MAIN FLOOR

Laund.

Stor.

STAIRS TO OPT. BSMT.

Garage
23⁰ x 19⁵

Bath

W.i.c.

STAIRS DN

Optional Bonus Room
11⁰ x 19²

OPT. BONUS FLOOR PLAN

Inviting Wrap-Around Porch

■ *Total living area 1,716 sq. ft.* ■ *Price Code B* ■

No. 93909

■ This plan features:

— Three bedrooms

— Two full baths

■ A warm and inviting welcome, achieved by a wrap-around Porch

■ A corner gas fireplace and two skylights highlighted in the Great Room

■ The Dining Room is naturally lighted by the sliding glass doors leading to a rear Deck

■ A well-appointed, U-shaped Kitchen separated from the Dining Room by a breakfast bar, contains a skylight

■ A luxurious Master Bedroom equipped with a plush Bath

■ Two additional Bedrooms share the full hall Bath and receive light from dormers

■ No materials list is available for this plan

Main floor — 1,716 sq. ft.

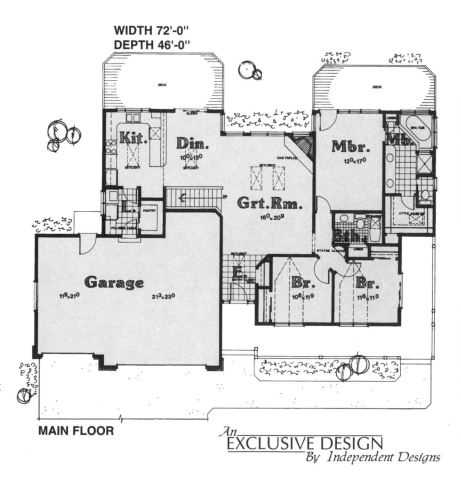

WIDTH 72'-0"
DEPTH 46'-0"

MAIN FLOOR

An
EXCLUSIVE DESIGN
By Independent Designs

Inviting Porch Adorns Affordable Home

■ *Total living area 1,243 sq. ft.* ■ *Price Code A* ■

No. 90682

■ **This plan features:**

— Three bedrooms

— Two full baths

■ A large and spacious Living Room adjoins the Dining Room for ease in entertaining

■ A private Bedroom wing offering a quiet atmosphere

■ A Master Bedroom with his-n-her closets and a private Bath

■ An efficient Kitchen with a walk-in Pantry

Main area — 1,243 sq. ft.
Basement — 1,103 sq. ft.
Garage — 490 sq. ft.

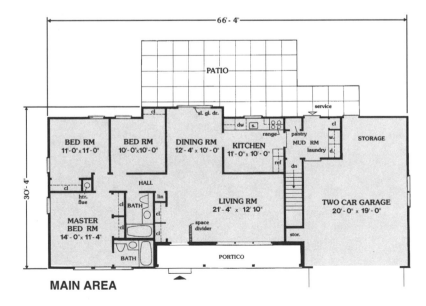

MAIN AREA

Easy Living

No. 93447

■ This plan features:

— Three bedrooms

— Two full baths

■ A covered front Porch shelters the entry to this home

■ The Family Room is enlarged by a vaulted ceiling and also has a fireplace

■ The Kitchen is L-shaped and includes a center island

■ The Dining Room is open to the Kitchen for maximum convenience

■ A covered walkway leads to the two car Garage

■ The Master Bedroom has a private bath, which has two building options

■ Both of the secondary Bedrooms have walk-in closets

■ No materials list is available for this plan

Main Floor — 1,474 sq. ft.
Garage — 454 sq. ft.
Width — 43'-0"
Depth — 42'-6"

■ Total living area 1,474 sq. ft. ■ Price Code A ■

An EXCLUSIVE DESIGN *By Greg Marquis*

MAIN FLOOR

Cozy Hideaway

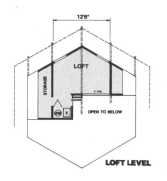

No. 94308

■ This plan features:

— One bedroom

— One full bath

■ Two levels of windows to enjoy the surroundings

■ Kitchen and Living Room with vaulted ceilings give a spacious feel

■ Efficient Kitchen layout which is highlighted by a corner sink

■ Living Room equipped with a sofa sleeper

■ Loft overlooks the Living Room with added storage

■ No materials list is available for this plan

Lower level — 511 sq. ft.
Loft — 148 sq. ft.

An EXCLUSIVE DESIGN *By Marshall Associates*

■ Total living area 659 sq. ft. ■ Price Code A ■

LOWER LEVEL

LOFT LEVEL

For a Narrow Lot

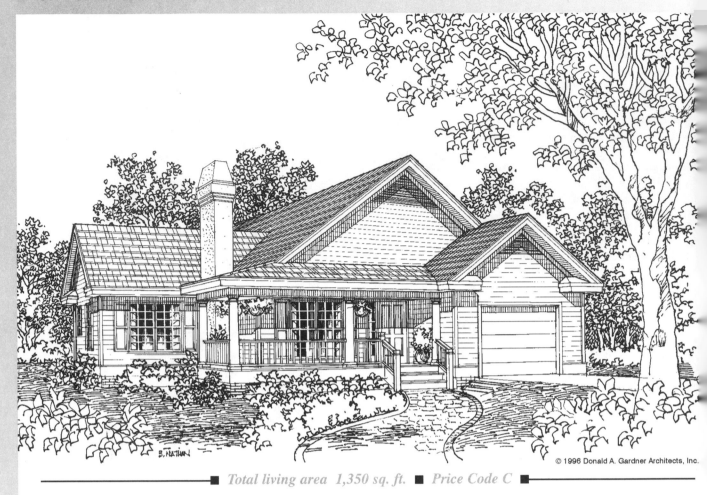

© 1996 Donald A. Gardner Architects, Inc.

■ Total living area 1,350 sq. ft. ■ Price Code C ■

No. 99868

■ **This plan features:**

— Three bedrooms

— Two full baths

■ A Great Room topped by a cathedral ceiling and accented by a fireplace

■ A convenient pass-through opening from the Kitchen

■ The Master Suite is loaded with luxuries, including a walk-in closet and a private Bath with a separate shower and garden tub

■ Two additional Bedrooms share a full Bath

Main floor — 1,350 sq. ft.
Garage & storage — 309 sq. ft.

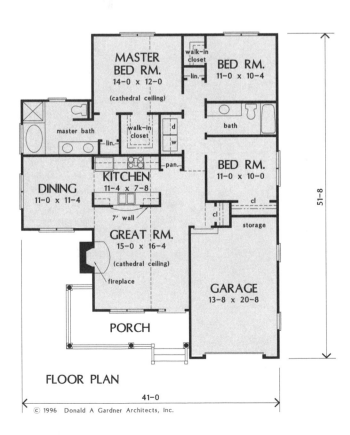

FLOOR PLAN

© 1996 Donald A Gardner Architects, Inc.

■ *Total living area 1,653 sq. ft.* ■ *Price Code B* ■

No. 92283

■ This plan features:

— Three bedrooms

— Two full baths

■ A sheltered Porch leads into an easy-care, tiled Entry

■ Spacious Living Room offers a cozy fireplace, triple window and access to Patio

■ An efficient Kitchen with a skylight, a work island, a Dining area, a walk-in Pantry and a Utility/Garage entry

■ Secluded Master Bedroom highlighted by a vaulted ceiling, access to Patio and a lavish Bath

■ Two additional Bedrooms, one with a cathedral ceiling, share a full Bath

■ No materials list is available for this plan

Main floor — 1,653 sq. ft.
Garage — 420 sq. ft.

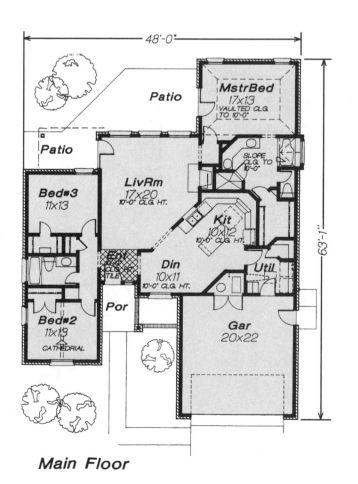

Main Floor

Two-Story Atrium

■ *Total living area 2,617 sq. ft.* ■ *Price Code F* ■

No. 26870

■ This plan features:

— Three bedrooms

— Two full and one half baths

■ A two-story Atrium entrance leading into open layout of Living, Family and Kitchen areas

■ A spacious Living Room with a quiet Dining Room nearby

■ A Family Room with a cozy fireplace and direct access to Deck and Kitchen

■ An airy Kitchen with a unique solar plant bay

■ A private Master Suite wing with a double vanity Bath

■ Two additional Bedrooms on upper level sharing a Balcony/ Study and full Bath

■ Loads of recreation space and Storage on lower level

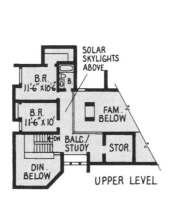

SOLAR SKYLIGHTS ABOVE

B.R. 11'-6" X 10'-6"

B.R. 11'-6" X 10'

FAM. BELOW

BALC./ STUDY

STOR.

DIN. BELOW

UPPER LEVEL

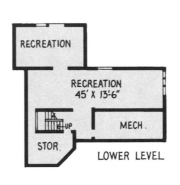

RECREATION

RECREATION 45' X 13'-6"

MECH.

STOR.

LOWER LEVEL

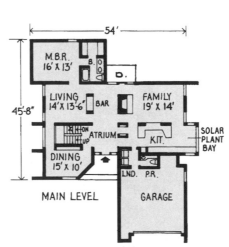

54'

M.B.R. 16' X 13'

LIVING 14' X 13'-6"

BAR

FAMILY 19' X 14'

45'-8"

ATRIUM

KIT.

SOLAR PLANT BAY

DINING 15' X 10'

LND. P.R.

MAIN LEVEL

GARAGE

Main level — 1,641 sq. ft.
Upper level — 976 sq. ft.
Lower level — 1,632 sq. ft.

A Nice Ranch Design

No. 90354

■ This plan features:

— Three bedrooms

— One full and one three-quarter baths

■ A vaulted ceiling in the Great Room, that also includes a fireplace and access to the rear Deck

■ A double door entrance leads into the Den/third Bedroom

■ The Kitchen and Breakfast Area have a vaulted ceiling and an efficient layout

■ The Master Suite is crowned by a vaulted ceiling and pampered by a private Bath and Dressing Area

■ A full hall Bath serves the two additional Bedrooms

Main area — 1,360 sq. ft.

■ Total living area 1,360 sq. ft. ■ Price Code A ■

MAIN AREA

Compact Home Design

No. 10455

■ This plan features:

— Three bedrooms

— Two full baths

■ An energy saving airlock Entry

■ The Living Room has an entire wall of windows, a fireplace, built-in bookcases, and a wetbar

■ The step-saver Kitchen has an abundance of storage and a convenient peninsula counter

■ The Master Bedroom has separate vanities and walk-in closets

Main area — 1,643 sq. ft.
Garage — 500 sq. ft.

■ Total living area 1,643 sq. ft. ■ Price Code B ■

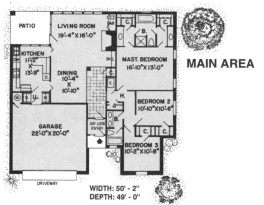

MAIN AREA

WIDTH: 50' - 2"
DEPTH: 49' - 0"

Backyard Views

■ Total living area 1,746 sq. ft. ■ Price Code B ■

Patio

Breakfast
10'10" x 12'

Great Room
16'2" x 18'4"

Master Bedroom
15' x 12'10"

Bath

walk-in closet

Kitchen
11'8" x 14' 4"

Dining Room
11' x 9'2"

Foyer

Hall

Bath

Laun.

Porch

Bedroom
11' x 12'6"

Bedroom
12'6" x 11'11"

slope ceiling   slope ceiling

Two-car Garage
22' x 20'8"

WIDTH: 65' - 10"
DEPTH: 56' - 0"

MAIN FLOOR

No. 92655

■ This plan features:

— Three bedrooms

— Two full baths

■ Front Porch accesses open Foyer, and spacious Dining Room and Great Room with sloped ceilings

■ Corner fireplace, windows and atrium door to Patio enhance Great Room

■ Convenient Kitchen with a pantry, peninsula serving counter for bright Breakfast Area and nearby Laundry/Garage entry

■ Luxurious Bath, walk-in closet and backyard view offered in Master Bedroom

▨ No materials list is available for this plan

Main floor — 1,746 sq. ft.
Garage — 480 sq. ft.
Basement — 1,697 sq. ft.

Total living area 1,884 sq. ft. ■ Price Code C ■

No. 98430

■ This plan features:

— Three bedrooms

— Two full and one half baths

■ Arched openings highlight the hallway accessing the Great Room

■ A French door to the rear yard and decorative columns at its arched entrance

■ Another vaulted ceiling topping the Dining Room

■ An expansive Kitchen features a center work island, a built-in Pantry and a Breakfast Area

■ The Master Suite has a tray ceiling and a lavish private Bath

■ An optional basement, slab or crawl space foundation — please specify when ordering

Main floor — 1,884 sq. ft.
Basement — 1,908 sq. ft.
Garage — 495 sq. ft.

© Frank Betz Associates

Main floor

OPT. BASEMENT STAIRS LOCATION

Southampton Style Cottage

■ Total living area 2,068 sq. ft. ■ Price Code C ■

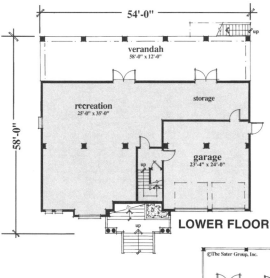

LOWER FLOOR

verandah
58'-0" x 12'-0"

recreation
25'-0" x 35'-0"

storage

garage
23'-4" x 24'-0"

up

54'-0"

58'-0"

Main floor — 2,068 sq. ft.
Basement — 1,402 sq. ft.
Garage — 560 sq. ft.

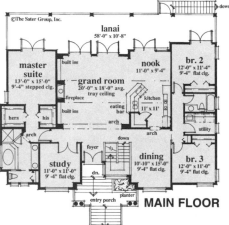

MAIN FLOOR

©The Sater Group, Inc.

lanai
58'-0" x 10'-8"

master
suite
13'-0" x 15'-0"
9'-4" stepped clg.

built ins

grand room
20'-0" x 18'-0" avg.
tray ceiling

fireplace

built ins

hers   his

arch

nook
11'-0" x 9'-4"

br. 2
12'-0" x 11'-4"
9'-4" flat clg.

kitchen
11' x 11'

eating
bar

arch

down

foyer

planter

study
11'-0" x 11'-0"
9'-4" flat clg.

dn.

dining
10'-10" x 15'-0"
9'-4" flat clg.

utility

br. 3
12'-0" x 11'-0"
9'-4" flat clg.

arch

entry porch

No. 94260

■ This plan features:

— Three bedrooms

— Two full baths

■ An arched opening leads into the Grand Room, which has a fireplace

■ Five French doors in various rooms open out onto the rear Lanai

■ Access the Dining Room from the Kitchen through an arched opening

■ The Kitchen has a walk-in Pantry located next to the Nook

■ On the opposite side of the home are a Study and the Master Suite

■ The space on the ground level can be finished into a Recreation Room

■ No materials list is available for this plan

Step Saving One Floor Living

No. 24320

This plan features:

— Three bedrooms

— Two full baths

■ A covered entrance leads to the Foyer and opens into the Living, Breakfast and Kitchen areas

■ A fireplace and corner windows in the Living Area

■ A galley Kitchen offers a breakfast bar, a built-in pantry and easy access to the covered Porch and Garage

■ The Master Bedroom features a double closet and a private bath

■ Two additional bedrooms sharing a full hall bath

■ No materials list is available for this plan

Main area — 1,235 sq. ft.
Garage — 425 sq. ft.

An EXCLUSIVE DESIGN *By Marshall Associates*

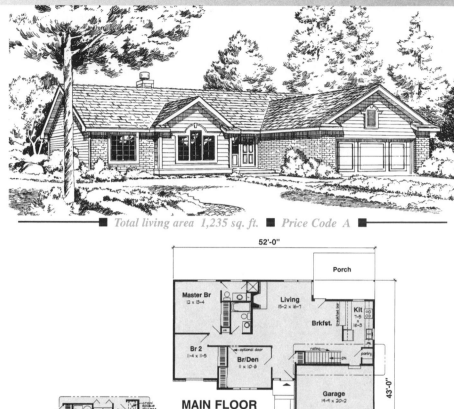
■ Total living area 1,235 sq. ft. ■ Price Code A ■

Attractive Tiled Entry

No. 94303

This plan features:

— Two bedrooms

— One full and one three-quarter baths

■ A tiled entry leads to an open Dining/Living Room area with a hearth fireplace and a wall of windows with an atrium door to the Terrace

■ An efficient Kitchen has a corner window and an eating bar adjoining the Dining Area, Garage and Terrace

■ The Master Bedroom has a walk-in closet, a private Bath and an atrium door to the Terrace

■ One additional Bedroom with ample closet space is near the full Bath

■ No materials list is available for this plan

Main floor — 1,013 sq. ft.
Garage — 390 sq. ft.

An EXCLUSIVE DESIGN *By Marshall Associates*

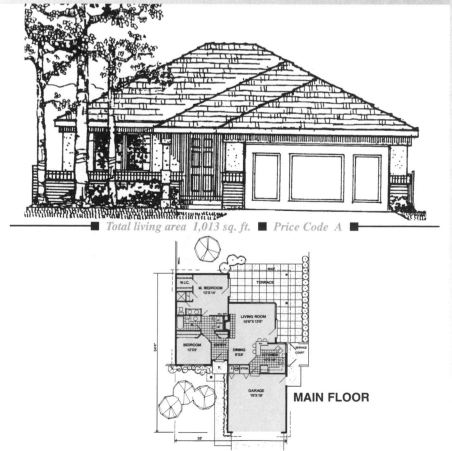
■ Total living area 1,013 sq. ft. ■ Price Code A ■

Formal Balance

■ *Total living area 1,476 sq. ft.* ■ *Price Code A* ■

No. 90689

■ This plan features:

— Three bedrooms

— Two full baths

■ A cathedral ceiling in the Living Room with a heat-circulating fireplace as the focal point

■ A bow window in the Dining Room adds elegance as well as natural light

■ A well-equipped Kitchen serves both the Dinette and the formal Dining Room efficiently

■ A Master Bedroom with three closets and a private Master Bath with sliding glass doors to the Master Deck with a Hot Tub

Main floor — 1,476 sq. ft.
Basement — 1,361 sq. ft.
Garage — 548 sq. ft.

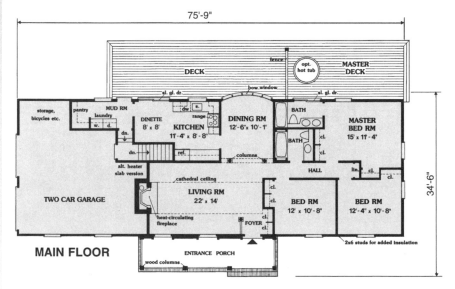

MAIN FLOOR

75'-9"

34'-6"

storage, bicycles etc.

pantry

MUD RM

laundry

w.   d.

DINETTE
8' x 8'

KITCHEN
11'-4" x 8'-8"

dw.   s.

range

ref.

dn.

dn.

DINING RM
12'-6" x 10'-1"

sl. gl. dr.

bow window

fence

opt.
hot tub

MASTER DECK

sl. gl. dr.

DECK

BATH

BATH

MASTER BED RM
15' x 11'-4"

cl.

cl.

HALL

lin.   cl.

cl.

columns

alt. heater
slab version

cathedral ceiling

TWO CAR GARAGE

LIVING RM
22' x 14'

heat-circulating fireplace

cl.

cl.

BED RM
12' x 10'-8"

BED RM
12'-4" x 10'-8"

cl.

FOYER

cl.

2x6 studs for added insulation

ENTRANCE PORCH

wood columns

© 1997 Donald A. Gardner Architects, Inc.

■ Total living area 1,246 sq. ft. ■ Price Code C ■

No. 96484

■ This plan features:

— Three bedrooms

— Two full baths

■ Open living spaces and vaulted ceilings create an illusion of spaciousness

■ Cathedral ceilings maximize space in the Great Room and Dining Room

■ The Kitchen features a skylight and breakfast bar

■ The well equipped Master Suite is located in the rear for privacy

■ Two additional Bedrooms in front share a full Bath

Main floor — 1,246 sq. ft.
Garage — 420 sq. ft.

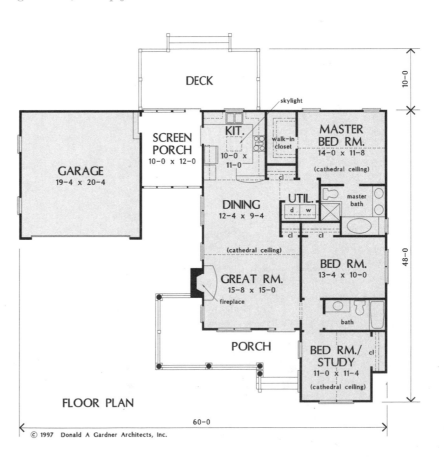

FLOOR PLAN

© 1997 Donald A Gardner Architects, Inc.

Compact Ranch Loaded with Living Space

■ *Total living area 1,092 sq. ft.* ■ *Price Code A* ■

No. 34328

■ **This plan features:**

— Three bedrooms

— One full bath

■ The central entrance opens to the Living Room, which has a fireplace and an abundance of windows

■ The Kitchen features a Breakfast Area with sliding doors to the backyard and an optional Deck

■ Three large Bedrooms share a full Bath

Main area — 1,092 sq. ft.
Basement — 1,092 sq. ft.

ALTERNATE FLOOR PLAN
for Crawl Space

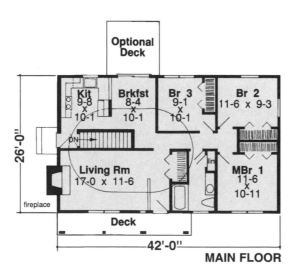

MAIN FLOOR

Exclusive Master Suite

No. 34031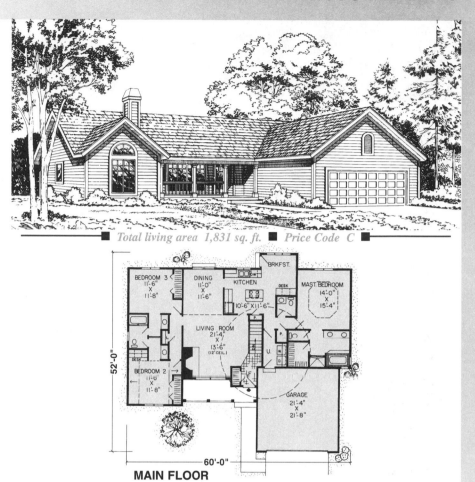

■ This plan features:

— Three bedrooms

— Two full and one half baths

■ Front Porch entry into Foyer and open Living and Dining Rooms

■ Huge fireplace and double window highlight Living Room

■ Convenient Kitchen with cooktop island/snackbar, pantry, and bright Breakfast area with backyard access

■ Corner Master Bedroom offers a decorative ceiling, walk-in closets and a double vanity Bath

■ Two additional Bedrooms with ample closets and private access to a full Bath

Main floor — 1,831 sq. ft.
Basement — 1,831 sq. ft.
Garage — 484 sq. ft.

■ Total living area 1,831 sq. ft. ■ Price Code C ■

MAIN FLOOR

Designed for Informal Life Style

No. 90325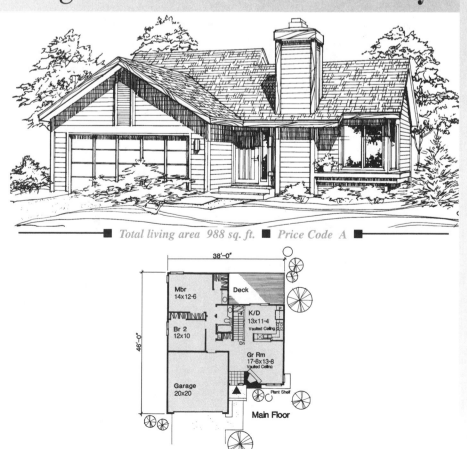

■ This plan features:

— Two bedrooms

— One full bath

■ A Great Room and Kitchen accented by vaulted ceilings

■ A conveniently arranged L-shaped food preparation center

■ A Dining Room overlooking a Deck through sliding doors

■ A Great Room highlighted by a corner fireplace

■ A Master Bedroom including a separate vanity and dressing area

Main floor — 988 sq. ft.
Basement — 988 sq. ft.
Garage — 400 sq. ft.

■ Total living area 988 sq. ft. ■ Price Code A ■

Main Floor

Small, But Not Lacking

■ *Total living area 1,546 sq. ft.* ■ *Price Code C* ■

No. 94116

■ **This plan features:**

— Three bedrooms

— One full and one three-quarter baths

■ Great Room adjoins the Dining Room for ease in entertaining

■ The Kitchen is highlighted by a peninsula counter/snack bar extends work space and offers convenience

■ Split-bedroom plan allows privacy for the Master Bedroom

■ Two additional Bedrooms share the full family Bath in the hall

■ Garage entry convenient to the Kitchen

Main floor — 1,546 sq. ft.
Basement — 1,530 sq. ft.
Garage — 440 sq. ft.

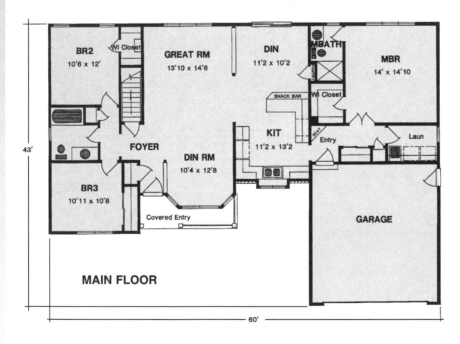

MAIN FLOOR

Traditional Beauty

© 1993 Donald A Gardner Architects, Inc.

■ *Total living area 1,576 sq. ft.* ■ *Price Code D* ■

No. 99802

■ This plan features:

— Three bedrooms

— Two full baths

■ Traditional beauty with large arched windows, round columns, covered Porch, brick veneer and an open floor plan

■ Clerestory dormers above covered Porch lighting the Foyer

■ Cathedral ceiling enhances the Great Room along with a cozy fireplace

■ Island Kitchen with Breakfast area accesses the large Deck with an optional spa

■ Tray ceiling over the Master Bedroom, Dining Room and Bedroom/Study

■ Dual vanity, separate shower, and whirlpool tub in the Master Bath

Main floor — 1,576 sq. ft.
Garage — 465 sq. ft.

FLOOR PLAN

© 1993 Donald A Gardner Architects, Inc.

Home on a Hill

■ *Total living area 1,908 sq. ft.* ■ *Price Code C* ■

No. 20501

■ This plan features:

— Three bedrooms

— Two full baths

■ Window walls combine with sliders to unite active areas with a huge outdoor Deck

■ Interior spaces flow together for an open feeling that is accentuated by the sloping ceilings and towering fireplace in the Living Room

■ An island Kitchen with easy access to the Dining Room

■ The Master Suite is complete with a garden spa, abundant closet space, and a balcony

First floor — 1,316 sq. ft.
Second floor — 592 sq. ft.

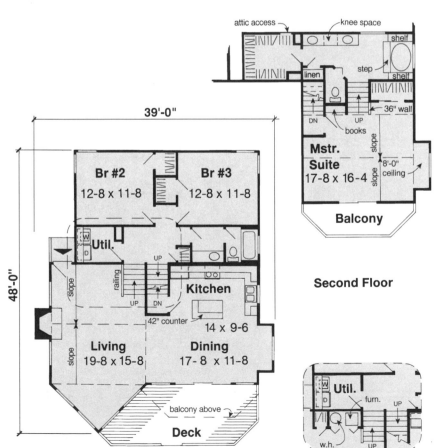

Second Floor

attic access — knee space
shelf
linen
step
shelf
36" wall
DN   UP
books
8'-0" ceiling
slope
slope
Mstr. Suite
17-8 x 16-4
Balcony

39'-0"

48'-0"

Br #2
12-8 x 11-8

Br #3
12-8 x 11-8

W D **Util.**
UP
railing
UP   DN
Kitchen
42" counter
14 x 9-6
slope
slope
Living
19-8 x 15-8
Dining
17-8 x 11-8
balcony above

Deck

First Floor

Pier/ Crawl Space Option

W D **Util.** furn.
UP
w.h.
UP

Ranch Provides Great Floor Plan

No. 34055

This plan features:

- Four bedrooms
- Two full baths
- A large Living Room and Dining Room flowing together into one open space for perfect entertaining
- A Laundry area, which doubles as a mudroom, off the Kitchen
- The Master Suite includes a private Bath
- A two-car Garage

Main area — 1,527 sq. ft.
Basement — 1,344 sq. ft.
Garage — 425 sq. ft.

Total living area 1,527 sq. ft. ■ Price Code B

70'-0"

28'-0"

| Ldry | Kit 12-4 x 8 | Dining Rm 11 x 13-6 | pantry | Br 4 11-8 x 11-2 | MBr 1 12 x 13-6 |

Garage 22 x 20

Living Rm 20-4 x 13-6

Br 3 12 x 10

Br 2 12 x 11-2

MAIN AREA

Dining 11-6 x 13-6 / pantry

Br 4 12 x 11-2

Alternate Plan w/ Crawlspace

High Impact Angles

No. 90357

This plan features:

- Three bedrooms
- Two full baths
- Soaring ceilings give this house a spacious, contemporary feeling
- A fireplaced Great Room adjoins the convenient Kitchen, with a sunny Breakfast Nook
- Sliding glass doors open onto an angular Deck
- A Master Suite with vaulted ceilings and a private Bath

Main area — 1,368 sq. ft.

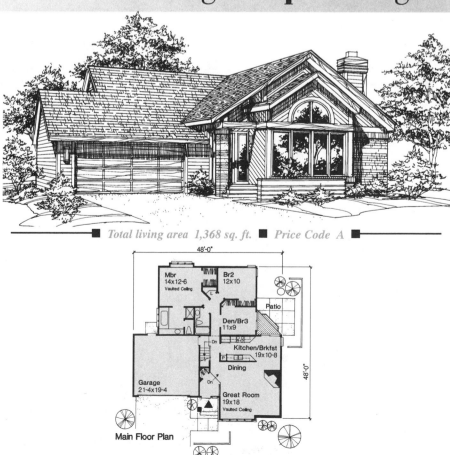

Total living area 1,368 sq. ft. ■ Price Code A

48'-0"

48'-0"

Mbr 14x12-6 Vaulted Ceiling

Br2 12x10

Patio

Den/Br3 11x9

Kitchen/Brkfst 19x10-8

Dining

Garage 21-4x19-4

Great Room 19x18 Vaulted Ceiling

Main Floor Plan

335

Outstanding Four-Bedroom

Total living area 1,945 sq. ft. ■ Price Code C

WIDTH 56'-6"
DEPTH 52'-6"

Bedroom 2
12⁵ x 11³

Vaulted Great Room
15³ x 22³

Vaulted Breakfast

Master Suite
13² x 16⁰

Kitchen

Vaulted M. Bath

Bedroom 3
11³ x 11⁵

Bath

Foyer
(15'-0" HIGH CLG.)

Dining Room
12⁵ x 11
(9'-0" HIGH CLG.)

Bedroom 4/ Study
12⁵ x 11⁰

W.i.c.

Stor.

Garage

MAIN FLOOR

© Frank Betz Associates

No. 98435

■ This plan features:

— Four bedrooms

— Two full baths

■ Radius window highlights the exterior and the formal Dining Room

■ High ceiling tops the Foyer for a grand first impression

■ Vaulted ceiling enhances the Great Room accented by a fireplace framed by windows on either side

■ Arched opening to the Kitchen from the Great Room

■ Breakfast Room topped by a vaulted ceiling and enhanced by an elegant French door to the rear yard

■ Tray ceiling and a five-piece compartmental Bath gives a luxurious presence to the Master Suite

■ Three additional Bedrooms share a full, double vanity Bath in the hall

■ An optional basement or crawl space foundation — please specify when ordering

Main floor — 1,945 sq. ft.

Gazebo Porch Creates Old-Fashioned Feel

Total living area 1,452 sq. ft. ■ Price Code A

67'-0"

47'-0"

Master Br
14-5 x 12-0

Great Rm
14-0 x 16-7

Porch
11-5 x 7-0

FURN.

Garage
23-8 x 23-4

Dining
11-5 x 9-3

2-SIDED F.P.

Kitchen
11-7 x 10-1

Br 2
11-0 x 10-0

Brkfst
11-7 x 7-8

Br 3
10-2 x 10-0

LEDGE

Porch

MAIN FLOOR

No. 24718

■ This plan features:

— Three bedrooms

— Two full baths

■ An old-fashioned welcome is created by the covered Porch

■ The Breakfast Area overlooks the Porch and is separated from the Kitchen by an extended counter

■ The Dining Room and the Great Room are highlighted by a two sided fireplace, enhancing the temperature as well as the atmosphere

■ The roomy Master Suite is enhanced by a whirlpool Bath with a double vanity and a walk-in closet

■ Each of the two secondary Bedrooms features a walk-in closet

■ No materials list is available for this plan

Main floor — 1,452 sq. ft.
Garage — 584 sq. ft.

For First Time Buyers

No. 93048

■ **This plan features:**

— Three bedrooms

— Two full baths

■ An efficiently designed Kitchen with a corner sink, ample counter space and a peninsula counter

■ A sunny Breakfast Room with a convenient hide-away laundry center

■ An expansive Family Room that includes a corner fireplace and direct access to the Patio

■ A private Master Suite with a walk-in closet and a double vanity Bath

■ Two additional Bedrooms, both with walk-in closets, that share a full hall Bath

■ No materials list is available for this plan

Main floor — 1,310 sq. ft.
Garage — 449 sq. ft.

Total living area 1,310 sq. ft. ■ *Price Code A* ■

WIDTH 49–10

MAIN FLOOR

© Larry E. Belk

Fireplace Center of Circular Living Area

No. 10274

■ **This plan features:**

— Three bedrooms

— One full and one three-quarter baths

■ A dramatically positioned fireplace is a focal point in the main Living Area

■ The Kitchen, Dining and Living Rooms form a circle that allows work areas to flow into living areas

■ Sliding glass doors access the wood Deck

■ A convenient Laundry Room located off the Kitchen

■ A double Garage provides excellent storage

Main area — 1,783 sq. ft.
Garage — 576 sq. ft.

Total living area 1,783 sq. ft. ■ *Price Code C* ■

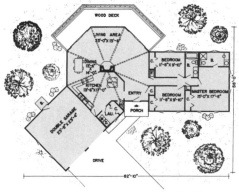

MAIN FLOOR

Everything You Need...
...to Make Your Dream Come True!

You pay only a fraction of the original cost for home designs by respected professionals.

You've Picked Your Dream Home!

You can imagine your new home situated on your lot in the morning sunlight. You can visualize living there, enjoying your family, entertaining friends and celebrating holidays. All that remains are the details. That's where we can help. Whether you plan to build it yourself, act as your own general contractor or hire a professional builder, your Garlinghouse Co. home plans will provide the perfect design and specifications to help make your dream home a reality.

We can offer you an array of additional products and services to help you with your planning needs. We can supply materials lists, construction cost estimates based on your local material and labor costs and modifications to your selected plan if you would like.

For over 90 years, homeowners and builders have relied on us for accurate, complete, professional blueprints. Our plans help you get results fast... and save money, too! These pages will give you all the information you need to order. So get started now... We know you'll love your new Garlinghouse home!

Sincerely,

President   Chief Executive Officer

EXTERIOR ELEVATIONS

Elevations are scaled drawings of the front, rear, left, and right sides of a home. All of the necessary information pertaining to the exterior finish materials, roof pitches, and exterior height dimensions of your home are defined.

CABINET PLANS

These plans, or in some cases elevations, will detail the layout of the kitchen and bathroom cabinets at a larger scale. This gives you an accurate layout for your cabinets or an ideal starting point for a modified custom cabinet design. Available for most plans. You may also show the floor plan without a cabinet layout. This will allow you to start from scratch and design your own dream kitchen.

TYPICAL WALL SECTION

This section is provided to help your builder understand the structural components and materials used to construct the exterior walls of your home. This section will address insulation, roof components, and interior and exterior wall finishes. Your plans will be designed with either 2x4 or 2x6 exterior walls, but most professional contractors can easily adapt the plans to the wall thickness you require.

FIREPLACE DETAILS

If the home you have chosen includes a fireplace, the fireplace detail will show typical methods to construct the firebox, hearth and flue chase for masonry units, or a wood frame chase for a zero-clearance unit. Available for most plans.

FOUNDATION PLAN

These plans will accurately dimension the footprint of your home including load bearing points and beam placement if applicable. The foundation style will vary from plan to plan. Your local climatic conditions will dictate whether a basement, slab or crawlspace is best suited for your area. In most cases, if your plan comes with one foundation style, a professional contractor can easily adapt the foundation plan to an alternate style.

ROOF PLAN

The information necessary to construct the roof will be included with your home plans. Some plans will reference roof trusses, while many others contain schematic framing plans. These framing plans will indicate the lumber sizes necessary for the rafters and ridgeboards based on the designated roof loads.

TYPICAL CROSS SECTION

A cut-away cross-section through the entire home shows your building contractor the exact correlation of construction components at all levels of the house. It will help to clarify the load bearing points from the roof all the way down to the basement. Available for most plans.

DETAILED FLOOR PLANS

The floor plans of your home accurately dimension the positioning of all walls, doors, windows, stairs and permanent fixtures. They will show you the relationship and dimensions of rooms, closets and traffic patterns. The schematic of the electrical layout may be included in the plan. This layout is clearly represented and does not hinder the clarity of other pertinent information shown. All these details will help your builder properly construct your new home.

STAIR DETAILS

If stairs are an element of the design you have chosen, the plans will show the necessary information to build these, either through a stair cross section, or on the floor plans. Either way, the information provides your builders the essential reference points that they need to build the stairs.

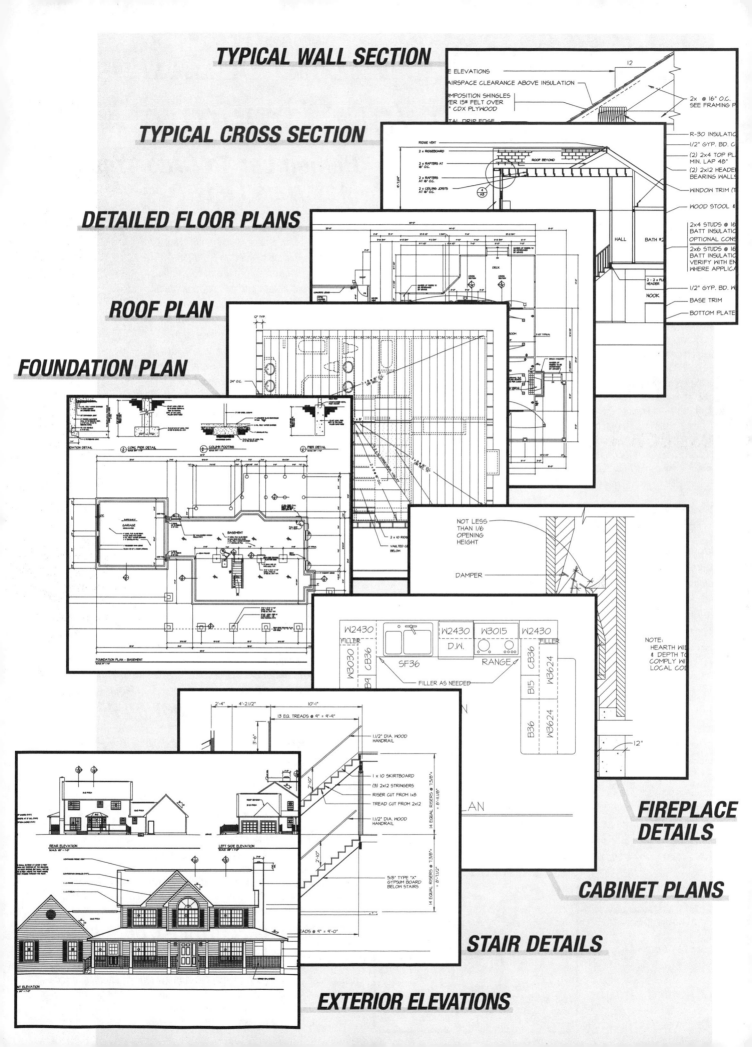

TYPICAL WALL SECTION

TYPICAL CROSS SECTION

DETAILED FLOOR PLANS

ROOF PLAN

FOUNDATION PLAN

FIREPLACE DETAILS

CABINET PLANS

STAIR DETAILS

EXTERIOR ELEVATIONS

Garlinghouse Options & Extras ...Make Your Dream A Home

Reversed Plans Can Make Your Dream Home Just Right!

"That's our dream home...if only the garage were on the other side!"

You could have exactly the home you want by flipping it end-for-end. Check it out by holding your dream home page of this book up to a mirror. Then simply order your plans "reversed." We'll send you one full set of mirror-image plans (with the writing backwards) as a master guide for you and your builder.

The remaining sets of your order will come as shown in this book so the dimensions and specifications are easily read on the job site...but most plans in our collection come stamped "REVERSED" so there is no construction confusion.

We can only send reversed plans with multiple-set orders. There is a $50 charge for this service.

As Shown   Reversed

Some plans in our collection are available in Right Reading Reverse. Right Reading Reverse plans will show your home in reverse, with the writing on the plan being readable. This easy-to-read format will save you valuable time and money. Please contact our Customer Service Department at (860) 659-5667 to check for Right Reading Reverse availability. (There is a $135 charge for this service.)

Specifications & Contract Form

We send this form to you free of charge with your home plan order. The form is designed to be filled in by you or your contractor with the exact materials to use in the construction of your new home. Once signed by you and your contractor it will provide you with peace of mind throughout the construction process.

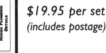

$19.95 per set
(includes postage)

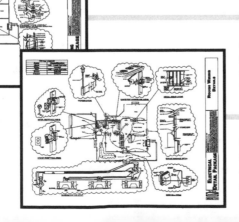

Remember To Order Your Materials List

It'll help you save money. Available at a modest additional charge, the Materials List gives the quantity, dimensions, and specifications for the major materials needed to build your home. You will get faster, more accurate bids from your contractors and building suppliers — and avoid paying for unused materials and waste. Materials Lists are available for all home plans except as otherwise indicated, but can only be ordered with a set of home plans. Due to differences in regional requirements and homeowner or builder preferences... electrical, plumbing and heating/air conditioning equipment specifications are not designed specifically for each plan. However, non-plan specific detailed typical prints of residential electrical, plumbing and construction guidelines can be provided. Please see below for additional information.

Detail Plans Provide Valuable Information About Construction Techniques

Because local codes and requirements vary greatly, we recommend that you obtain drawings and bids from licensed contractors to do your mechanical plans. However, if you want to know more about techniques — and deal more confidently with subcontractors — we offer these remarkably useful detail sheets. These detail sheets will aid in your understanding of these technical subjects. **The detail sheets are not specific to any one home plan and should be used only as a general reference guide.**

RESIDENTIAL CONSTRUCTION DETAILS

Ten sheets that cover the essentials of stick-built residential home construction. Details foundation options — poured concrete basement, concrete block, or monolithic concrete slab. Shows all aspects of floor, wall and roof framing. Provides details for roof dormers, overhangs, chimneys and skylights. Conforms to requirements of Uniform Building code or BOCA code. Includes a quick index and a glossary of terms.

RESIDENTIAL PLUMBING DETAILS

Eight sheets packed with information detailing pipe installation methods, fittings, and sized. Details plumbing hook-ups for toilets, sinks, washers, sump pumps, and septic system construction. Conforms to requirements of National Plumbing code. Color coded with a glossary of terms and quick index.

RESIDENTIAL ELECTRICAL DETAILS

Eight sheets that cover all aspects of residential wiring, from simple switch wiring to service entrance connections. Details distribution panel layout with outlet and switch schematics, circuit breaker and wiring installation methods, and ground fault interrupter specifications. Conforms to requirements of National Electrical Code. Color coded with a glossary of terms.

Modifying Your Favorite Design, Made *EASY!*

OPTION #1

Modifying Your Garlinghouse Home Plan

Simple modifications to your dream home, including minor non-structural changes and material substitutions, can be made between you and your builder by marking the changes directly on your blueprints. However, if you are considering making significant changes to your chosen design, we recommend that you use the services of The Garlinghouse Design Staff. We will help take your ideas and turn them into a reality, just the way you want. Here's our procedure!

When you place your Vellum order, you may also request a free Garlinghouse Modification Kit. In this kit, you will receive a red marking pencil, furniture cut-out sheet, ruler, a self addressed mailing label and a form for specifying any additional notes or drawings that will help us understand your design ideas. Mark your desired changes directly on the Vellum drawings. NOTE: Please use only a **red pencil** to mark your desired changes on the Vellum. Then, return the redlined Vellum set in the original box to us. **IMPORTANT**: Please **roll** the Vellums for shipping, **do not fold** the Vellums for shipping.

We also offer modification estimates. We will provide you with an estimate to draft your changes based on your specific modifications before you purchase the vellums, for a $50 fee. After you receive your estimate, if you decide to have us do the changes, the $50 estimate fee will be deducted from the cost of your modifications. If, however, you choose to use a different service, the $50 estimate fee is non-refundable. (Note: Personal checks cannot be accepted for the estimate.)

Within 5 days of receipt of your plans, you will be contacted by the Design Staff with an estimate for the design services to draw those changes. A 50% deposit is required before we begin making the actual modifications to your plans.

Once the design changes have been completed to your vellum plan, a representative will call to inform you that your modified Vellum plan is complete and will be shipped as soon as the final payment has been made. For additional information call us at 1-860-659-5667. Please refer to the Modification Pricing Guide for estimated modification costs.

OPTION #2

Reproducible Vellums for Local Modification Ease

If you decide not to use Garlinghouse for your modifications, we recommend that you follow our same procedure of purchasing our Vellums. You then have the option of using the services of the original designer of the plan, a local professional designer, or architect to make the modifications to your plan.

With a Vellum copy of our plans, a design professional can alter the drawings just the way you want, then you can print as many copies of the modified plans as you need to build your house. And, since you have already started with our complete detailed plans, the cost of those expensive professional services will be significantly less than starting from scratch. Refer to the price schedule for Vellum costs.

IMPORTANT RETURN POLICY: Upon receipt of your Vellums, if for some reason you decide you do not want a modified plan, then simply return the Kit and the unopened Vellums. Reproducible Vellum copies of our home plans are copyright protected and only sold under the terms of a license agreement that you will receive with your order. Should you not agree to the terms, then the Vellums may be exchanged, less the shipping and handling charges, and a 20% exchange fee. For any additional information, please call us at 1-860-659-5667.

MODIFICATION PRICING GUIDE

CATEGORIES	ESTIMATED COST
KITCHEN LAYOUT — PLAN AND ELEVATION	$175.00
BATHROOM LAYOUT — PLAN AND ELEVATION	$175.00
FIREPLACE PLAN AND DETAILS	$200.00
INTERIOR ELEVATION	$125.00
EXTERIOR ELEVATION — MATERIAL CHANGE	$140.00
EXTERIOR ELEVATION — ADD BRICK OR STONE	$400.00
EXTERIOR ELEVATION — STYLE CHANGE	$450.00
NON BEARING WALLS (INTERIOR)	$200.00
BEARING AND/OR EXTERIOR WALLS	$325.00
WALL FRAMING CHANGE — 2X4 TO 2X6 OR 2X6 TO 2X4	$240.00
ADD/REDUCE LIVING SPACE — SQUARE FOOTAGE	QUOTE REQUIRED
NEW MATERIALS LIST	QUOTE REQUIRED
CHANGE TRUSSES TO RAFTERS OR CHANGE ROOF PITCH	$300.00
FRAMING PLAN CHANGES	$325.00
GARAGE CHANGES	$325.00
ADD A FOUNDATION OPTION	$300.00
FOUNDATION CHANGES	$250.00
RIGHT READING PLAN REVERSE	$575.00
ARCHITECTS SEAL (Available for most states.)	$300.00
ENERGY CERTIFICATE	$150.00
LIGHT AND VENTILATION SCHEDULE	$150.00

Questions?

Call our customer service department at 1-860-343-5977

"How to obtain a construction cost calculation based on labor rates and building material costs in your Zip Code area!"

ZIP-QUOTE!
HOME COST CALCULATOR

ZIP QUOTE
HOME COST CALCULATOR

WHY?

Do you wish you could quickly find out the building cost for your new home without waiting for a contractor to compile hundreds of bids? Would you like to have a benchmark to compare your contractor(s) bids against? *Well, Now You Can!!,* with **Zip-Quote** Home Cost Calculator. Zip-Quote is only available for zip code areas within the United States.

HOW?

Our new **Zip-Quote** Home Cost Calculator will enable you to obtain the calculated building cost to construct your new home, based on labor rates and building material costs within your zip code area, without the normal delays or hassles usually associated with the bidding process. Zip-Quote can be purchased in two separate formats, an itemized or a bottom line format.

"How does **Zip-Quote** actually work?" When you call to order, you must choose from the options available, for your specific home, in order for us to process your order. Once we receive your **Zip-Quote** order, we process your specific home plan building materials list through our Home Cost Calculator which contains up-to-date rates for all residential labor trades and building material costs in your zip code area. "The result?" A calculated cost to build your dream home in your zip code area. This calculation will help you (as a consumer or a builder) evaluate your building budget. This is a valuable tool for anyone considering building a new home.

All database information for our calculations is furnished by Marshall & Swift, L.P. For over 60 years, Marshall & Swift L.P. has been a leading provider of cost data to professionals in all aspects of the construction and remodeling industries.

OPTION 1

The **Itemized Zip-Quote** is a detailed building material list. Each building material list line item will separately state the labor cost, material cost and equipment cost (if applicable) for the use of that building material in the construction process. Each category within the building material list will be subtotaled and the entire Itemized cost calculation totaled at the end. This building materials list will be summarized by the individual building categories and will have additional columns where you can enter data from your contractor's estimates for a cost comparison between the different suppliers and contractors who will actually quote you their products and services.

OPTION 2

The **Bottom Line Zip-Quote** is a one line summarized total cost for the home plan of your choice. This cost calculation is also based on the labor cost, material cost and equipment cost (if applicable) within your local zip code area.

COST

The price of your **Itemized Zip-Quote** is based upon the pricing schedule of the plan you have selected, in addition to the price of the materials list. Please refer to the pricing schedule on our order form. The price of your initial **Bottom Line Zip-Quote** is $29.95. Each additional **Bottom Line Zip-Quote** ordered in conjunction with the initial order is only $14.95. **Bottom Line Zip-Quote** may be purchased separately and does NOT have to be purchased in conjunction with a home plan order.

FYI

An **Itemized Zip-Quote** Home Cost Calculation can ONLY be purchased in conjunction with a Home Plan order. The **Itemized Zip-Quote** can not be purchased separately. The **Bottom Line Zip-Quote** can be purchased separately and doesn't have to be purchased in conjunction with a home plan order. Please consult with a sales representative for current availability. If you find within 60 days of your order date that you will be unable to build this home, then you may exchange the plans and the materials list towards the price of a new set of plans (see order info pages for plan exchange policy). The **Itemized Zip-Quote** and the **Bottom Line Zip-Quote** are NOT returnable. The price of the initial **Bottom Line Zip-Quote** order can be credited towards the purchase of an **Itemized Zip-Quote** order only. Additional **Bottom Line Zip-Quote** orders, within the same order can not be credited. Please call our Customer Service Department for more information.

Itemized Zip-Quote is available for plans where you see this symbol. 🆁

Bottom Line Zip-Quote is available for all plans under 4,000 square feet.

SOME MORE INFORMATION

Itemized and Bottom Line Zip-Quotes give you approximated costs for constructing the particular house in your area. These costs are not exact and are only intended to be used as a preliminary estimate to help determine the affordability of a new home and/or as a guide to evaluate the general competitiveness of actual price quotes obtained through local suppliers and contractors. However, Zip-Quote cost figures should never be relied upon as the only source of information in either case. Land, sewer systems, site work, landscaping and other expenses are not included in our building cost figures. Garlinghouse and Marshall & Swift L.P. can not guarantee any level of data accuracy or correctness in a Zip-Quote and disclaim all liability for loss with respect to the same, in excess of the original purchase price of the Zip-Quote product. All Zip-Quote calculations are based upon the actual blueprints and do not reflect any differences or options that may be shown on the published house renderings, floor plans, or photographs.

Ignoring Copyright Laws Can Be
A $1,000,000 Mistake

Recent changes in the US copyright laws allow for statutory penalties of up to **$100,000** per incident for copyright infringement involving any of the copyrighted plans found in this publication. The law can be confusing. So, for your own protection, take the time to understand what you can and cannot do when it comes to home plans.

••• WHAT YOU CANNOT DO •••

You Cannot Duplicate Home Plans

Purchasing a set of blueprints and making additional sets by reproducing the original is **illegal**. If you need multiple sets of a particular home plan, then you must purchase them.

You Cannot Copy Any Part of a Home Plan to Create Another

Creating your own plan by copying even part of a home design found in this publication is called "creating a derivative work" and is **illegal** unless you have permission to do so.

You Cannot Build a Home Without a License

You must have specific permission or license to build a home from a copyrighted design, even if the finished home has been changed from the original plan. It is **illegal** to build one of the homes found in this publication without a license.

What Garlinghouse Offers

Home Plan Blueprint Package

By purchasing a multiple set package of blueprints or a vellum from Garlinghouse, you not only receive the physical blueprint documents necessary for construction, but you are also granted a license to build one, and only one, home. You can also make simple modifications, including minor non-structural changes and material substitutions, to our design, as long as these changes are made directly on the blueprints purchased from Garlinghouse and no additional copies are made.

Home Plan Vellums

By purchasing vellums for one of our home plans, you receive the same construction drawings found in the blueprints, but printed on vellum paper. Vellums can be erased and are perfect for making design changes. They are also semi-transparent making them easy to duplicate. But most importantly, the purchase of home plan vellums comes with a broader license that allows you to make changes to the design (ie, create a hand drawn or CAD derivative work), to make an unlimited number of copies of the plan, and to build one home from the plan.

License To Build Additional Homes

With the purchase of a blueprint package or vellums you automatically receive a license to build one home and only one home, respectively. If you want to build more homes than you are licensed to build through your purchase of a plan, then additional licenses may be purchased at reasonable costs from Garlinghouse. Inquire for more information.

IMPORTANT INFORMATION TO READ BEFORE YOU PLACE YOUR ORDER

How Many Sets Of Plans Will You Need?

The Standard 8-Set Construction Package

Our experience shows that you'll speed every step of construction and avoid costly building errors by ordering enough sets to go around. Each tradesperson wants a set — the general contractor and all subcontractors; foundation, electrical, plumbing, heating/air conditioning and framers. Don't forget your lending institution, building department and, of course, a set for yourself. * Recommended For Construction *

The Minimum 4-Set Construction Package

If you're comfortable with arduous follow-up, this package can save you a few dollars by giving you the option of passing down plan sets as work progresses. You might have enough copies to go around if work goes exactly as scheduled and no plans are lost or damaged by subcontractors. But for only $60 more, the 8-set package eliminates these worries. * Recommended For Bidding *

The Single Study Set

We offer this set so you can study the blueprints to plan your dream home in detail. They are stamped "study set only-not for construction", and you cannot build a home from them. In pursuant to copyright laws, it is _illegal_ to reproduce any blueprint.

An Important Note About Building Code Requirements:

All plans are drawn to conform to one or more of the industry's major national building standards. However, due to the variety of local building regulations, your plan may need to be modified to comply with local requirements — snow loads, energy loads, seismic zones, etc. Do check them fully and consult your local building officials.

A few states require that all building plans used be drawn by an architect registered in that state. While having your plans reviewed and stamped by such an architect may be prudent, laws requiring non-conforming plans like ours to be completely redrawn forces you to unnecessarily pay very large fees. If your state has such a law, we strongly recommend you contact your state representative to protest.

The rendering, floor plans, and technical information contained within this publication are not guaranteed to be totally accurate. Consequently, no information from this publication should be used either as a guide to constructing a home or for estimating the cost of building a home. Complete blueprints must be purchased for such purposes.

Order Form

Plan prices guaranteed until 4/1/02— After this date call for updated pricing

Order Code No. **CHP21**

_____ set(s) of blueprints for plan #_____ $_____

_____ Vellum & Modification kit for plan #_____ $_____

_____ Additional set(s) @ $30 each for plan #_____ $_____

_____ Mirror Image Reverse @ $50 each $_____

_____ Right Reading Reverse @ $135 each $_____

_____ Materials list for plan #_____ $_____

_____ Detail Plans @ $19.95 each
    ❏ Construction ❏ Plumbing ❏ Electrical $_____

_____ Bottom line ZIP Quote @ $29.95 for plan #_____ $_____

_____ Additional Bottom Line Zip Quote
    @ $14.95 for plan(s) #_____
      $_____

_____ Itemized ZIP Quote for plan(s) #_____ $_____

Shipping (see charts on opposite page) $_____

Subtotal $_____

Sales Tax   CT residents add 6% sales tax $_____

TOTAL AMOUNT ENCLOSED $_____

Send your check, money order or credit card information to:
(No C.O.D.'s Please)

Please submit all United States & Other Nations orders to:

Garlinghouse Company
174 Oakwood Drive
Glastonbury, CT. 06033

ADDRESS INFORMATION:

NAME: _____

EMAIL ADDRESS: _____

STREET: _____

CITY: _____

STATE: _____ ZIP: _____

DAYTIME PHONE: _____

TERMS OF SALE FOR HOME PLANS: All home plans sold through this publication are copyright protected. Reproduction of these home plans, either in whole or in part, including any direct copying and/or preparation of derivative works thereof, for any reason without the prior written permission of Garlinghouse, Inc., is strictly prohibited. The purchase of a set of home plans in no way transfers any copyright or other ownership interest in it to the buyer except for a limited license to use that set of home plans for the construction of one, and only one, dwelling unit. The purchase of additional sets of that home plan at a reduced price from the original set or as a part of a multiple set package does not entitle the buyer with a license to construct more than one dwelling unit.

Payment must be made in U.S. funds. Foreign Mail Orders: Certified bank checks in U.S. funds only

Credit Card Information

Charge To: ❏ Visa   ❏ Mastercard

Card # | | | | | | | | | | | | | | | | |

Signature _____ Exp. ____/____

ORDER TOLL FREE — 1-800-235-5700
Monday-Friday 8:00 a.m. to 8:00 p.m. Eastern Time
or FAX your Credit Card order to 1-860-659-5692
All foreign residents call 1-800-659-5667

Please have ready: 1. Your credit card number   2. The plan number   3. The order code number ⇨ CHP21

Garlinghouse 2001 Blueprint Price Code Schedule   *Additional sets with original order $30*

	1 Set	4 Sets	8 Sets	Vellums	ML	Itemized ZIP Quote
A	$350	$395	$455	$550	$60	$50
B	$390	$435	$495	$600	$60	$50
C	$430	$475	$535	$650	$60	$50
D	$470	$515	$575	$700	$60	$50
E	$510	$555	$615	$750	$70	$60
F	$555	$600	$660	$800	$70	$60
G	$600	$645	$705	$850	$70	$60
H	$645	$690	$750	$900	$70	$60
I	$690	$735	$795	$950	$80	$70
J	$740	$785	$845	$1000	$80	$70
K	$790	$835	$895	$1050	$80	$70
L	$840	$885	$945	$1100	$80	$70

Shipping — (Plans 1-59999)

	1-3 Sets	4-6 Sets	7+ & Vellums
Standard Delivery (UPS 2-Day)	$25.00	$30.00	$35.00
Overnight Delivery	$35.00	$40.00	$45.00

Shipping — (Plans 60000-99999)

	1-3 Sets	4-6 Sets	7+ & Vellums
Ground Delivery (7-10 Days)	$15.00	$20.00	$25.00
Express Delivery (3-5 Days)	$20.00	$25.00	$30.00

International Shipping & Handling

	1-3 Sets	4-6 Sets	7+ & Vellums
Regular Delivery Canada (7-10 Days)	$25.00	$30.00	$35.00
Express Delivery Canada (5-6 Days)	$40.00	$45.00	$50.00
Overseas Delivery Airmail (2-3 Weeks)	$50.00	$60.00	$65.00

Our Reorder and Exchange Policies:

If you find after your initial purchase that you require additional sets of plans you may purchase them from us at special reorder prices (please call for pricing details) provided that you reorder within 6 months of your original order date. There is a $28 reorder processing fee that is charged on all reorders. For more information on reordering plans please contact our Customer Service Department.

Your plans are custom printed especially for you once you place your order. For that reason we cannot accept any returns.

If for some reason you find that the plan you have purchased from us does not meet your needs, then you may exchange that plan for any other plan in our collection. We allow you sixty days from your original invoice date to make an exchange. At the time of the exchange you will be charged a processing fee of 20% of the total amount of your original order plus the difference in price between the plans (if applicable) plus the cost to ship the new plans to you. Call our Customer Service Department for more information. Please Note: Reproducible vellums can only be exchanged if they are unopened.

Important Shipping Information

Please refer to the shipping charts on the order form for service availability for your specific plan number. Our delivery service must have a street address or Rural Route Box number — never a post office box. (PLEASE NOTE: Supplying a P.O. Box number *only* will delay the shipping of your order.) Use a work address if no one is home during the day.

Orders being shipped to APO or FPO must go via First Class Mail.

For our International Customers, only Certified bank checks and money orders are accepted and must be payable in U.S. currency. For speed, we ship international orders Air Parcel Post. Please refer to the chart for the correct shipping cost.

Thank you.

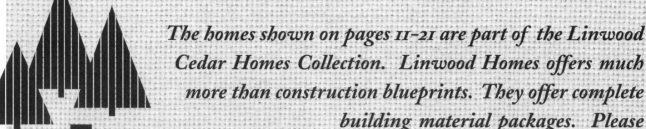

The homes shown on pages 11-21 are part of the Linwood Cedar Homes Collection. Linwood Homes offers much more than construction blueprints. They offer complete building material packages. Please take a moment to read how Linwood can help you to make your dream home become a reality. ▲

For over thirty years, Linwood has succeeded in business by recognizing that satisfied customers are the key to our future. It is that commitment to quality and service that has brought many of our customers back to build another Linwood Cedar home. Experience has shown us that there is no short cut to success. That is why we offer all the elements needed to produce the desired result - Your Dream Home!

There are no construction blueprints available for our homes. We offer a complete construction package, which includes all of the necessary materials and labor (if desired) to build your home. Here is what we offer:

HIGH QUALITY CONSTRUCTION MATERIALS — All cedar siding and interior

components are manufactured by Linwood. We operate our own sawmill to control the quality of our Western Red Cedar from the log to the finished product. We manufacture a wide range of components to customized patterns resulting in higher performance standards than commonly available in the market.

All framing lumber is high quality kiln dried material from the forests of Western Canada. This lumber is certified by the North American Lumber Grading Association and is generally acknowledged as the best on the market.

All construction materials and components are supplied by major brand name manufacturers. We put our buying power to work for you to obtain superior products at an advantageous price. These products include architectural laminated beams, plywood, windows, doors, and roofing material that are certified to national home building standards. This means that your Linwood Home package provides the widest possible selection of options at a uniformly high quality standard, to give you many years of maintenance free usage.

FULL WARRANTY PROGRAM — Linwood has a full structural warranty on all home

packages good for ten years. Our warranty is in turn supported by individual warranties of all our suppliers. This powerful combination provides our customers with one of the strongest warranty programs available in the industry today.

WORLDWIDE SHIPPING EXPERTISE — The company has shipped home packages

all over the world for decades. Our destinations include Germany, Switzerland, Japan, Korea, Australia, New Zealand, Chile and Lithuania as well as Canada and the United States. We specialize in hard to reach destinations where it is important that everything needed for construction is included in the package. Our products have been delivered to the final building site by truck, container, barge, even helicopter. You can depend on us to get the package exactly where you want it.

CONSTRUCTION SUPPORT — You can use our builder or yours. In addition, we offer a variety of levels of construction support. As an option, we even panelize wall units for rapid and easy assembly. All our builders are qualified members of the Linwood Home Builders Association. You only have to select the program that best suits your budget.

BASIC ASSISTANCE PROGRAM — This program allows you to act as your own general contractor. You receive both factory and local assistance in selecting contractors, receiving and evaluating quotes, obtaining planning permits, and monitoring on-site job performance by the selected sub-trades.

Contractor Assistance Program - Contractors not experienced in post and beam construction can contact our factory to receive detailed instruction in the fastest and most efficient method of assembling a post and beam house. A toll-free hotline number is also available for immediate assistance in dealing with construction questions.

FULL CONSTRUCTION MANAGEMENT — We will manage your project under the supervision of a qualified authorized Linwood builder. Once foundations are in place, a building team can completely assemble an average two thousand square foot Linwood home package in approximately four weeks.

Your new home will have siding, a roof, windows installed, doors in place, and the whole structure weatherproofed. You can then complete the interior finishing of the home according to your own timetable and budget. If necessary we can also assist you in this finishing process.

Now that you have heard an overview of what Linwood has to offer we invite you to find out even more. If you are interested in the homes on pages 11-21 or would like to see more of the homes that Linwood has available please call 1-800-235-5700. A Garlinghouse Telesales representative will take down some information that will be forwarded to Linwood Homes. A representative from Linwood Homes will call you to discuss your building project. Please note that only the homes on pages 11-21 are available through Linwood Homes. All of the other plans in this publication are available as blueprints through The Garlinghouse Company. The Garlinghouse Company does not sell building material packages for their home plans.

LINWOOD
custom cedar homes

 **Materials List Available**   **Zip Quote Available**   **R** **Right Reading Reverse**

Options legend: ML = Materials List, ZQ = Zip Quote, RR = Right Reading Reverse

Plan#	Page#	Price Code	Square Footage	Options
1074	59	A	1040	ML RR
1078	87	A	1024	ML
9107	50	C	2051	ML RR
9964	308	C	1956	ML RR
10012	95	C	2108	ML RR
10054	313	A	1174	ML RR
10220	123	A	888	ML
10228	139	A	1289	ML
10274	337	C	1783	ML
10306	103	A	408	ML
10328	127	B	1600	ML
10396	64	D	2228	ML
10455	323	B	1643	ML
10464	86	D	2222	ML
10515	2	C	2015	ML ZQ
10542	72	F	2624	ML
10548	120	B	1688	ML
10549	106	E	2280	ML
10569	146	C	1840	ML
10583	4	K	3903	ML ZQ
10594	143	B	1565	ML
10619	36	E	2352	ML
10674	89	B	1600	ML ZQ
10745	80	B	1643	ML
10748	124	B	1540	ML
10839	32	B	1738	ML ZQ RR
20001	37	A	1255	ML
20002	60	A	728	ML
20062	43	A	1500	ML ZQ RR
20066	73	C	1850	ML
20075	183	B	1682	ML RR
20083	285	B	1575	ML ZQ
20087	79	B	1568	ML ZQ
20089	138	B	1588	ML
20095	84	E	2477	ML
20100	31	B	1737	ML ZQ RR
20104	171	B	1686	ML
20110	110	C	1786	ML RR
20150	151	B	1638	ML ZQ RR
20156	52	A	1359	ML ZQ RR
20161	27	A	1307	ML ZQ RR
20164	30	A	1456	ML ZQ RR
20180	122	B	1592	ML
20191	159	B	1606	ML
20198	23	C	1792	ML ZQ
20204	75	B	1532	ML
20220	161	B	1568	ML ZQ
20403	304	B	1734	ML ZQ
20501	334	C	1908	ML ZQ
24240	63	A	964	ML
24250	104	B	1700	ML ZQ RR
24301	132	C	1957	ML RR
24302	156	A	988	ML ZQ
24303	155	A	984	ML ZQ
24304	223	A	993	ML
24305	99	A	984	ML
24306	135	A	1330	ML
24308	255	A	823	ML
24309	185	A	897	ML
24310	191	A	888	ML
24311	219	A	1127	ML ZQ
24312	207	A	1298	ML
24313	251	A	1210	ML
24314	140	C	1850	ML
24315	162	F	2545	ML
24317	178	B	1620	ML ZQ
24318	279	A	1398	ML RR

Plan#	Page#	Price Code	Square Footage	Options
24319	29	B	1710	ML ZQ
24320	327	A	1235	
24321	194	C	1961	
24322	216	F	2667	
24323	230	E	2500	
24324	238	C	1800	
24325	248	C	1816	
24326	201	B	1505	ML ZQ
24327	315	A	1266	ML ZQ
24402	250	A	1346	ML ZQ RR
24651	262	C	1821	
24700	22	A	1312	ML ZQ
24701	33	B	1625	ML ZQ
24704	280	C	1855	
24708	264	B	1576	ZQ
24709	67	A	1330	
24714	298	C	1771	
24717	290	B	1642	
24718	336	A	1452	
24721	54	B	1539	
24723	299	A	1112	
26110	263	A	1469	ML
26111	10	A	1341	ML
26112	147	A	1487	ML ZQ
26113	275	A	1338	ML
26114	267	A	1112	ML
26740	271	B	1512	ML
26760	296	C	2023	ML
26810	306	G	2843	ML
26870	322	F	2617	ML
34003	88	A	1146	ML ZQ RR
34011	49	B	1672	ML ZQ RR
34029	34	B	1686	ML ZQ RR
34031	331	C	1831	ML ZQ RR
34043	29	B	1583	ML ZQ RR
34054	44	A	1400	ML ZQ RR
34055	335	B	1527	ML ZQ RR
34075	131	A	576	ML ZQ
34150	55	A	1492	ML ZQ RR
34154	67	A	1486	ML ZQ RR
34328	330	A	1092	ML ZQ RR
34600	26	A	1328	ML ZQ RR
34601	33	A	1415	ML ZQ RR
34602	35	B	1560	ML ZQ
34625	199	A	1231	ML ZQ RR
35005	155	A	1484	ML
84020	203	A	768	
84056	38	B	1644	
84058	87	A	1298	
84330	215	A	1114	
90004	275	A	1285	ML
90007	283	C	1830	ML
90048	97	A	1274	ML
90288	259	A	1387	ML
90307	315	A	1187	ML
90309	303	A	1039	ML
90324	243	A	1016	ML
90325	331	A	988	ML
90348	267	A	1149	ML
90354	323	A	1360	ML
90357	335	A	1368	ML
90360	95	A	1283	ML
90390	235	A	1231	ML
90398	247	B	1630	ML
90407	40	C	1950	ML
90409	133	B	1670	ML
90412	169	A	1454	ML

Plan#	Page#	Price Code	Square Footage	Options
90418	227	B	1607	ML
90423	192	C	1773	ML
90433	220	A	928	ML
90441	233	C	1811	ML
90476	254	C	1804	ML
90601	276	B	1613	ML
90611	47	B	1732	ML
90613	251	A	1432	ML
90620	99	A	1476	ML
90623	139	A	1474	ML
90629	56	C	2176	ML
90630	283	A	1207	ML
90633	115	B	1583	ML
90638	127	A	1042	ML
90669	111	A	1332	ML
90680	301	A	1393	ML
90682	318	A	1243	ML
90684	199	B	1590	ML
90689	328	A	1476	ML
90692	147	A	1492	ML
90821	131	A	796	ML
90822	287	A	1263	ML
90844	61	B	1552	ML
90847	93	A	1360	ML
90855	211	A	1186	ML
90859	223	B	1611	ML
90869	66	C	1766	ML
90905	101	A	1314	ML
90930	125	B	1702	ML
90934	141	A	884	ML
90941	74	F	2651	ML
90983	154	A	1396	ML
90986	173	B	1731	ML
90990	188	A	1423	ML
90995	82	A	1011	ML
91021	177	A	1295	ML
91026	39	A	1354	ML
91031	193	A	880	ML
91033	24	A	1249	ML
91063	311	A	1207	
91071	255	B	1671	
91304	92	E	2312	ML
91319	217	H	3192	ML
91340	228	A	1111	ML
91342	249	A	1345	ML
91349	215	B	1694	ML
91418	257	B	1665	ML
91545	128	A	1420	ML
91704	144	C	1837	ML
91722	195	A	1249	ML
91731	274	C	1857	ML
91753	239	A	1490	
91785	247	B	1680	ML
91797	231	A	1485	ML
91807	281	A	1410	ML
92026	167	A	863	ML
92220	292	C	1830	ZQ
92238	310	B	1664	ZQ
92239	71	A	1198	
92281	187	A	1360	
92283	321	B	1653	
92400	108	A	1050	
92405	71	B	1564	
92502	31	A	1237	ML
92503	112	A	1271	ML
92516	126	C	1887	ML
92523	137	A	1293	ML

INDEX INDEX INDEX

Materials List Available | Zip Quote Available | R Right Reading Reverse

Plan#	Page#	Price Code	Square Footage	Options
92525	148	A	1484	ML
92527	164	B	1680	ML
92528	179	A	1363	ML
92531	181	C	1754	ML
92536	202	C	1869	ML
92544	213	C	1987	ML
92552	237	C	1873	ML
92556	168	B	1556	ML
92557	246	A	1390	ML
92560	261	B	1660	ML
92562	123	C	1856	ML
92617	289	C	1955	
92625	27	B	1746	ZIP
92630	314	C	1782	ZIP
92649	58	B	1508	ZIP
92655	324	B	1746	ZIP
92660	118	C	1964	
92705	145	C	1849	
92801	176	A	1440	ML
92802	295	B	1505	ML
92803	45	B	1600	ML
92804	175	B	1686	ML
92805	186	C	1768	ML
92806	196	C	1841	ML
93000	170	C	1862	
93015	189	A	1087	
93017	209	A	1142	
93018	307	A	1142	
93021	241	A	1282	
93027	187	A	1500	
93030	269	C	1955	
93048	337	A	1310	
93061	159	B	1742	
93073	287	A	1202	
93104	204	C	1756	ZIP R
93133	98	C	1761	ZIP R
93143	130	C	1802	
93161	157	B	1540	ZIP
93165	75	A	1472	
93171	205	B	1642	
93191	224	C	1756	
93222	253	A	1292	ML ZIP R
93261	277	C	1778	ML ZIP
93279	293	A	1388	ML ZIP
93447	319	A	1474	
93909	317	B	1716	
94116	332	B	1546	ML
94204	8	C	1764	
94240	307	B	1647	
94248	90	C	1853	
94249	212	C	1876	
94250	232	B	1706	
94251	242	C	1838	
94252	252	J	3714	
94253	260	F	3285	
94255	270	F	3296	
94256	299	B	1684	
94257	286	F	2594	
94258	300	C	1824	
94259	312	F	2520	
94260	326	C	2068	
94261	41	G	2957	
94262	25	C	1792	
94263	28	A	1288	
94280	6	H	3244	
94300	291	A	950	
94301	46	C	1871	

Plan#	Page#	Price Code	Square Footage	Options
94302	83	A	1137	
94303	327	A	1013	
94304	135	A	1377	
94305	179	A	1025	
94306	167	A	1012	
94307	102	A	786	
94308	319	A	659	
94309	303	A	1215	
94310	119	B	1513	
94311	107	A	1370	
94312	191	A	1024	
94313	62	C	1836	
94314	70	C	1951	
94315	163	B	1550	
94316	311	B	1524	
94800	59	A	1199	ML
94801	121	A	1300	ML
94917	129	C	1782	ML
94921	239	B	1651	ML
94923	184	B	1666	ML
94966	197	C	1911	ML
94970	295	A	1385	ML
94972	63	B	1580	ML
94982	291	A	1360	ML R
94985	79	A	1279	ML R
94986	218	B	1604	ML
96405	210	E	1903	ML R
96417	225	D	1561	ML ZIP R
96418	115	C	1452	ML R
96419	243	D	1541	ML R
96452	266	C	1475	ML R
96458	78	D	1512	ML R
96468	305	D	1864	ML R
96484	329	C	1246	ML R
96493	96	D	1770	ML R
96506	116	B	1654	ML
96509	134	A	1438	ML
96510	91	A	1372	ML
96511	85	A	1247	ML
96513	158	B	1648	ML
96519	174	A	1243	
96522	221	B	1515	ML
97108	94	C	1794	
97124	119	A	1416	
97233	172	B	1743	
97254	198	B	1692	
97702	171	B	1601	
98005	190	D	1542	ML R
98014	200	D	1859	ML R
98020	222	E	1795	ML R
98316	236	C	1859	ML
98408	226	C	1856	ML
98411	244	A	1373	ML
98412	276	B	1553	ML
98414	258	B	1575	ML
98415	278	A	1429	ML
98423	294	B	1671	ML
98425	316	C	1845	ML
98430	325	C	1884	ML
98432	288	B	1670	ML
98434	109	A	1346	ML
98435	336	C	1945	ML
98441	263	B	1502	
98443	271	A	1359	
98456	117	B	1715	ML
98460	142	B	1544	
98464	48	C	1779	

Plan#	Page#	Price Code	Square Footage	Options
98479	57	B	1575	
98498	183	A	1135	
98503	152	C	1876	
98522	107	B	1528	
98709	103	A	1380	ML
98714	160	C	2017	ML
98743	182	C	1958	
98747	229	A	1280	ML
98804	91	A	1372	ML
98805	175	A	1089	ML
98807	68	A	1487	ML
98912	245	A	1345	ML
98915	265	A	1208	ML
99081	163	B	1590	
99208	282	C	1830	ML
99241	211	A	1366	ML
99303	195	A	1421	ML
99321	143	A	1368	ML
99324	76	A	1307	ML
99345	207	A	1325	ML
99487	81	C	1806	ML
99610	83	B	1528	ML
99633	208	C	1798	ML
99635	259	B	1650	ML
99639	309	A	1367	ML
99701	111	A	1260	ML
99705	240	C	2091	ML
99707	219	A	1476	ML
99719	203	A	1266	ML
99745	235	A	1482	ML
99801	302	G	2188	ML ZIP R
99802	333	D	1576	ML ZIP R
99803	105	E	1977	ML ZIP R
99804	153	E	1815	ML ZIP R
99805	165	E	1787	ML ZIP R
99806	297	C	1246	ML R
99807	113	E	1879	ML ZIP R
99808	149	E	1832	ML ZIP R
99809	77	C	1417	ML ZIP R
99810	51	D	1685	ML R
99811	42	D	1699	ML R
99812	100	C	1386	ML ZIP R
99813	114	E	1959	ML R
99815	65	E	1912	ML ZIP R
99826	136	C	1346	ML R
99828	256	C	1298	ML R
99830	150	C	1372	ML ZIP R
99831	69	D	1699	ML R
99834	227	D	1575	ML R
99835	53	D	1515	ML R
99840	268	D	1632	ML R
99844	231	D	1737	ML R
99845	166	E	1954	ML ZIP R
99849	151	C	1322	ML R
99856	279	C	1310	ML R
99857	180	E	1865	ML R
99858	206	C	1253	ML ZIP R
99860	214	C	1498	ML R
99864	284	C	1426	ML R
99868	320	C	1350	ML R
99871	234	D	1655	ML R
99878	272	E	1864	ML ZIP R

CRE▲TIVE HOMEOWNER®

How-To Books for...

REMODELING BASEMENTS, ATTICS & GARAGES

Cramped for space? This book shows you how to find space you may not know you had and convert it into useful living areas. 40 colorful photographs and 530 full-color drawings.

BOOK #: 277680   192pp.   8½"x10⅞"

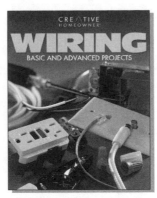

WIRING: Basic and Advanced Projects
(Conforms to latest National Electrical Code)

Included are 350 large, clear, full-color illustrations and no-nonsense step-by-step instructions. Shows how to replace receptacles and switches; repair a lamp; install ceiling and attic fans; and more.

BOOK #: 277049   256pp.   8½"x10⅞"

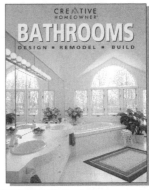

BATHROOMS: Design, Remodel, Build

Shows how to plan, construct, and finish a bathroom. Remodel floors; rebuild walls and ceilings; and install windows, skylights, and plumbing fixtures. Specific tools and materials are given for each project. Includes 90 color photos and 470 color illustrations.

BOOK #: 277053   192pp.   8½"x10⅞"

The Smart Approach to BATH DESIGN

Everything you need to know about designing a bathroom like a professional is explained in this book. Creative solutions and practical advice about space, the latest in fixtures and fittings, and safety features accompany over 150 photographs.

BOOK #: 287225   176pp.   9"x10"

BUILD A KIDS' PLAY YARD

Here are detailed plans and step-by-step instructions for building the play structures that kids love most: swing set, monkey bars, balance beam, playhouse, teeter-totter, sandboxes, kid-sized picnic table, and a play tower that supports a slide. 200 color photographs and illustrations.

BOOK #: 277662   144 pp.   8½"x10⅞"

CABINETS & BUILT-INS

26 custom cabinetry projects are included for every room in the house, from kitchen cabinets to a bedroom wall unit, a bunk bed, computer workstation, and more. Also included are chapters on tools, techniques, finishing, and materials.

BOOK #: 277079   160 pp.   8½"x10⅞"

DECKS: Planning, Designing, Building

With this book, even the novice builder can build a deck that perfectly fits his yard. The step-by-step instructions lead the reader from laying out footings to adding railings. Includes three deck projects, 500 color drawings, and photographs.

BOOK #: 277162   192pp.   8½"x10⅞"

FURNITURE REPAIR & REFINISHING

From structural repairs to restoring older finishes or entirely refinishing furniture: a hands-on step-by-step approach to furniture repair and restoration. More than 430 color photographs and 60 full-color drawings.

BOOK #: 277335   240pp.   8½"x10⅞"

HOUSE FRAMING

Written for those with beginning to intermediate building skills, this book is designed to walk you through the framing basics, from assembling simple partitions to cutting compound angles on dormer rafters. More than 400 full-color drawings.

BOOK #: 277655   208pp.   8½"x10⅞"

the Home Planner, Builder & Owner

KITCHENS: Design, Remodel, Build

This is the reference book for modern kitchen design, with more than 100 full-color photos to help homeowners plan the layout. Step-by-step instructions illustrate basic plumbing and wiring techniques; how to finish walls and ceilings; and more.

BOOK #: 277065   192pp.   8½"x10⅞"

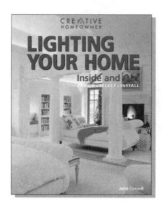

LIGHTING YOUR HOME: Inside and Out

Lighting should be selected with care. This book thoroughly explains lighting design for every room as well as outdoors. It is also a step-by-step manual that shows how to install the fixtures. More than 125 photos and 400 drawings.

BOOK #: 277583   176pp.   8½"x10⅞"

MASONRY: Concrete, Brick, Stone

Concrete, brick, and stone choices are detailed with step-by-step instructions and over 35 color photographs and 460 illustrations. Projects include a brick or stone garden wall, steps and patios, a concrete-block retaining wall, a concrete sidewalk.

BOOK #: 277106   176pp.   8½"x10⅞"

The Smart Approach to KITCHEN DESIGN

Transform a dated kitchen into the spectacular heart of your home. Learn how to create a better layout and more efficient storage. Find out about the latest equipment and materials. Savvy tips explain how to create style like a pro. More than 150 color photos.

BOOK #: 279935   176 pp.   9"x10"

PLANNING YOUR ADDITION

Planning an addition to your home involves a daunting number of choices, from choosing a contractor to selecting bathroom tile. Using 280 color drawings and photographs, architect/author Jerry Germer helps you make the right decision.

BOOK #: 277004   192pp.   8½"x10⅞"

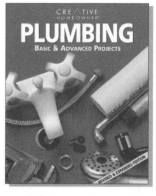

PLUMBING: Basic & Advanced Projects

Take the guesswork out of plumbing repair and installation for old and new systems. Projects include replacing faucets, unclogging drains, installing a tub, replacing a water heater, and much more. 500 illustrations and diagrams.

BOOK #: 277620   176pp.   8½"x10⅞"

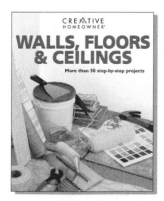

WALLS, FLOORS & CEILINGS

Here's the definitive guide to interiors. It shows you how to replace old surfaces with new professional-looking ones. Projects include installing molding, skylights, insulation, flooring, carpeting, and more. Over 500 color photos and drawings.

BOOK #: 277697   176pp.   8½"x10⅞"

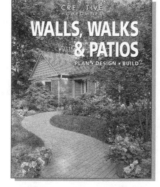

WALLS, WALKS & PATIOS

Learn how to build a patio from concrete, stone, or brick and complement it with one of a dozen walks. Learn about simple mortarless walls, landscape timber walls, and hefty brick and stone walls. 50 photographs and 320 illustrations, all in color.

BOOK #: 277994   192pp.   8½"x10⅞"

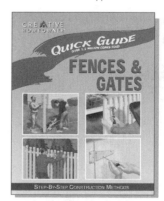

QUICK GUIDE: FENCES & GATES

Learn how to build and install all kinds of fences and gates for your yard, from hand-built wood privacy and picket fences to newer prefabricated vinyl and chain-link types. Over 200 two-color drawings illustrate step-by-step procedures.

BOOK #: 287732   80pp.   8½"x10⅞"

Place Your Order ....

WORKING WITH TILE

Design and complete interior and exterior tile projects on walls, floors, countertops, shower enclosures, more. 425 color illustrations and over 80 photographs.

BOOK #: 277540   176pp.   8½"x10⅞"

COLOR IN THE AMERICAN HOME

Find out how to make the most of color in your home. Over 150 photographs of traditional and contemporary interiors.

BOOK #: 287264   176pp.   9"x10"

The Smart Approach to HOME DECORATING

Learn how to work with space, color, pattern, and texture with the flair of a professional designer. More than 300 color photos.

BOOK #: 279667   256pp.   9"x10"

CREATIVE HOMEOWNER®

BOOK ORDER FORM   *Please Print*

SHIP TO:

Name:

Address:

City: State: Zip: Phone Number:

(Should there be a problem with your order)

Quantity	Title	Price	CH #	Cost
	375 Southern Home Plans	$9.95	277037	
	380 Country & Farmhouse Home Plans	9.95	277035	
	400 Affordable Home Plans	9.95	277012	
	508 One-Story Home Plans	9.95	277030	
	508 Two-Story Home Plans	9.95	277031	
	600 Most Popular Home Plans	9.95	277029	
	Adding Value to Your Home	16.95	277006	
	Advanced Home Gardening	24.95	274465	
	Annuals, Perennials, and Bulbs	19.95	274032	
	Bathrooms: Design, Remodel, Build	19.95	277053	
	Better Lawns, Step by Step	14.95	274359	
	Bird Feeders	10.95	277102	
	Build a Kids' Play Yard	14.95	277662	
	Cabinets & Built-Ins	14.95	277079	
	Color in the American Home	19.95	287264	
	Complete Guide to Wallpapering	14.95	278910	
	Complete Guide to Water Gardens	19.95	274452	
	Complete Home Landscaping	24.95	274615	
	Creating Good Gardens	16.95	274244	
	Custom Closets	12.95	277132	
	Decks: Planning, Designing, Building	16.95	277162	
	Decorating with Paint & Paper	19.95	279723	
	Decorating with Tile	19.95	279824	
	Decorative Paint Finishes	10.95	287371	
	Drywall: Pro Tips for Hanging & Finishing	14.95	278315	
	Easy-Care Guide to Houseplants	19.95	275243	
	Fences, Gates & Trellises	14.95	277981	
	Furniture Repair & Refinishing	19.95	277335	
	Gazebos & Other Outdoor Structures	14.95	277138	
	Home Book	40.00	267855	
	Home Landscaping: California Reg.	19.95	274267	
	Home Landscaping: Mid-Atlantic Reg.	19.95	274537	
	Home Landscaping: Midwest Reg./S Can.	19.95	274385	
	Home Landscaping: Northeast Reg./SE Can.	19.95	274618	
	Home Landscaping: Southeast Reg.	19.95	274762	
	House Framing	19.95	277655	
	Kitchens: Design, Remodel, Build (New Ed.)	16.95	277065	
	Lighting Your Home Inside & Out	16.95	277583	
	Lyn Peterson's Real Life Decorating	27.95	279382	
	Masonry: Concrete, Brick, Stone	16.95	277106	
	Mastering Fine Decorative Paint Techniques	27.95	279550	
	Planning Your Addition	16.95	277004	
	Plumbing: Basic and Advanced Projects	14.95	277620	
	Remodeling Basements, Attics & Garages	16.95	277680	
	Smart Approach to Bath Design	19.95	287225	
	Smart Approach to Home Decorating	24.95	279667	
	Smart Approach to Kitchen Design	19.95	279935	

Quantity	Title	Price	CH #	Cost
	Smart Approach to Window Decor	$19.95	279431	
	Trees, Shrubs & Hedges for Home Landscaping	19.95	274238	
	Walls, Floors & Ceilings	16.95	277697	
	Walls, Walks & Patios	16.95	277994	
	Wiring: Basic and Advanced Projects	19.95	277049	
	Working with Tile	16.95	277540	
	Yard and Garden Furniture (Plans & Projects)	19.95	277462	

Quick Guide Series

Quantity	Title	Price	CH #	Cost
	Quick Guide - Attics	$7.95	287711	
	Quick Guide - Basements	7.95	287242	
	Quick Guide - Ceramic Tile	7.95	287730	
	Quick Guide - Decks	7.95	277344	
	Quick Guide - Fences & Gates	7.95	287732	
	Quick Guide - Floors	7.95	287734	
	Quick Guide - Garages & Carports	7.95	287785	
	Quick Guide - Gazebos	7.95	287757	
	Quick Guide - Insulation & Ventilation	7.95	287367	
	Quick Guide - Interior & Exterior Painting	7.95	287784	
	Quick Guide - Masonry Walls	7.95	287741	
	Quick Guide - Patios & Walks	7.95	287778	
	Quick Guide - Plumbing	7.95	287863	
	Quick Guide - Ponds & Fountains	7.95	287804	
	Quick Guide - Pool & Spa Maintenance	7.95	287901	
	Quick Guide - Roofing	7.95	287807	
	Quick Guide - Shelving & Storage	7.95	287763	
	Quick Guide - Siding	7.95	287892	
	Quick Guide - Stairs & Railings	7.95	287755	
	Quick Guide - Storage Sheds	7.95	287815	
	Quick Guide - Trim (Crown Molding, Base & more)	7.95	287745	
	Quick Guide - Walls & Ceilings	7.95	287792	
	Quick Guide - Windows & Doors	7.95	287812	
	Quick Guide - Wiring, Fourth Edition	7.95	287884	

Number of Books Ordered _____   Total for Books _____

NJ Residents add 6% tax _____

Prices subject to change without notice.   Subtotal _____

Postage/Handling Charges _____
$3.75 for first book / $1.25 for each additional book

Total _____

Make checks (in U.S. currency only) payable to

CREATIVE HOMEOWNER®
P.O. BOX 38, 24 Park Way
Upper Saddle River, New Jersey 07458-9960

Please visit us at our Web site: **www.creativehomeowner.com**